ALSO BY DAVID GRAFTON

Red, Hot and Rich:
An Oral History of Cole Porter

THE SISTERS

THE SISTERS

BABE MORTIMER PALEY,
BETSEY ROOSEVELT WHITNEY,
MINNIE ASTOR FOSBURGH

The Lives and Times of the Fabulous Cushing Sisters

DAVID GRAFTON

VILLARD BOOKS

1992

LIBRARY OF CONGRESS CATALOGING-IN-PUBLICATION DATA
Grafton, David.
The sisters: Babe Mortimer Paley, Betsey Roosevelt Whitney,
Minnie Astor Fosburgh: the lives and times of the fabulous Cushing
sisters / David Grafton.—1st ed.
p. cm.
Includes index.
ISBN 0-394-58416-3
1. Paley, Babe Mortimer.   2. Whitney, Betsey Cushing Roosevelt.
3. Fosburgh, Minnie Astor.   4. Cushing family.   5. Women—
United States—Biography.   6. Sisters—United States—Biography.
7. Upper classes—United States—Social life and customs—20th
century.   I. Title.
CT3260.G72   1992
929'.2'0973—dc20   91-50061

Manufactured in the United States of America
9 8 7 6 5 4 3 2
First Edition

FOR:

GUILLERMO "GUILLO" CARDONA

DARYL WILLIAMS, D.D.S.

EVE HEFFER

All history is gossip.
—*John F. Kennedy*

ACKNOWLEDGMENTS

A writer likes to think that a book is all his own. But that is clearly not the case with any literary effort, especially biography, and I'm indebted to hundreds of people, not all of whom I'll be able to mention. Foremost among them is Agnes Birnbaum, my agent, who saw me safely through a number of years of frustration and occasional heartache. She has never failed to offer me comforting words, as well as her own good judgment, and she has seen me to the finish line on more than one occasion. And with saintly patience my editorial assistant, Martha Leff, plowed through transcripts and original manuscripts to provide me with a wonderfully clean and readable final copy.

At Villard Books, I was supremely guided and protected by one of the most talented editors in publishing, Diane Reverand, whose undaunted patience was remarkable. And the vigilance of her highly efficient assistants, Amy Einhorn and Jason Kaufman, kept me moving along during the final stages of this project. Thanks also to Heather Kilpatrick, the able legal counsel at Villard Books who provided sound advice on all matters legal. I regret that I can offer no more than a mention to many of those who follow, some of whom have given me hours of their time: Diana Edkins, Jean Cook Barkhorn, Sibilla Clark, Brooke Astor, Boaz Mazor, Helen Bernstein, Liza Fosburgh, Kitty Carlisle Hart, Tex McCrary, Alexander Liberman, Jeanne Murray Vanderbilt, Patricia Linden, Archibald Gillies, William H. Hutton, Dorothy Hart Hearst Paley Hirshon, the late Jerome Zerbe, Eleanor Lambert, Natalie Davenport, Taki, Pat Kerr, James Bloodworth, Michael Thomas, Dorothy Dillon Eweson, Millicent H. Fenwick, William Norwich, Janice Braun (Yale University Historical Library), Patrick McCarthy, Albert Hadley, Paul Sheridan, Cayetana de Alba (La Duquesa de Alba), Doris and Lowell Zollar, Maureen Smith, Pedro and Margarita Vincenty, Gael Love, Lawrence Minard, Ann Gerber, Bill Zwecker, Carol Vining, Vincent F.M. Catanzano, Megan McKinney Whitfield, Luis Ortiz, Roque Cutie, Hope Daniels, Nikki Zollar and William Von Hoene, Pat Ray, Donna Hodge, Charles C. Bricker, Jr., Marcy Maker, Linda Cardona, Jean-Jacques Naudet, Pedro Vincenty, Jr., George Chapman, David Sinkler, Florence Stern, Earl Blackwell, Liz Smith, Judy Niedermaier, Tanya Rhinelander, Raymond Teichman (FDR Library), Don Dadas, Chaneta Matthews, Mabel Munger, Joy Bell, Juan C. Booker, Chris Hjelm, Miguel Hinujosa, Susan Magrino, Ruben and Nina Terzian, and Sugar Rautbord.

FOREWORD

Ideas, especially ideas that translate into books, are like dear friends; they bring an enrichment to our lives. And like friends, they are not arrived at easily.

And such was the case with *The Sisters*, my biography of the glamorous Cushing sisters. My involvement with those outstanding ladies began in 1985, when I first began to gather every ounce of material I could put my hands on relating to their careers as the most luminous society beauties of their day. This initial step also included contacting the sole surviving sister, Betsey Cushing Roosevelt Whitney, as well as family and friends.

But research alone didn't put the book together. I'd been aware of the Cushing sisters all of my life from family, friends, and certainly the media. In their day, which stretched from the 1930s through the late 1970s, they had the same effect on the American public as the British Royal Family has on the British populace.

And with this biography, which details the lives of these three re-markable women, I hope that in some small way I've presented their story in a fair and well-rounded manner.

David Grafton
September 2, 1991

CONTENTS

THE SISTERS

1

HAPPY DAYS ARE HERE

*O*N a sweltering day in June of 1930, the comely Betsey Cushing and the dashing young James Roosevelt joined hands in holy wedlock, launching front-page news throughout the eastern United States and even garnering national and international media attention. The bride was the second daughter of Harvard's preeminent neurosurgeon Henry Cushing and the formidable, social Katherine "Kate" Crowell Cushing. The groom was the eldest son of Eleanor and Franklin Delano Roosevelt, then First Lady and governor of New York and probably the most popular American political couple of the era.

Among the most luminous of the season's social events, the June 4 wedding took place in Brookline, Massachusetts, at the stately St. Paul's Episcopal Church. Five hundred prominent members of Boston's and New York's social, political, and medical elite crowded into the church, while more than a thousand Depression-weary onlookers gathered outside, braving hours in the hundred-degree heat to catch glimpses of the glamorous bridal party and celebrated guests.

The bride, scorning traditional white satin, had chosen a magnificent floor-length gown of silver lamé, fashioned in the Grecian style, with a long square train flowing from the waist and full angel sleeves of translucent mignonette. On her head, Betsey wore a pearl-encrusted band of braided silver and a filmy mignonette veil, and in her hands she carried a bouquet of majestic calla lilies. Petite and lovely, she was every bit the fairy-tale princess as she entered the magical kingdom of America's most aristocratic political dynasty.

Betsey's older sister, Mary "Minnie" Cushing, served as maid of honor, while her fifteen-year-old little sister, Barbara "Babe," was one of the bevy of society bridesmaids. These included Frances Bennet Endres, of Brookline, and Emily Ingersoll, of Penllyn, Pennsylvania—both classmates of the bride at the Westover School—and the groom's sister, Anna Eleanor Roosevelt Dall, of Tarrytown, New York. All carried small bouquets of spring flowers and wore long, full gowns of aquamarine organdy, accessorized with wide-brimmed straw hats trimmed in matching fabric.

The ushers, decked out in white tie, tails, and silk top hats, included Jimmy Roosevelt's Harvard classmates William Hutton, of New York, and Morris R. Brownell, Jr., of Philadelphia; and brothers Franklin D. Roosevelt, Jr., and John A. Roosevelt, both of Hyde Park, New York. Elliott Roosevelt served as his brother's best man.

Governor and Mrs. Roosevelt made a spectacular entrance, arriving at the church under the protection of a large contingent of New York state troopers attired in ceremonial dress. The crowd of onlookers gave the senior Roosevelts a warm welcome as they slipped in through a side entrance, Eleanor holding the hand of their tiny granddaughter, Sistie Dall. Both Kate Cushing and Eleanor Roosevelt were attired in elegant gowns of dove-gray silk.

Dr. Cushing gave his daughter away in the tradition-laden ceremony, which was jointly performed by Dr. Endicott Peabody, famed headmaster of Groton (the groom's prep school alma mater), and the Reverend William L. Clark, rector of St. Paul's. When the bridal party and distinguished guests emerged from the church, they were greeted by the enthusiastic crowds and the New York state troopers, who created an even greater sensation by providing a motorcycle escort to the Cushing home for the reception.

There, at 305 Walnut Street in Brookline, five hundred additional guests descended on the handsome yellow colonial. The house, situated on almost three acres of land, with magnificent formal gardens and landscaped grounds, was a perfect setting for the festivities. The newly-weds and their respective families formed a receiving line in front of the large bay window of the Cushings' spacious living room. After passing through the line, the thousand guests gathered outside beneath a massive marquee for lavish refreshments and in an equally large tent to dance to the music of Ruby Newman's orchestra, a great favorite along the Ivy League circuit.

The gymnasium over the combination barn-garage appeared more like one of Boston's exclusive shops than the site of the Cushing sisters' rough-and-tumble childhood play. Three long tables, stretching from one end of the gym to the other, almost groaned audibly under the weight of the dazzling array of wedding gifts, carefully arranged for viewing. There were heavy silver tea services, fragile imported china of several different patterns, massive antique trays and silver hollowware, enough lamps to light a small country inn, and various and sundry other treasures. One entire wall was hung with valuable artwork, and around another was a splendid display of clocks. Furniture of every description and priceless Oriental rugs completed the princely offerings.

As impressive as the gifts themselves were the names on the accompanying cards. Former New York governor, Al Smith had given the young couple a pair of porcelain candelabra and a set of elegant silver sauce dishes. Dr. William Mayo's gift was another set of sauce dishes, this one an exquisite antique. Mrs. Corinne Roosevelt Robinson had sent a magnificent seventeenth-century Spanish mirror, and the governor and First Lady of Puerto Rico, Theodore Roosevelt and Mrs. Roosevelt, had presented Betsey and Jimmy with a Wedgewood demitasse set. The judges of New York's court of appeals had joined in sending a handsome silver bowl, while Mrs. Nathaniel Thayer and Mrs. Robert Lovett had together presented an heirloom set of maple bedroom furniture. Helen Huntington Astor, wife of Vincent Astor, had given the young Roosevelts a pair of blue and white Lowestoft porcelain cups and saucers.

These were but a few of the prestigious names on a guest list that read like a veritable *Who's Who* of the era. Among those in attendance were

Mrs. Alfred E. Smith, former First Lady of New York (although her husband was not able to attend); Mr. and Mrs. Henry Morgenthau; General Clarence R. Edwards, retired wartime commander of the famed Yankee Division; Mrs. Hugh D. Scott; Richard C. Adlrich; Mr. and Mrs. Fellows-Gordon; Mr. and Mrs. Ogden Potter-Palmer; future Supreme Court justice Felix Frankfurter and his wife; and Louis Howe, a wisp of a man who, despite unprepossessing looks, a bland personality, and a decided lack of popularity among the Roosevelts and their inner political circle, would provide the brilliant campaign strategy to guide Franklin Delano Roosevelt into the White House. And last but certainly not least was Sara Delano Roosevelt, FDR's suspicious, possessive mother, who was hostile toward everyone close to her son—even Eleanor, Jimmy, and the other children. Sara had, upon meeting Betsey, put the young woman firmly in her place, saying, "I understand your father is a surgeon. Surgeons always remind me of my butcher." Nevertheless, with her $ 2 million fortune, Sara was an absolutely indispensable guest.

Betsey's was hardly a rags-to-riches story, and despite Sara's snobbery, the Cushing-Crowell lineage was eminently suitable for a Roosevelt alliance. But the fact remained that Betsey was "marrying up," from the *haute bourgeosie* into the closest thing the Depression-torn United States had to royalty. She was not from a moneyed family in the grand traditional mold of railroad-fortune heiresses Consuelo Vanderbilt and Anna Gould or Chicago department-store heiress Mary Field. Betsey's father had achieved the status of Harvard faculty and had firmly established his reputation as the father of modern brain surgery; he had earned a substantial living from his life's work and had even built up a sizable investment portfolio, but by the time his middle daughter, Betsey, married into the wealthy, aristocratic Roosevelt family, the Depression had wiped out most of his fortune. Although Betsey's mother had come from a socially prominent Cleveland family, the Cushings could not lay claim to the exalted status of the grand Boston Brahmin clans, such as the Peabodys, the Cabots, and the Gardiners. Yet Betsey had snared the prime catch on the marriage mart, thus achieving what would be the first of many brilliant marriages for the three Cushing sisters. Little wonder that these three women, living out the ultimate fantasies of the poverty-stricken, glamour-starved American public, would capture its collective imagination, become the embodiment of its aspirations and dreams, set its fashion and cultural trends, and provide vicarious escape from the dreary reality of dust bowls and breadlines.

2

BUILDING A LEGACY

$\mathcal{I}T$ was no accident that the Cushing sisters married so well. In fact, Betsey's marriage to Jimmy Roosevelt had fallen a bit short of her mother's lifelong ambitions, for as Kate Cushing had once confided to a New York gossip columnist, she fully expected her girls "to marry into the highest level of European nobility or into America's moneyed aristocracy." While the Roosevelts were aristocratic enough, Sara held the purse strings and her $2 million fortune was certainly not in a league with the enormous wealth of the Astors or the Whitneys, who would become later Cushing conquests. Still, Betsey's first trip to the altar was an eminently respectable start, hardly an embarrassment to the enterprising Kate.

Both Kate Crowell and Harvey Cushing had always been highly motivated individuals who knew exactly what they wanted and how to go about getting it, no matter how long or arduous the quest. Kate had, in fact, endured a seemingly endless ten-year courtship while Harvey had worked murderous hours and traveled extensively to hone his professional skills. From her earliest childhood, Kate was strong-willed and goal-oriented, but as a well-bred Victorian young lady, she soon learned to sublimate her strong feelings and mask her steely determination when it suited her to do so. Harvey, on the other hand, showed no such reticence when it came to his ambitions; he attacked his career with all the aggressive tenacity of a terrier sinking its teeth into a particularly juicy bone.

Harvey Cushing was born at home on April 8, 1869, in his family's large house on Euclid Avenue, in Cleveland, Ohio. He was the tenth and last child of Betsey Maria and Dr. Henry Kirke Cushing. While the senior Dr. Cushing's successful practice provided his wife and numerous offspring with all the material comforts, Harvey's mother served as the family's spiritual mentor. Betsey Maria had an understanding nature and a keen sense of humor, coupled with an ardent belief in domestic responsibility. She also had a great love of music and literature, which she passed on to all her children—especially to her youngest, Harvey, for whom she recited poetry each night as she put him to bed.

Harvey attended primary school in Cleveland and then the city's Central High School. Good at his studies and a superb athlete, excelling in baseball and gymnastics, he was also known for his fiery temper, which would stay with him throughout his life. In fact, his brother Alleyne and cousin Perry Harvey frequently taunted him with a popular refrain of the day: "Pepper Pot, Pepper Pot, when you were young, They tell me you had a most fiery tongue."

From Central High, Harvey proceeded to Yale University, where he found the traditional, exclusive Ivy League ambience very much to his liking. There he went out for the "varsity nine," playing baseball throughout his undergraduate years despite his father's snobbish aversion and strenuous objections to his involvement with the team. In fact, one of Harvey's greatest moments was Yale's victory over the Harvard baseball team. He also gained admittance to the prestigious secret society Scroll and Key, but he did not make Phi Beta Kappa. Henry Kirke, who had attained this exalted academic status in his undergraduate years, was sorely disappointed. Still, on June 24, 1891, Harvey did graduate in the upper third of his class. Harvard Medical School had accepted him, and he eagerly anticipated entering in the fall.

In the meantime, he went home to Cleveland for the summer, dividing his time between family and friends and spending most days and occasional evenings boating on Lake Erie. It was during this summer idyll that he began to take serious notice of Katherine Crowell, whose parents were long-standing friends of Betsey Maria and Henry Kirke. The Crowells were spending the season at their vacation home, Breezy Point, near Cleveland. The twenty-year-old Kate was beautiful and high-spirited, a popular member of Cleveland's young social set. Even though Harvey was strongly attracted to Kate, he was not yet ready to commit himself to any woman. As the summer wore on, he began to think more and more of the arduous studies that lay ahead and less and less of serious involvement with Kate.

Late in September of 1891, Harvey Cushing left Cleveland for Boston, where he threw himself into the heavy academic demands of medical school. Despite his massive work load, he always managed to find time for visits to New Haven. No sooner would he set foot on the Yale campus than his heart would lighten, difficult medical studies forgotten as he reminisced about his carefree undergraduate days.

Meanwhile Kate was attending boarding school in Connecticut. Early the following spring, she and her friend Mary Goodwillie visited Boston, hoping to enjoy a day with Harvey. By then Harvey was not only immersed in his studies but spending considerable time at Massachusetts General Hospital, working with his closest friend and fellow medical student, Amory Codman. The only chance Kate had to see her busy beau was when he escorted her and Mary back to the train station for the trip home. Certainly, this must have been a discouraging, if not infuriating, episode in what would prove to be an extremely long and not terribly romantic courtship. But Kate had decided that Harvey Cushing was the man she would marry, and to this end she was willing to bide her time, suppressing her own strong will and deepest feelings.

As Harvey accelerated his studies, he even gave up going home for the Christmas holidays, much to Kate's dismay. The situation was not to improve in the near future, for as Harvey's years at Harvard drew to a close, he applied for and received an internship at Mass General. The grueling schedule at the hospital kept him so inundated with work that he did not even find time to attend his own commencement in June 1895.

Nevertheless, he graduated *cum laude* from Harvard Medical School—a far more impressive academic record than he had achieved in his undergraduate days.

With the aid of Amory Codman, the young intern succeeded in having Mass General acquire and install a fantastic new invention—the X-ray machine, which had first been used at the University of Würzburg in Germany. Thus Cushing and Codman began pioneer work in an entirely new field of medical technology, a field that would soon prove indispensable in diagnostic procedures. Harvey was clearly thrilled with the machine, which he described in a letter to his mother as "great sport—very useful in the out-patient clinic, to locate needles, etc. We could," he added, "look through the chest readily this morning, count the ribs, see the heart, the edge of the liver. It is positively uncanny." Throughout his internship Harvey persisted in the study and work habits that he had acquired during his Harvard years. He was an utter workaholic, as his long-suffering family and sweetheart already knew all too well.

As his internship came to an end, Harvey had to face some hard decisions regarding his career—whether to go abroad to study with some of the finest medical men on the Continent or opt for a prestigious position at another great teaching hospital in the United States. Always a careful man, he weighed his options for weeks. Unfortunately for Kate Crowell, it was highly unlikely that any consideration of their relationship entered into his decision-making process. Nevertheless, Kate remained resolute in her intention to marry him. By this time she was "Harvey's girl," a status that could hardly have provided her with great satisfaction but one that at least saved her from the stigma of spinsterhood.

Harvey finally decided to write to Dr. William Osler, chief clinician at Johns Hopkins University Hospital in Baltimore, in the hope of obtaining a staff position alongside the well-known, highly respected physician. As it happened, there was no opening in Osler's department, but the clinician referred the young man to Dr. William S. Halsted, chief of surgery, who offered him the position of assistant resident surgeon. While this was not the job Cushing had wished for, he was well aware of the great strides Johns Hopkins was making in all areas of medicine and so was quick to accept. The hospital was famed for its high standards of service, its research, its therapeutic achievements—and even its nearly spotless halls and wards, a rarity in turn-of-the-century American medical institutions.

So it was that Harvey Cushing arrived in Baltimore in October of 1896. He was twenty-seven years old, with enormous energy, great confidence in his own abilities, and an all-consuming desire to succeed in his chosen field. Slim and handsome, with an erect carriage and deep-set blue eyes in a narrow face, he had an aristocratic appearance. Self-discipline was perhaps his greatest asset, a quality that he would later pass on to all three of his daughters. With unrelenting dedication and hard work throughout murderous eighteen-hour days, he refined his surgical skills and, exposed to some of the most advanced medical minds of the late nineteenth century, shaped his future genius.

No doctor at Hopkins made a greater impression on Cushing than William Halsted. Brilliant but erratic, Halsted could be enormously hard on those working under him, especially on young Dr. Cushing. Some of the chief surgeon's demands were simply his way of showing the great esteem and affection that he felt for Harvey. There was another reason, far more serious and ultimately far more devastating, why Halsted leaned so heavily on his relatively inexperienced new assistant. The esteemed surgeon was addicted to cocaine. Thus his not-yet-thirty-year-old protégé found himself handling most of the major surgical procedures. It was a tremendous burden on such a young man in such a new, largely experimental field of medicine. At this extraordinarily stressful and precarious time, Harvey was most fortunate to come under the guiding hand of Dr. William Osler, whom he had originally sought as his mentor. In fact, it was Osler who first recognized Harvey's unique talents in the emerging field of neurosurgery, a medical specialty that was only then beginning to receive the attention of the great European medical geniuses. Osler saw to it that the young assistant surgeon became aware of all the medical innovations, both at home and abroad.

And so, with the consent of his superiors at Johns Hopkins, Harvey decided to take off for a fourteen-month sojourn in Europe, combining study in London, Paris, and Bern with all the sights and pleasures of a young gentleman's grand tour. By this time Harvey and Kate—and their respective families—had come to an informal understanding. At last the young couple was indeed, though not publicly, engaged. What torment Kate must have endured over Harvey's latest career move we will never know. She remained loyal and stoical, despite frequent taunts about the seemingly endless courtship. Even if she had wanted to break off the loose-knit relationship after so many years, she could not have done so—at least not without being relegated by turn-of-the-century social conventions to eternal spinsterhood. At twenty-nine years of age and after nine years of courtship, Kate was already beyond a marriageable age, as was Harvey at thirty-one. The jilting of a fiancé, however elusive and uncommitted, would have created a highly scandalous situation, irreparably damaging to a young lady's reputation. Kate remained in Cleveland, hoping desperately that she would soon be able to make a formal announcement of Harvey's intention to marry her.

But Harvey was still otherwise occupied. On July 2, 1900, he landed at Liverpool, immediately proceeding to the London home of Dr. Victor Horsley, the great pioneer in the still fledgling field of brain surgery. After introducing his guest to the Horsley family, the British surgeon took Harvey to see just how brain surgery should be performed. Horsley's speed and almost devil-may-care attitude stunned the young American doctor, but he could not help but admire the neurosurgeon's pioneering spirit.

As it happened, Dr. Osler was also spending the summer of 1900 in England. Once Harvey met up with his Johns Hopkins mentor, the intellectual Osler took him in hand, and together they toured London's museums, bookshops, and outstanding hospitals. Osler was a man of medium build, with a huge mustache, large, piercing eyes, and a swarthy complexion. Yet despite his rather daunting appearance, he exuded an almost godlike charisma. His students, interns, and nurses at Johns Hopkins worshiped him—and Harvey Cushing was no exception.

Osler took his youthful protégé everywhere, to dinner meetings and professional banquets, where Harvey met some of the best-known surgeons in Great Britain as well as equally prominent scientists, writers, and statesmen. While visiting the great London hospitals, Harvey's critical eye took in everything—both good and bad. His diary was filled with sharp criticisms of the "miserable laboratories" and "dreadfully careless techniques." A perfectionist by nature, he was always perfectly dressed even in the operating room. His incessant faultfinding and harsh rebukes, lifelong habits, would never endear him to his colleagues.

Harvey spent weekends with the Oslers, boating and picnicking along the Thames with the illustrious doctor, his wife, Grace, and their young son, Revere. On occasion they would go to the Oslers' seaside summer place at Dorset, with its wonderful view of the Isle of Wight. Commenting on this phase of his time abroad, Cushing wrote, "It's a treat to go about with Dr. Osler. He's a big man here, even bigger than in his own country, and just as nice."

Late in July Harvey and Dr. Osler went to the Thirteenth International Medical Congress in Paris, at which doctors and scientists from every corner of the globe presented papers on the latest medical advances. For the most part, though, Harvey found the meetings disappointing; soon he turned to sight-seeing, thus beginning his lifelong love affair with the French capital. From Paris he set out alone for Switzerland and Italy, finally returning to the United States in August of 1901.

Harvey Cushing had by this time formulated his plans for a bold course of action in his chosen field. Almost immediately upon his return to Johns Hopkins, he appealed to Dr. Halsted to open a separate department of brain surgery. Halsted refused. Like almost everyone in the medical profession at that time, he considered neurosurgery to be an unproven, extremely dangerous specialty. Harvey persisted. After weeks of badgering the chief of surgery, he won Halsted's reluctant consent. The young would-be neurosurgeon was exultant, although he feared that if he failed in his attempts at the riskiest of all surgical procedures, his career would be in grave jeopardy. His self-confidence, however, equaled his medical genius.

Kate undoubtedly expected to be able to make a formal announcement of her plans to wed Harvey in the near future. Once again, she found she would have to bide her time, for Harvey set up bachelor quarters in Baltimore with two other young colleagues from Johns Hopkins, Thomas B. Futcher and Henry Barton Jacobs. Shiny brass plates for all three doctors went up over the front door of the rooming house at 3 West Franklin Street, in Baltimore. It was glaringly apparent that Harvey had no immediate intention of moving into his own home and starting a family.

Approaching her thirtieth birthday, Kate was an attractive young woman of medium build, a little on the plump side, with radiant skin and brown hair and eyes. She was witty and outgoing, with strong opinions and a quick temper that matched that of Harvey Cushing. Kate corresponded with Harvey, sharing news of their families and bringing him up to date on Cleveland social life. Harvey responded on a monthly basis, but his letters were filled with news of his professional progress and little if anything about his social life or the Osler family. During all the years of their long courtship, never once did Kate admonish her intended.

The three doctors agreed to share the household chores, but not surprisingly, Harvey failed to hold up his end of the bargain. He was simply too immersed in medicine. As always, his personal life took a back seat to his profession. Fortunately for the three young bachelors, their rooms adjoined the home of the Oslers, and Grace Osler provided a motherly presence, welcoming the trio for tea, an occasional dinner, and lively, stimulating conversation. These were wonderful days for Harvey. Still, the time was coming when he would have to make a choice between permanent self-absorbed bachelorhood and the more settled, responsible life of a husband and father.

3

THE CHOICE

$\mathcal{B}$Y the beginning of 1902, Harvey Cushing finally reached a decision regarding his personal life. At thirty-three, he must have realized that it was "now or never." If he didn't marry soon, he would probably remain a bachelor forever, a choice he had often considered during the many years of his professional formation. He had established his medical reputation and set up a practice in Baltimore, and he was, quite simply, running out of excuses for postponing his formal commitment to Kate Crowell. The steely yet eternally patient young woman had waited ten very long years for her big moment. She had hung on, as "Harvey's girl," while he completed his studies, then his internship, then his residency. She had sat at home while he had spent fourteen months abroad. And she had tolerated the frustrating months of his Baltimore bachelorhood. Whether Harvey opted for marriage out of pity or love, out of a sense of duty or a real desire to settle down with his intended, only Harvey and Kate would ever know. In February 1902 the couple at last announced their engagement, setting the date for June 10 of that year.

The long-awaited wedding took place in a country setting, near Cleveland, a quiet affair with only family and close friends in attendance. By the first week of July, the newlyweds were in Baltimore, settling into Harvey's former bachelor quarters on West Franklin Street, which his roommates, Drs. Futcher and Jacobs, had vacated for other accommodations in the rooming house. Grace Osler instantly "adopted" Kate, taking the new bride under her ever-motherly wing. As Dr. Osler had been Harvey's mentor, his kindly wife became Kate's, helping her to cultivate the art of keeping a doctor happy without crowding him.

Kate learned her lessons well. Harvey's friends and colleagues were unanimous in the belief that his marriage was a stroke of pure genius. Over the years their opinion remained unchanged. Kate proved to be the perfect wife for the single-minded physician. Devoting herself to his comfort and his concerns, she managed to raise their five children almost single-handedly and to entertain his friends, colleagues, and students with noteworthy graciousness and style.

Like a duck to water, Kate quickly took to the staid, tradition-bound, ever-so-proper city of Baltimore, with its heavy overtones of both southern and British gentility. Even that many years after the Civil War, the city was predominantly Confederate in its attitudes and customs. While the turn-of-the-century skies were beginning to blacken with the smoke spewing forth from the ever-growing number of industrial chimneys, most of Baltimore was cloaked in a mantle of leisure, ease, and genteel comfort. The residents still referred to their front doorsteps as "pleasure porches" and the beaches along Chesapeake Bay as the "pleasure shore." The wide, tree-shaded streets of handsome brick houses surrounding a lovely, well-manicured park lent an air of unhurried elegance to the increasingly urban port city. Coexisting with this southern charm was a decidedly British influence. In fact, entire sections of Baltimore—with typically English-sounding street names, such as Featherbed Lane, Lovely Lane, Johnny Cake Road, and April Alley—seemed more a part of eighteenth-century London than twentieth-century America.

Kate was certainly a well-bred young woman, but the ultra-refined atmosphere of her new home made a lasting impression on her. Throughout her life Kate would exude a highly aristocratic charm and carry herself with all the refined dignity of a lady "to the manor born."

This demeanor would of course influence her entire family, especially Betsey, whose regal style would become legendary.

On August 4, 1903, only a little over a year after her arrival in Baltimore, Kate gave birth to her first child, a boy named William Harvey. The joy surrounding the arrival of the Cushings' firstborn was marred by sad news from Cleveland. Harvey's mother, Betsey Maria, was gravely ill. With Kate and the baby in tow, Harvey rushed home to his mother's bedside. At the sight of her fifth grandchild—the son of her favorite child—Betsey Maria seemed to rally. The young family soon returned to Baltimore. Within the month Harvey had to return to Cleveland, where his beloved mother quietly passed away on October 21, 1903.

Betsey Maria's death was a real tragedy for Harvey, whose life was already beset with grave difficulties. He had entered a long and painful period of professional frustration and failure. Although knowledge of the human brain was slowly increasing through physiological and pathological experiments and through the persistent efforts of a few great pioneer neurosurgeons like Cushing himself, there were no established methods, no basic procedures, for removing brain tumors. Harvey was forced to improvise, to invent all his own instruments, and even to occasionally imperil his patients' lives in his zealous desire to save them. During a period of more than six years, Harvey had a very hard time finding patients, for not many were willing to undergo such dangerous experimental surgery, and an even harder time curing them. The terrible truth was that among the pitifully small number who did submit to the drastic operation, few survived. Between 1901 and 1903, Harvey performed only seven brain-tumor operations—all unsuccessful. The four he performed the following year proved equally fatal.

The stress from this risky and apparently futile struggle to save lives must have been terrible indeed for the young doctor—especially given the highly skeptical attitude of most of his colleagues, who continued to question his motives and methods. A lesser man would undoubtedly have given up and chosen a safer specialty, but Harvey Cushing was very determined. He simply refused to give up. His curiosity, his need to find new answers and develop definitive procedures, never diminished. Certainly personal ambition played a part in his tenacity, but Harvey also felt a strong sense of moral obligation to serve humanity—a grave responsibility he had assumed from the first moment he took scalpel in hand. Despite his repeated failures, he remained convinced that brain surgery could and would make a dramatic contribution to both medicine and humankind. Added to these feelings was a totally unshakable belief that plain, old-fashioned hard work would eventually ensure success in any endeavor, no matter how impossible it might seem.

Even as his operations failed, Harvey managed to push his way to the forefront of his field. His pioneer work began to establish his reputation far beyond Johns Hopkins, and he was soon receiving frequent invitations to speak at other universities, as well as a number of job offers. The University of Maryland wanted him, as did his alma mater, Yale, but he wisely rejected such offers and set about raising funds for the Johns Hopkins University Medical Center and for his research in neurosurgery.

For all the funds he raised for Hopkins, Harvey realized no real personal gain. In fact, during his entire tenure at the growing hospital, he never earned more than five hundred dollars per month, even with the income from his writing and speaking engagements. Possibly in part for this reason—his family was growing by leaps and bounds—and more particularly because he finally realized that it would take decades for Johns Hopkins to reach the status of a first-class teaching institution, Harvey became restless. No matter how much money he brought in from generous benefactors or how far and wide his reputation was heralded, the hospital was still in its adolescence, proving itself little by little. Having gotten his start and established his reputation, Harvey was now ready and eager to practice his specialty on a far larger stage, one with its reputation on solid ground and its resources firmly ensconced. And so it was that he at last decided to accept the flattering offer to teach at his alma mater, Harvard Medical School, and to become surgeon in chief at the Peter Bent Brigham Hospital.

The Baltimore years had been a time of growth for Harvey Cushing and his rapidly expanding family. Mary "Minnie" Benedict Cushing had been born on January 27, 1906; Betsey Maria arrived on May 18, 1908, and a second son, Henry Kirke, made his appearance on May 22, 1910. Now it was time for the Cushings to move on. Kate too was ready for a larger stage on which to perform her highly ambitious social and maternal roles.

4

THE CIRCLE WIDENS

*A*S Harvey familiarized himself with his new surroundings, Kate settled the family into the large, comfortable house at 305 Walnut Street, in the prestigious Boston suburb of Brookline. The substantial pale yellow colonial, with its green shutters, white picket fence, and lovely grounds, had all the amenities that a large and growing family could possibly want. It was exactly the right sort of prosperous setting for the now solidly upper middle-class Cushings. A Hopkins colleague, upon receiving a photograph in the Cushings' first Christmas card from Boston, wrote, "What a bully house, what a nice yard and what a solid fence. I can just see the way in a few years the Boston *jeunesse dorée* and *cultivée* will be sidling up to the fence, cussing the distance from the house and trying to catch a glimpse of the Cushing girls."

Kate decorated her spacious new home with great skill, combining her love of color with her appreciation of quality materials and her ever-present sense of utility and function. Treasured family antiques and heirlooms lent the house an air of dignity, while her choice of colors and fabrics created a stylish yet comfortable homey atmosphere that exuded graciousness and charm.

Harvey's life, not surprisingly, centered around his work. In fact, he devoted more time to his students and assistants than he did to his own children. For him medicine was everything. He did make a few moments for tennis, however, and indeed became an avid player. It was up to Kate to create a harmonious, hospitable backdrop for her busy husband's professional activities, perfecting her skills as a hostess while raising her large family. Like Betsey Maria before her, Kate took on the real burden of parenting and came to understand its great joys and frequent heartaches.

On July 15, 1915, Kate gave birth to her fifth and last child. She and Harvey named the baby girl Barbara, but she would forever after be known as Babe. Even as Kate tended to the infant, she saw the older children off to private day school, all their books in order, every pencil sharpened to a fine point, every uniform immaculately pressed and in perfect condition. Minnie and Betsey, who attended Miss May's School, were always turned out in starched middy blouses and intricately pleated skirts, accompanied by wide-brimmed hats that were changed according to the season. Once a week a seamstress came to the house to sew and repair the family wardrobe, and Kate was not above lending her expert help, especially with the delicate silks and laces. Most important, Kate served as her children's—particularly her daughters'—closest adviser and confidante.

Although Harvey was almost never at home, his presence was always felt. And as socialite and former New Jersey congresswoman Millicent Fenwick explained in a recent interview, "One could sense that everything was done there to make life comfortable for this great man." The Cushing household revolved around his every whim. Harvey seemed almost a guest in his own home, a personable and frequent guest, to be sure, one whose brilliant conversation and intelligence contributed much to the overall atmosphere and whose preferred status earned him the privilege of a household intimate. He might even parcel out an occasional bit of advice, or scold or discipline the family members from time to time. But then, after participating, he would make a speedy exit and go back to the true core of his existence—medicine.

Clearly, Harvey Cushing was no ordinary husband or parent. When the children voiced objections to his preoccupation with his career, it was up to Kate to explain as best she could and to fill the void left by her husband's absence. No doubt she herself would have liked to claim more of his attention, but being the highly disciplined individual that she was, she never gave any outward sign of unhappiness. Only a few intimates of the family, such as Dr. Lewis Weed, when helping Kate put the children to bed, or Dr. Gilbert Horrax, walking with her on the beach on a summer evening when Harvey chose to remain at home in Brookline, came close to guessing her loneliness and disappointment.

Meanwhile, Kate eagerly embraced the social climate of Boston, which was far more formal than that of either Cleveland or Baltimore. Soon members of the old Brahmin families numbered among the many guests who frequently visited the Cushing home. Richard Henry Dana, Jr.; Louis Agassiz; A. Lawrence Lowell; M. A. De Wolfe Howe, editor of *The Atlantic Monthly;* Harvard's former president Charles W. Eliot; and the wives of these distinguished Bostonians welcomed the Cushings into their midst with open arms. In Kate's shrewd estimation, she and her growing brood—especially her girls—were socially on their way.

Harvey had developed a tendency to drag home unexpected guests— eminent colleagues and favored students alike—at all hours. Kate always managed to be prepared. Everyone who entered the Cushings' front door, whether by invitation or Harvey's whim, could be assured of a warm welcome from Kate, the children, and even the servants, who assumed the hospitable manner of the family they served. Invariably the Cushings' daily ritual of afternoon tea became a social occasion, including any number of guests, even though the host, generally engrossed in an experiment or case, seldom appeared. In fair weather, tea was served out by the tennis court; otherwise, family and guests gathered in front of a cozy fire in the house.

As the children grew older, Kate gave them chores. The boys worked on the yard with Gus, the unconventional family handyman, gardener, and jack-of-all-trades. Gus also served as Harvey's driver after the doctor was involved in a traffic accident that, through no fault of his own, resulted in a woman's death. Gus and his employer were devoted to each other despite their habit of arguing and exchanging sharp words.

The girls, under Kate's unerringly critical eye, soon learned to sew, create menus, cook at least a little, and especially to master the fine art of entertaining. In addition to assisting their mother at the tea table, they helped her make the frequent visitors feel welcome and comfortable. So it was that, early on, the Cushing sisters learned to entertain and cater to the comforts of an eclectic mix of personalities, many of whom were masters of their own medical or social fiefdoms. This special learning experience was a far cry from the limited and unchallenging exposure permitted to most young girls of the era. Even then Kate was beginning to groom her daughters for their future starring roles in the world of wealth, power, and social standing. To this end she was willing to bide her time, submerging her great strengths and ambitions in the role of "the little woman" dedicated to the preeminence of her husband. Certainly, as witnessed by her stoicism during her strange, interminable courtship, Kate was exceedingly patient and determined. Even while she was devoting her energies to entertaining Harvey's colleagues and students, her discerning eye was separating those who could be useful to her cause from those who were merely to be tolerated for the sake of her husband's career. She worked extremely hard and with untiring dignity to create a diverse but highly social atmosphere in which her gifted children might grow and develop.

Of course the atmosphere of the Cushing household was not always gracious and serene, for Kate could not forever mask her strong character and quick temper, traits that in every way matched those of her husband. This may indeed have proved to be the salvation of their marriage, for it is unlikely that Harvey would have respected a less dynamic woman. The two shared an abiding love. As a close family friend and neighbor, Mrs. Albert Bigelow, observed, "It is not possible to write about Harvey and not write about Kate also. She not only forestalled all his needs but was in every way the perfect companion for him, for not only did she have a mind and character but she carried herself well and had a beauty of face and expression that well matched his distinguished appearance when they went about together." According to Cushing's biographer, Elizabeth Thomson, the great salvation of their marriage was "the love for one another that was longstanding and deep-running and strong enough to withstand the impact of two highly motivated individuals working out a life together."

Mrs. Bigelow added insight into the life that Harvey and Kate arranged for themselves when she said,

I think another way in which Kate helped Harvey was being just as decided as he was. I don't believe she put up with irritable moods; she probably discouraged them by not being oversympathetic but helped instead all she could by providing cheer and comforts. I supposed it was a fault that he was so absorbed by his work that, although he loved his children, he had little time to take responsibility for them, and I believe he leaned on Kate far more than she did on him. This is all speculation; yet in painting a portrait, that is what the artist has to go by to bring out the character of his subject . . . It is probably far from easy to live with a tense, sensitive, brilliant being, such as Harvey was, but I know Kate superbly achieved her role in guarding his strength to enrich the world and in helping him fulfill his destiny.

It is a fact that Harvey Cushing was devoted to his wife and drew great emotional support from her—far more than anyone suspected. Under Harvey and Kate's leadership, the Cushing household may not always have been a sea of tranquility, but it was a spirited and happy environment.

When, on April 6, 1917, the United States declared war on Germany, Harvey Cushing immediately decided to go to the front in France, thus completely absenting himself from his family for an extended period of time. He departed early in May, stopping in London only long enough to pay his respects to the Oslers. Harvey learned from Sir William and Lady Grace (for Dr. Osler had by this time been knighted) that their only son, Revere, was serving with a British artillery unit in France.

After nearly a year of service under British command, Harvey was summarily ordered to appear before the British commanding general at Tours in May of 1918. The hardworking doctor arrived, confidently expecting to receive a promotion in rank, only to find himself the object of an investigation. The British censors had found a report containing harsh criticisms of a high-ranking English surgeon in one of Harvey's letters. This was not his first offense; he had received a prior warning for sending home to Kate a few amusing words that he had lifted from a British soldier's letter. The current charges, however, were far more serious; in fact, the command staff was even considering a court martial. Had the authorities been aware of the hundreds of pictures, along with detailed descriptions of military matters, that filled Harvey's diary, he might well have faced a firing squad.

Fortunately, the American military authorities learned of Harvey's shocking predicament and came to his defense. Given his position and exalted reputation, the situation was an extremely delicate one. The American and British military staffs began top-level negotiations, and ultimately the latter dropped all charges. Cushing was quietly transferred to the American command in France, where he promptly received a promotion to the rank of lieutenant colonel.

With this promotion came increased duties with the large numbers of wounded soldiers who were flooding field hospitals from the Battle of Argonne. Working grueling eighteen- to twenty-hour days, deprived of meals and sleep, and constantly exposed to the raw elements, Harvey seriously jeopardized his own health. In August of 1918 he contracted a life-threatening case of influenza. To make matters worse, he disregarded the orders of the chief medical officer and returned to the field units within a matter of days, only to collapse with a far more serious condition developing. This time Harvey had no choice but to remain in the hospital. After many weeks of treatment and complete rest, his health improved, but the illness left him with chronic polyneuritis of the legs. This massive inflammation of the nerves of the legs would cause him a great deal of suffering throughout his life, particularly in his later years.

Harvey Cushing returned home from the war in February 1919. Apparently having forgotten or forgiven his indiscretions, the British government presented him with the Order of Bath, and General John J. Pershing, commander of the American forces in Europe, cited Harvey "for exceptional meritorious and conspicuous service as Director of Base Hospital Number Five." Years later, in 1926, the year in which Harvey would win a Pulitzer prize for his biography of Sir William

Osler, the United States Army would belatedly award him the Distinguished Service Medal.

Despite his long absence from home, Harvey was less inclined than ever to allot time to family matters. Exceedingly anxious to put into practice all the advances and discoveries made in neurology and psychiatry during the war years, he actually accelerated his career at Harvard Medical School and his staff duties at the Peter Bent Brigham Hospital. Kate was still very much the single parent, with almost total responsibility for familial duties. Seldom during those postwar years did Harvey find time to go with his wife and children to their summer home at Little Boar's Head, that sliver of New Hampshire that meets the sea. While the family vacationed, he remained at home, immersed in his work.

One summer Harvey accidentally stumbled upon his first intense taste of parenting, for his son Bill took a summer job that kept him in Brookline. With Kate and the other children away, Harvey had little choice but to assume a parental role. This brief close contact with his oldest child seemed to make a profound impression on Harvey. He began to realize that he had not always provided as much influence in the raising of his children as he might have liked. He also began to realize that they had somehow along the way developed strikingly distinct personalities. As they approached adulthood, they were beginning to make demands upon him as a parent. From time to time he would parcel out precious moments from his overloaded professional life to lend an ear to a problem or to give counsel. Despite—or perhaps because of—his infrequent appearances, his children adored him. When he was around them, he was witty, buoyant, and even clownishly silly, qualities that endeared him to his offspring.

Babe, the child who most closely resembled Harvey both in coloring and bone structure, longed for more of her father's attention. "Dear Papa," she wrote at the age of eight, "Stay at home with me and don't go earning money. We'll just do something funny, I'll give you my pennies and I give you my shiney Buckle. I'll arange all for you."

However, it was for Bill that Harvey Cushing reserved most of his devotion and parental concern, possibly because, like many parents, he had the highest hopes for his firstborn. Also in time-honored tradition, Harvey was probably hardest on his oldest child. Indeed, he was often highly critical of the extremely handsome and very headstrong youth, who in turn could be quite rebellious.

Bill first attended Milton Academy and then transferred to Andover at his father's insistence. The senior Cushing was convinced that Andover was the more prestigious school and therefore placed his son among boys who just might prove useful in later life. By 1925 Bill was at Yale. He was not a brilliant college student, but then Harvey had not really excelled in his undergraduate years either. Bill, like his father, did love books; when at home during school breaks, he would barricade himself in the family library, devouring whatever there was to read. Unfortunately, this dedication did not carry over to his studies. At school he was caught up in the "rah-rah" social life so typical in the Ivy League of the era. As he matured, Bill learned to be more tactful in his dealings with his father, and a newfound relationship began to develop between them.

This relationship, however, was to be very short-lived. On the morning of June 12, 1926, just as Harvey was preparing to leave home for the hospital, he received an urgent telephone call. As he listened to the voice on the other end of the line, his face froze and tears came to his eyes. He replaced the receiver, continued on to the hospital, and performed a scheduled surgery. That early-morning call had informed him that Bill had died instantly in an automobile accident near Guilford, Connecticut. Upon completing the surgery, Cushing telephoned Kate at their Little Boar's Head summer home and told her of the tragedy; she made plans to return home. Bill's death was a blow from which Harvey never fully recovered. He was filled with tremendous remorse for not having given his son more companionship, attention, and acceptance in the short time they had had together. That they had at least reconciled their differences and reached some sort of understanding was a small source of comfort to the grieving doctor. Harvey could not transfer any of his strong feelings for Bill to Henry, the sole surviving Cushing son. In a family of go-getters and achievers, Henry seemed almost a changeling. He never did manage to capture a fair share of his father's affections.

Kate was shattered by Bill's death. Perhaps the only thing that saved her was her almost obsessive zeal to launch her daughters into society. As the girls reached their teens and blossomed into the ranks of Boston debutantes, Kate was finally coming into her own, orchestrating their emergence into the rarefied social and financial ambience that would enhance their opportunities and ultimately seal their fates. Gone were the exuberant, carefree days of roughhousing with their brothers, of playing basketball in the gymnasium and baseball and ice hockey on the extensive lawns of their home, with Kate acting as referee in the long-since-accepted absence of their father.

Now that the girls were becoming young women, Harvey's only role was to lay down a few general limits. As Millicent Fenwick explained, it was up to Kate to see to it that the children followed these dicta to the very letter. Kate had once confided to Fenwick that she would never dare tell her husband that the children often broke the strict ten-o'clock curfew he had imposed on them all. The girls were not even allowed to entertain their beaux in the drawing room beyond that hour. Undoubtedly, Harvey had issued this edict at least in part because of his habit of sitting down to his writing in the adjoining study at ten. His belief that any self-respecting young man should go home by that advanced hour was probably more a result of his desire for peace and quiet than of any real Victorian convictions. He was, however, adamantly opposed to the girls' smoking, despite his own two- or three-pack-a-day habit. He absolutely forbade them to drink, which in his opinion was totally improper for young ladies of quality. If the girls ever did smoke or drink, it had to be on the sly.

Harvey greatly valued education. While he did not oppose Kate's decision to send the girls to Westover, a finishing school in Connecticut, he did insist that they take "constructive courses," so that they would know how to do something useful in case they ever had to earn their own living.

In all other matters Kate assumed complete control over her daughters' lives, preparing them in deadly earnest for their stellar futures. According to Millicent Fenwick, she was "the most pivotal person in their lives, certainly as it related to their prominence in the world." This "formidable" woman, Fenwick continued,

> instilled in them the dictum that nothing could stop them in their
> goal to attain whatever it was they wanted in life. She drilled into

them that they were wonderful . . . each of the girls and especially Babe entered the world convinced that they were the most attractive young women in the world, combining both beauty and brains.

Clearly, Kate had her work cut out for her, and it would not always be easy, for each of the girls was an individual and, in her own way, as strong-willed and determined as her mother. Only Betsey, so much like Kate in appearance and temperament and so much like Harvey in character, would prove to be a quick study. From earliest childhood Betsey knew exactly what she wanted and never hesitated to go straight to the point to get it. Once her mind was made up, she never permitted anything or anyone to stand in her way. She also shared her father's desire to help others—and her sense of family was almost dynastic. Of all the sisters, Betsey was the one who most enjoyed being with her mother's contemporaries and who most willingly adopted her mother's manners and aspirations, probably because they were so compatible with her own inclinations and ambitions.

Minnie, without a doubt the brainiest of the trio and the most like her father in intellect, love of literature, and sense of humor, was far more difficult for Kate to control. Minnie loved to listen to her brilliant father as he expounded on scientific subjects and the intricate surgical procedures that he employed. Harvey and his colleagues, in turn, were delighted by the inquiring mind of this eager young woman. Of all the Cushing children, she was probably closest to her father. She was a voracious reader with a great passion for the arts, rarely missing an exhibit at the Baltimore and Boston museums. Not alone in her intelligence and interests, Minnie developed a wide circle of young women friends who sought her out for counsel and direction. But the eligible young bachelors who were in constant attendance at the Cushing home were less enthralled, for Minnie was so tall, so intelligent, and so witty that she generally managed to intimidate them. Such mental and aesthetic keenness was not necessarily considered a virtue for a woman in that era. Much to the distress of her ever-watchful mother, this very independent young woman seemed to have no success in establishing meaningful relationships with her male contemporaries. In fact, on more than one occasion Kate despaired of Minnie's ever making a suitable match.

Babe, so like her father in looks, was known for her generosity. Once she became socially viable, she found herself far more attuned to Minnie and her activities than to the dictates of their mother or the model provided by middle sister Betsey. Nine years Babe's senior, Minnie—both by example and direction—had a tremendous role in forming the youngest sister's character. Babe had a natural curiosity about literature and the arts, and as she grew older, Minnie was only too happy to introduce her younger sister to contemporary classics. The strong bond between these two sisters developed early in childhood and continued throughout their entire lives.

All three sisters were close, often exchanging confidences with one another, but it was obvious from the beginning that Minnie and Babe shared a special closeness. In fact, a very subtle lifelong rivalry was developing between Betsey and Babe. Of the trio Betsey was the one most likely to seek her mother's advice on a personal issue, to bring Kate in to resolve a problem and render the final word. Minnie and Babe, on the other hand, were more likely to follow their own inclinations once they had decided on a course of action. Little did it matter if these inclinations ran contrary to the values and expectations of their mother or middle sister. Needless to say, this made for some very heated discussions among the Cushing women, but for all their disagreements, they never lost respect for one another. While Kate might have acquiesced in a particular battle, especially if she felt that by so doing she was better preparing her daughters for the world beyond the Cushing household, she quite obviously won the war. The girls may have approached the world on their own terms and in their own individual manners, but approach it they did—and in a way that ultimately did Kate's goals and strategies proud. True, they never won the coronets Kate had envisioned, but their glamorous marriages and the phenomenal fortunes that accompanied them made all three sisters legendary figures in the world of international society.

5

THE FAVORITE

*I*T was not surprising that Betsey should have been the first of the Cushing sisters to arrive at the altar. It was, however, somewhat puzzling that she, the one who most heartily embraced her mother's marital ambitions, should have chosen a nearly penniless groom. Certainly, James Roosevelt's lineage and social credentials were impeccable, his father's political status and immense popularity thrilling, and his own popularity and personal charm undeniable. But Jimmy had not finished his education, and his prospects for a large inheritance—with so many relatives vying for Sara's sizable but finite fortune—were virtually nil. The stooped, prematurely balding Jimmy was not even particularly handsome, although his height and fairness, coupled with his social prominence and finesse, made him extremely attractive to an impressive number of young debutantes.

In all probability, Betsey truly fell in love with Jimmy Roosevelt. That, at least, was the consensus among his friends. According to William Hutton, Jimmy's Harvard classmate and an usher at the wed-

ding, the Cushing-Roosevelt alliance was a love match from the start.
In fact, Hutton commented, after meeting Betsey, Jimmy simply seemed
to disappear from the Harvard social scene in which he had always been
so active. His friends rarely even saw him around the Cambridge campus except when he was actually attending classes.

It was also possible that Betsey assumed he possessed more wealth
and glamour than he did, when actually, beyond the Roosevelts' public
image, his was a rather dull, ordinary day-to-day existence. Or perhaps
Betsey was caught up in the thrill of the chase, for Jimmy—fortune or
no fortune—was undeniably a great marital catch. Or maybe, since the
Depression had claimed a sizable portion of Harvey Cushing's nest egg,
the basic financial security that went along with Jimmy's status as scion
of the aristocratic Roosevelt clan was sufficient enticement. Even though
he could not boast enormous wealth, he and his bride of choice would
surely never go hungry. And Jimmy was capable and ambitious, with a
background that was guaranteed to open doors for him; there was no
reason why he should not become a success in his own right. Apparently, that prospect was good enough for Betsey Cushing.

Jimmy, like his father before him, had prepped at the exclusive
Groton School, then—to please FDR and to uphold family tradition—
had gone on to Harvard in spite of his personal preference for the less
snobbish Williams College. Once in Cambridge, he threw himself into
Harvard life with a vengeance, becoming a prominent member of the
class of 1930. He was president of Phillips Brooks House, a fraternity
devoted to charitable activities, as well as a member of Fly Club and
Hasty Pudding, two of the university's most prestigious societies.
Though a trick knee prevented him from going out for running or
contact sports, young Roosevelt was able to row on the Harvard crew.
Jimmy had earned, as his father had, a formidable reputation as a ladies'
man, squiring about far more than his fair share of the socially elite
young women attending the nearby Seven Sisters colleges. Until he met
Betsey.

Once Betsey Cushing caught Jimmy Roosevelt's eye, all the other
debs were forgotten. He fell head over heels in love with this slip of a
girl with brown hair, unusually large blue eyes, and an exceedingly
proper Boston upbringing. Although he was still in his junior year at

Harvard, the couple announced their engagement almost immediately. Not long thereafter, during a school break, Betsey received a distraught call from her future mother-in-law, Eleanor. Jimmy was desperately ill and was calling for his fiancée. "Will you come?" his frantic mother pleaded.

Of course, Betsey hurried to the governor's mansion, where she found Jimmy bedded down with a severe case of pneumonia. Governor and Mrs. Roosevelt received her cordially, but Sara Delano Roosevelt's welcome was noticeably cooler. Apparently, the autocratic, possessive dowager saw Betsey not as an ideal wife for her eldest grandson but as yet another threat to her matriarchal dominance over the Roosevelt men. This reaction was not at all unusual, for Sara felt much the same way about Eleanor—and in fact about anyone who got too close to her son or grandsons. Although Jimmy's manipulative grandmother was a major force to be reckoned with, Betsey was not dissuaded from her matrimonial plans. Her fiancé soon recovered and returned to Harvard. Just two days after his graduation, the wedding came off without a hitch. This may, unfortunately, have been the high point of the ill-fated marriage.

After a glamorous two-month honeymoon in Europe, undoubtedly financed by Sara Roosevelt, Jimmy and Betsey met up with their first taste of reality—a command to appear before the matriarch at her Hyde Park estate. Jimmy's grandmother expected the young couple to give a full accounting of just how they planned to chart their married life, what they planned to live on while Jimmy, in time-honored family tradition, attended law school. To his credit, Jimmy refused any financial aid from "Granny," although he did at first accept an allowance from his parents and temporary lodgings from his in-laws. So it was that the young Roosevelts began married life in the Cushing home with Betsey's family while Jimmy studied law at Boston University Law School. The apparent serenity of this arrangement pleased both the Cushings and the senior Roosevelts but soon proved too dull for Jimmy, or "Rosie," as Betsey called him. It was not long before he rebelled against living on his parents' money and under his in-laws' roof.

As a young man, Jimmy Roosevelt had three major ambitions common to most of the men in his family—to marry young, to gain financial independence, and to become president of the United States. Having already attained his first goal, he was eager to achieve the second. When friends introduced him to a Boston insurance agent named Victor de Gerard, an exiled Russian aristocrat and former officer in the czar's army, Jimmy immediately seized the opportunity and entered the insurance business with his newfound emigré friend. The part-time work proved so lucrative that soon Jimmy left law school without even a backward glance—much to his father's consternation. FDR's unerring political instincts warned him that his son's entanglement in an industry so rife with influence peddling would prove to be a distinct political liability.

Jimmy, however, was determined. As an insurance agent, he was an overnight success—no mean feat during the Depression. Soon he and Betsey were able to move into their own home, at 19 College Hill Road, in Cambridge, which they completely furnished with their profusion of lavish wedding gifts. The de Gerard connection did not last; Jimmy almost immediately moved on to form a partnership with a very shrewd Harvard man named John Sargent. Roosevelt and Sargent formed an immensely profitable insurance agency, and in its first year Jimmy personally raked in commissions totaling around $67,000. Thus he not only gained his much-coveted financial independence but became the wealthiest member of the entire Roosevelt clan—with the exception of his grandmother, Sara.

Once the insurance money began to pour in, Jimmy and Betsey purchased a 140-acre property known as Tory Row, in Framingham, Massachusetts. The young couple settled into the 150-year-old house, with its four chimneys and abundant charm, and began making plans for a family of their own. Soon Betsey gave birth to their first child, a daughter, whom (not surprisingly) they named Sara. Even then Jimmy was beginning to work toward goal number three, becoming chief of Massachusetts political patronage. Clearly, he was looking forward to the day when the voters of the Bay State might consider him for elective office; his sights were set on the governorship. In fact, long after he and Betsey had moved on to Washington, D.C., he was careful to maintain his official residence in Massachusetts. It seemed that Betsey's faith in

Jimmy's potential, if not his romantic appeal, was quickly being rewarded.

As the young Roosevelts were making the transition into married life, Franklin Delano Roosevelt was taking the nation by storm, charging headlong toward the highest political office in the land. Although first and foremost an aristocrat and most comfortable among his own kind, FDR possessed an unprecedented populist appeal. So great was this appeal that it would sweep him into the presidency not once or twice but four times.

Saturday, March 4, 1933—inauguration day—marked the dawning of the New Deal. It was a cold, dreary day in the nation's capital. The trees were stark and leafless, and the city's flags were at half-mast in mourning for Senator Thomas J. Walsh, of Montana, who had died on his honeymoon just days earlier. Not an auspicious beginning for the presidency that would irrevocably change the face of American politics. Betsey and Jimmy, along with all the other members of the large Roosevelt clan, were at the new president's side as he took office with all the pomp and circumstance due to his position. Tradition was the order of the day, beginning with a service conducted by Endicott Peabody, of Groton, at Washington's St. John's Episcopal Church. The Bible that Peabody used for the occasion was the venerable Dutch one that had recorded Roosevelt births and deaths for more than two hundred years. Then Jimmy, as the president's eldest son, led his father to the inaugural podium.

Many hours later, as dusk fell over the District of Columbia and the masses of humanity continued to file down Pennsylvania Avenue, the thirty-second president of the United States entered the White House. Tea was being served on the main floor for literally thousands of guests, including even some high-ranking officials from the Hoover administration. Avoiding the hordes, FDR and his immediate family went straight up to the second-floor presidential study, where the new cabinet, confirmed only a few hours earlier by the Senate, had gathered to be sworn in by Supreme Court justice Benjamin Cardozo. After this relatively private ceremony, the chief executive presented each new cabinet secretary with a freshly signed presidential commission and a hearty handshake, then shouted, "Just a family party—and a good show!" In an instant he was gone, having descended to the Red Room to keep an old promise. There he personally greeted thirteen Warm Springs children with varying degrees of paralysis.

That night seventy-two Roosevelts and other close relatives, including the Cushings, dined at the White House. Even Republican Alice Roosevelt Longworth, daughter of former president Theodore Roosevelt, was there to break bread with her Democratic fifth cousin on this momentous occasion. Then, when the family dinner party was over, the First Lady took five carloads of relatives to the inaugural ball. Her youngest son, John, escorted eighteen-year-old Babe Cushing to the festivities, where over six thousand dancers shuffled around the dance floor while another two thousand of the more sedate guests looked on from the surrounding boxes. All the proceeds from the sumptuous ball went to Roosevelt-designated charities.

Meanwhile, the president remained closeted in his upstairs study, for the "infantile paralysis," or polio, that had stricken him in 1921 made dancing an impossibility. Instead, he spent the time with his longtime political confidant and closest adviser, Louis Howe, discussing the events of the historic day—the day that would mark the beginning of vast political and economic reforms and would also irrevocably alter the personal lives of every member of the Roosevelt family.

The upheaval attending Eleanor and Franklin's ascent to the White House was more psychological than socioeconomic. In contrast to many of their predecessors and successors, the Roosevelts were quite at home in their luxurious new surroundings and at ease in their exalted new roles. In fact, the presidential lifestyle was merely an expansion of their former personal and political existence. Their aristocratic background and years as governor and First Lady of New York stood them in good stead. Even so, the enormous new responsibilities and constant glare of the media limelight were bound to take their toll—not only on the president and First Lady but on their children, in-laws, and grandchildren. Perhaps most profoundly affected were Betsey and James Roosevelt.

Doors opened almost magically to the young couple. While Jimmy was wheeling and dealing, taking full advantage of being the favorite son of the president of the United States, Betsey took to Boston's social scene, hosting and attending all the most important events in the exclusive, Brahmin-dominated society. It was she, not the no-longer-affluent senior Cushings, who staged Babe's lavish debut, presenting her in a dinner dance for nearly five hundred people at the Ritz-Carlton Hotel.

A scant two years after his father had taken office, Jimmy decided that his insurance agency was well enough established to allow him to address his political ambitions. Envisioning an official position within the White House, he moved his family to Washington, settling into an unremarkable house in Georgetown. But Jimmy had not anticipated the interference of the gnomelike Louis Howe, whose political savvy had for many years been FDR's guiding light and who continued to choreograph the president's executive strategies. Howe firmly believed that FDR's high-flying eldest son, with all his politically alarming insurance deals, would be a serious threat to the credibility of the administration. Thus the political mastermind was dead-set against Jimmy's serving in any sort of official capacity, particularly one as sensitive as that of a White House aide. In fact, Howe was determined to place as much distance as possible between Jimmy and the presidency. For a seemingly endless and frustrating time, FDR's closest adviser managed to foil all the young man's plans.

Upon Howe's death in 1936, blood proved thicker than politics. Jimmy succeeded his father's mentor as top presidential aide, with both personal and professional access to the Oval Office. It took months for FDR to spell out his son's precise duties to the press, but at last the nation learned that James Roosevelt would act as a clearinghouse for the problems of twenty-three different government agencies. While this rhetoric made Jimmy sound important enough, it in no way reflected the true power of his role—that of unofficial assistant president of the United States, with all the duties that had previously been the venue of the astute Louis Howe. Young Roosevelt's political instincts were quite good, but his personal judgment was often less than perfect. While he served as his father's top aide, he continued to rake in huge profits from Roosevelt and Sargent—profits thinly veiled from the public eye by being placed in Betsey's name. It was not long before even such old Roosevelt stalwarts as secretaries James A. Farley and Frances Perkins were dispensing less and less patronage—and Jimmy was dispensing more and more. He had become "the man to see" in the White House.

By 9:30 each day, Jimmy was at his father's bedside, along with secretaries Steve Early and Marvin McIntyre, ready to receive the daily orders. Jimmy's appointments began by 10:00, continuing throughout the day and often into the early evening. Almost every night he and Betsey dined at the White House. After dinner they went upstairs to the knickknack-filled second-story study adjoining the president's bedroom.

Once a Washington reporter asked a venerable politician just how much influence James Roosevelt really wielded in the affairs of the nation. "Well," drawled the old-timer, "Jimmy is the last man to see the president of the United States at night." That about summed it up.

Eleanor Roosevelt, too, played a key role in her husband's adminis-tration. As official White House hostess, she was expected to entertain important guests—and entertain she did, both formally and informally, with luncheons, teas, dinners, casual Sunday suppers, and weekend-long festivities. In a seemingly effortless style, she created an elegant yet comfortably hospitable atmosphere for every event, no matter how grand or casual. Of course, the well-bred First Lady drew a firm line between official and unofficial social functions and would never have dreamed of making public the names of the guests who attended the latter. Nevertheless, it was simply a matter of time until word leaked out and the huge number and wide variety of people invited to the White House became common knowledge. The nation's capital was really in many ways a small town, one in which everyone knew everyone else's business—and that business was inevitably politics. Neither Eleanor nor her fascinated public ever lost sight of the fact that any social gathering at the White House, even the smallest, most informal get-together, was in essence a political event and that each and every guest was in some way of political value to the Roosevelt administration. As time went on, Eleanor's role became more substantive. Franklin's paralysis made travel extremely difficult for him. Before long Eleanor was traveling extensively on his behalf, serving as his personal emissary.

As Jimmy's and Eleanor's duties increased, so too did Betsey's own. During her early days in Washington, she had devoted herself to her home and children, serving only as "window dressing" for the Roosevelt administration by attending the obligatory rounds of political and social events. Her appearances were no more or less frequent, no more or less demanding, than those of her sisters-in-law. Even before Jimmy had secured a position in the administration, Betsey was watching out for her sisters' interests. In time-honored tradition she, as the first to marry, felt a strong sense of obligation to see her sisters creditably established. In 1935, once she was firmly established in Washington, Betsey not only gave a second coming-out party, a glittering tea dance at the White House, for Babe, but managed to throw Minnie together with the astronomically wealthy real estate tycoon and FDR's longtime friend and Hudson Valley neighbor, Vincent Astor.

Betsey and Jimmy occasionally entertained at their home in Georgetown. It was at one of these parties that Betsey found the opportunity to introduce her still-unmarried sister Minnie to Vincent. Although Astor had been married to his first wife, Helen Huntington, for well over twenty years, their cool relations and separate lives were no secret. Astor occupied himself with his multitude of business interests and in every spare moment indulged in the great passion of his life—sailing throughout the world aboard his magnificent yacht, the *Nourmahal,* often conducting oceanographic studies on his voyages. Helen, on the other hand, was one of the prime movers and great patrons of New York's classical music scene.

Betsey had no compunction about introducing her sister to this particular married man. In fact, Betsey had very carefully orchestrated the introduction, and she was absolutely delighted by the taciturn Astor's reaction. He was instantly smitten with the bright, vivacious Minnie, whose intelligence was, in his eyes, not a threat but a great asset. Although Minnie was infuriatingly blasé about the brief encounter, Betsey felt certain she had lent a hand in the fulfillment of their mother's ambitious prophecy—and had diminished or at least partially atoned for what she might have begun to perceive as her own marital failure.

While Jimmy was waiting backstage for his starring political role, he and Betsey led a rather dull, ordinary life. In 1936 she gave birth to a second daughter, whom they named Kate. Even after Jimmy's appointment as presidential aide, Betsey tried hard to maintain a semblance of normalcy in their home. Each morning they ate together with the children and then Jimmy would go off to work, dropping his daughter Sara at the Potomac School on the way to "the office." This daily ritual, so much like that of thousands of other well-to-do Washington families, differed only in the mode of transportation. For Jimmy and little Sara were chauffeured in the White House Packard, accompanied by a contingent of Secret Service agents.

Even through the inevitable barrage of publicity that plagued the First Family, Betsey fiercely protected her daughters from the public eye, minimizing their contact with the press. In fact, whenever possible they were absent from the highly visible White House functions. Unlike Anna Roosevelt Dall's children, Buzzy and Sistie, who had become human props for the White House press corps and whose popularity was approximately equal to that of child star Shirley Temple, Sara and Kate Roosevelt were rarely on view. Betsey restricted her daughters' role to private visits with their grandparents and infrequent command performances, where tradition decreed that all the president's children and grandchildren be present—family Christmas celebrations, the annual Easter egg roll on the White House lawn, and an occasional unavoidable campaign appearance.

For a while Betsey was able to maintain her own relatively low profile, but it soon became apparent that she was FDR's favorite daughter-in-law. She lacked the wealth of Franklin, Jr.'s bride, Ethel Du Pont; the youth of John's fiancée, Anne Clark; and the athletic ability of Elliott's second wife, Ruth Googins. But FDR was totally captivated by Betsey's air of quiet, ladylike charm. Eleanor's frequent and prolonged absences left a definite void in the White House. Without the First Lady, all entertaining came to a halt. Then, as now, presidential social events were a political necessity, a means of courting, flattering, thanking, and appeasing key individuals and their spouses—benefitting the party in power and the nation as a whole. An invitation to the White House was a coveted prize, one that created or paid off numerous political chits, which the president might want or need to cash in or repay at any time. Fearing that the administration would suffer for want of an official hostess, the president elevated his favorite daughter-in-law to this position whenever Eleanor was away. As well prepared for this role as her mother-in-law, Betsey nevertheless recoiled from the political scheming it entailed—the machinations on which Eleanor thrived.

Although Betsey might have disliked politics, when it came to entertaining, she was right in her element. Polished from the top of her sleekly
coiffed head to the tips of her immaculately manicured fingernails and
daintily shod toes, she was everything Franklin Roosevelt could have
wished for in a hostess; she was well-bred, with an aristocratic but not
supercilious demeanor, expensively but never flashily dressed, lovely,
graceful, and charming. Most important, she managed to exude all these
virtues without threatening other women or intimidating men—a valuable political skill. In fact, Betsey possessed a unique ability to put
people of great wealth and power completely at ease, massaging their
often massive yet fragile egos with comfortable, relaxing conversation
that most often focused on their talents and abilities. Her earnest attentiveness made every guest feel as if he or she were the most important—
if not the only—person in the room. Betsey pleased the president, as well
as the numerous and varied White House guests.

Unfortunately, as Jimmy's and Betsey's influence in the White House
skyrocketed, their marriage plummeted, probably more because of neglect and tension than because of any outside romantic entanglements.
In effect, their high public profiles created a heady atmosphere that
allowed for few personal intimacies. If ever America had its own Prince
of Wales, it was James Roosevelt, number-one son of the most popular
politician of the twentieth century. And Betsey was a natural for the role
of princess. Little wonder that the fascinated press and the adoring
public should watch the couple's every move with rapt attention. Betsey
and Jimmy were forever in the limelight, which instantly converted
every detail of their lives into front-page news. They could not even
indulge in an affectionate gesture or engage in a minor spat without
making headlines. Few marriages would hold up well to such close
public scrutiny. As it turned out, none of FDR's children managed to
"live happily ever after" in marriage.

Betsey could never really adjust to the highly politicized and publicized Roosevelt lifestyle. She instinctively detested the necessity of garnering votes at every social gathering and was outraged by the
indignities of their fishbowl existence. Not that she was averse to her
exalted financial and social position—or to her publicly acknowledged
status as the president's favorite. In fact, she wholeheartedly returned
his affection with deep and abiding respect and love. Neither did Betsey

despise all the pomp and circumstance, the glamorous trappings of her elevated place in America's First Family. It was probably this fact, above all else, that prevented her from seriously considering divorce. After all, her mother had groomed her for a lofty position in society, and Betsey had never doubted that this would be her destiny. She did not need to be told that, as long as there was a Roosevelt in the White House, any thoughts of leaving Jimmy were out of the question. Such a move would have created a tremendous scandal and would have robbed her of her treasured status. Nor did she need to be told how her mother would have reacted. Kate would have been adamantly opposed, for she was not only intolerant of divorce and horrified by scandal but enamored of the immensely pleasurable perks that she had accrued as mother-in-law to the president's heir apparent.

Betsey was also well aware of Eleanor Roosevelt's outspoken views on divorce. The First Lady had all too often spelled them out privately for her daughters-in-law and publicly for the press and the population at large.

> I am one of those who believe that in almost everything we do in life, prevention is preferable to cure. I feel that a better understanding of the things which make marriage successful and a few more difficulties and safeguards thrown around this very serious step in the lives of young people might be helpful and sometimes prevent the necessity for divorce. If you and your partner in this marital contract do not share the same interests and the same enjoyments, you are not going to find life together very agreeable.

So spoke the woman whose own marital happiness had frequently been called into question. Even as Eleanor traversed the world on her husband's behalf, making every attempt to perpetuate the myth that theirs had been a love match, their true relationship was one of Washington's worst-kept secrets. The consensus was that their marriage had begun as a calculated alliance and evolved into a hard-nosed political partnership.

In any event, it was a little late for Betsey to be thinking in terms of prevention, and there was no real cure for what ailed her relationship with Jimmy. For the time being, she had no choice but to put on the best face possible and to play the role that her mother, the president and First Lady, and indeed the general public expected of her. Like Kate, Betsey was strong-willed enough to be able to suppress her personal feelings in support of her family. And so it was that she continued to act as substitute White House hostess and to make the almost frantic round of teas, luncheons, banquets, ship christenings, and openings of parks and buildings, to maintain the highly pleasing image of a harmonious First Family.

In actual fact, the First Family was anything but harmonious. Ironically, the more Betsey excelled in her role of "first daughter-in-law," the more miserable her life became. By making herself indispensable to the president and by winning his affection, she soon found herself enmeshed in a tangled web of petty family intrigue and jealousy. That these undercurrents should have existed in the White House was not particularly surprising, since they echoed almost exactly the entire mosaic of Roosevelt family life, as dictated by the clan matriarch. Sara Delano Roosevelt had long since mastered the fine art of familial manipulation through tight control of the purse strings. Never one to mince words, she openly disliked and mistrusted anyone who got too close to her most successful son. She brooked no interference from Eleanor, whom she openly humiliated at every available opportunity. When Betsey became a member of the clan, and then FDR's special favorite, the grande dame of Hyde Park constantly upbraided her, too. Eleanor, undoubtedly relieved to have Betsey succeed her at the bottom of the Roosevelt pecking order, closely followed Sara's example by continually berating the latest female upstart. Also like Sara, Eleanor proved to be extremely jealous and protective of what she deemed to be her personal and political territory.

As the First Lady's travels absented her from the White House more often and for longer periods of time, Betsey took up the slack, seeing to her father-in-law's comforts. With his consent and indeed his encouragement, she began to make inroads into the actual management of the White House domestic staff, which, according to Ted Morgan in *FDR,* she thought deplorable—"the worst in the world." One evening, when the family had dined on quail, the president expressed a desire to have quail hash for breakfast the following morning. Betsey immediately proceeded to speak to the cook, Henrietta Nesbit, who informed her that the staff had finished all the leftovers. Later Nesbit reported the incident to the First Lady, complaining that Betsey was constantly giving the staff orders. Eleanor, always more interested in the political ramifications of a social gathering than in the guests' enjoyment of the occasion—and undoubtedly resentful of her daughter-in-law's encroachment on what was properly the First Lady's sphere of influence—gave Betsey a sharp and definite set-down, decreeing that Nesbit would continue to reign supreme in the kitchen. Thus the cook kept on serving up menus that were totally lacking in imagination and gustatory appeal, even at the most important of state dinners in honor of visiting dignitaries. Betsey, so well schooled in the art of pleasing guests, was appalled but nevertheless wisely conceded defeat in this area.

Even so, she continued to cater to the president's every whim, frequently pouring his afternoon tea, accompanying him in his almost daily therapeutic swims, propping his feet on a hassock during the showing of a film at the White House, and even taking him to see his doctor about his sinus condition. No matter how busy her schedule might be, Betsey always managed to share a late-afternoon cocktail with her father-in-law. Here, too, her best efforts met with jealousy and resentment—not only from Eleanor but from Jimmy, who became especially annoyed when his father asked Betsey, as he almost always did, to stay on for a while longer as the others were leaving.

The situation deteriorated rapidly. Eleanor's pique began to surface in the letters that she wrote to her daughter, Anna. The final straw was when FDR arranged for Betsey to accompany him to Warm Springs without fully explaining the plans to Eleanor. After the First Lady found out about the trip, she became almost openly hostile toward her daughter-in-law. From that point on, what had at best been a lukewarm cordiality between the two women was a controlled but nevertheless very disturbing antipathy.

As Anna once explained to writer Bernard Asbell, the president's and Betsey's great fondness for each other triggered a continuous series of annoyances for Eleanor. In Anna's opinion, her mother "was apprehensive" of anyone who earned FDR's attention and affection. "Betsey would come in and sit with father," Anna stated,

> and this would annoy Mother because she felt that Betsey was trying to usurp some sort of position with father. . . . She'd say, "Betsey thinks she owns him, you know. . . ." Betsey would say, "Pa says he wants so-and-so after dinner," and Mother's feeling would be, "Well, Pa should have asked me himself."

In any event, Eleanor had never really warmed to this particular daughter-in-law, who seemed too snobbish and uppity for her taste. The First Lady frankly disliked Betsey's "pretenses" of glamour and the emphasis she placed on social decorum—a lesson she had learned perhaps a little too well from Kate. Eleanor prided herself on her own free and easy style, which never for a moment lost sight of who she was and yet never burdened other people with this awareness. Betsey's aristocratic manner struck her mother-in-law as a bit too heavy-handed, as acquired rather than "inborn."

Betsey, for her part, had never managed to grow fond of her larger-than-life mother-in-law. The two women were simply too strong and too different in personal style and social preferences. In fact, the ever-proper young Bostonian was deeply shocked and offended by Eleanor's friendships with two avowed lesbians, who had become powerbrokers in the New Deal. Influential journalist Lorena Hickok frequently slept in the antechamber of Eleanor's bedroom at the White House, giving rise to a great deal of speculation and rumor. Also very close to Eleanor was New York literary agent and theater producer Elizabeth "Bessie" Marbury, who had produced Cole Porter's very first Broadway show, *See America First,* and who had risen to the highest echelons of Democratic party circles. Only the strong hand of the president himself kept the two lesbians from engaging in open warfare for Eleanor's favor.

That Betsey was frankly embarrassed by her mother-in-law is blatantly evident from a story she recounted to author Ted Morgan. Once, at a White House party for Tallulah Bankhead, who, as usual, was late to arrive, Eleanor asked Betsey to dance. The young woman was positively mortified, particularly "when Eleanor raised her arm, displaying a thick tuft of armpit hair." Still, Betsey could not gracefully decline the invitation, and so she awkwardly struggled through a dance.

When the music stopped, Eleanor chided her: "Betsey," she said, "the boys say you're a very good dancer, but you've stepped on my feet twice."

"Oh, no," said Betsey, "I'm not a good dancer at all, but Missy [Marguerite LeHand, the president's longtime personal secretary] is a very good dancer." Eleanor, Betsey concluded, did not like to dance nearly so much as to *lead*.

As if family politics weren't complicated enough, Jimmy's envy and pettiness made life even more difficult for everyone. He jealously guarded the door to his father's office, often forcing even the closest relatives to wait for appointments. And Jimmy was extremely bitter over FDR's obvious preference for Betsey's company. As the friction between the young couple intensified, their marriage began to come apart at the seams. It was not long before everyone in the White House—and indeed throughout Washington—was aware of their marital woes. Betsey did her level best to protect Sara and Kate from the taint of scandal.

Betsey and Jimmy began to move in very different circles—she among the socially prominent figures who had drifted into Washington on the coattails of the New Deal, he among the high-powered political players who might prove useful once he made his bid for public office. Among Betsey's newfound friends were the aristocratic individuals who, while committed to the implementation of the New Deal, did not spend every waking moment talking politics. To the Anthony J. Drexel Biddles, the Averell Harrimans, and the Mellons, among others, Betsey was grateful for this respite from "shop talk."

Before long Betsey and Jimmy were bickering publicly over even the most trivial things. In the waning days of their marriage, Betsey had only one real friend in the White House—the president of the United States. FDR did his best to smooth over the difficulties and keep the marriage afloat, but it was sinking fast. As Betsey continued to rise in her father-in-law's esteem, Jimmy became ever more critical, finding fault with absolutely everything she did. He carped at the way she had engaged in battle with the White House staff, who, she felt, did not adequately provide for the comforts and needs of America's first citizen. Jimmy was openly hostile about the way she was "taking over" his mother's role. And of course his complaints reflected a great deal of self-interest, since he did not think his wife was taking adequate care of *him*. In fact, Jimmy was once quoted as saying, "I wanted more of her for myself. I was selfish. I never thought about what I should do for her, only about what she could do for me. I wanted her to do for me, not for Father." These attitudes, coupled with the all-encompassing atmosphere of rivalry, strife, and intrigue, and the constant glare of the political spotlight, would finally bring an end to the marriage.

Although the president tried to keep Betsey and Jimmy together, he was at least partly responsible for the highly charged atmosphere that was tearing them asunder. Certainly he was not above manipulating the members of his family by playing them against one another, a strategy that had proved highly effective in his dealings with his political cronies. A consummate politician at all times, FDR never failed to seize the opportunity to make himself the center of political and personal attention, with any number of people vying for his favor. In this way he always managed to keep control, and it was perhaps this very skill that had boosted him up the political ladder from his relatively humble first step, as a New York state assemblyman, to the very top rung—the presidency.

Franklin Roosevelt was very fond of his clever, attractive, refined daughter-in-law. Yet no matter how high she rose in his esteem, no matter how great a share she gained of his affection, the fact remained that she was a pawn in his game of family politics. In effect, his mother, wife, children, and numerous other family members were mere pieces on Roosevelt's chessboard.

It was only natural that his children would rebel against this highhanded, hurtful paternal manipulation, and most often their rebellion took the form of disastrous marriages and messy divorces. In response to what he considered to be a lack of parental love, Elliott practically made a career of such marriages and divorces, along with equally disastrous, messy business ventures. Anna, Eleanor's devout partisan, also took to multiple marriages, with roughly the same success as her brother, Elliott. Franklin, Jr., wound up making a total of three trips to the altar. And John set the longevity record, remaining married to Anne Clark Roosevelt for twenty-seven years before obtaining a Mexican divorce in 1965 and marrying Irene Boyd McAlpin. By that time he was a wealthy Wall Street stockbroker—and a Republican, the only one of the Hyde Park branch of the Roosevelt family to carry rebellion to such an extreme. Jimmy would soon be joining his sister and brothers on the marital carousel, with a total of four marriages to his credit, before finally settling down with his fourth wife, Mary Winskill.

At one point, while agonizing over her disintegrating relationship with Jimmy and the welfare of their daughters, Betsey consulted with her brother-in-law Franklin, Jr. "You knew when you married Jimmy," he said not very reassuringly, "you had your fingers crossed." So much for brotherly counsel. Jimmy had once told his brother John that he found all pregnant women repulsive. This remark had circulated throughout the family and eventually reached Betsey's ears, wounding her deeply.

As the decade of the thirties was drawing to a close, so too was Betsey's marriage. Jimmy was spending more and more time away from the family hearth, and Betsey, at FDR's urging, was valiantly trying to put her marital difficulties on the back burner and to carry out her duties both in her own home and at the White House. Although her life was a shambles, she had decided to bide her time, going through the motions of a marriage that had all but ceased to exist. It was fortunate for FDR that she did. Even then the political clouds over Europe were beginning to darken alarmingly. Hitler had already cast a menacing eye beyond the borders of his own nation, and his booted storm troopers were about to begin their inexorable march. FDR was preparing for the worst possible global scenario and the beginnings of America's lend-lease program to Great Britain. His never robust physical strength was taxed to its very limits. Eleanor was traveling almost nonstop, carrying the president's message of solidarity to America's allies. Soon Betsey, with help from Anna, found herself shouldering almost full responsibility for the White House social functions. In addition, as Franklin Delano Roosevelt became the first president in the history of the United States to seek a third term in office, he needed Betsey to manage the many obligatory fundraisers.

These final days before World War II were the headiest times of all, and Betsey rose admirably to the occasion, throwing herself into all the social and political events with a vengeance. The frenzied round of activity barely gave her time even to think about her marital woes. She received great satisfaction from the knowledge of how greatly she was helping her beloved father-in-law. Unfortunately, the stressful times, the constant media coverage, and the frenetic pace did not help to unite the Roosevelt clan. Rather it tore them even farther apart, raising their constant bickering to a feverish pitch.

Despite these trying circumstances, Betsey had the once-in-a-lifetime opportunity to shine as she never had before. In those final prewar days, she became the most visible and most gracious member of the First Family during the historic visit of Britain's King George VI and his lovely Scottish-born consort, Queen Elizabeth. The entire country was enthralled by the royal tour, for this was the first time a British monarch had ever set foot on U.S. soil.

President Roosevelt was at the railroad station to meet the silver and blue royal train. "At last I greet you," said FDR almost humbly as King George and Queen Elizabeth alighted onto the platform.

To which the king replied, "Mr. President, it is indeed a pleasure for Her Majesty and myself to be here."

Thus began one of the most momentous official visits ever to take place in the United States. Despite the intense ninety-plus-degree heat, the president and his family entertained the king and queen in befittingly royal style. The entire Roosevelt clan turned out to celebrate the occasion, with matriarch Sara Delano Roosevelt casting herself in the role of America's Queen Mother—every bit as formidable as the British dowager Queen Mary. Also present were the First Lady, daughter Anna, and all the Roosevelt sons and daughters-in-law, among whom Betsey Cushing Roosevelt emerged as the star player. In her own regal yet gracious and charming manner, she captivated both King George and Queen Elizabeth. This meeting proved to be the beginning of a lifelong friendship with the queen (today's beloved Queen Mother).

The round of elegant Washington entertainments paled by comparison with the Hyde Park picnic that the president hosted on June 11, 1939. This event—complete with hot dogs and cold drafts of Rupert's

beer—captured the imagination of the entire nation, whose many impoverished citizens heartily approved of the unpretentious activity and
humble cuisine. To the nation's delight, the king even spilled mustard
on his waistcoat.

At the wheel of his Ford touring car, specially adapted with manual
pedals, the president whisked the king and queen around the extensive
grounds of the Hyde Park estate. Although this carefree, informal tour
gave Scotland Yard palpitations, it greatly pleased the royal couple and
the American public. At one point, when Betsey's large picture hat flew
off, the king, seated next to her, asked the president to stop the car and
then graciously got out to retrieve it.

Meanwhile, Sara Roosevelt had quite different ideas about entertaining royalty, and it was well reported in the nation's press. The Roosevelt
matriarch gave a formal dinner for the royal couple at her Hyde Park
home. The president, to her displeasure, had drinks brought in before
dinner. It has been reported that the president said to the king, "My
mother thinks you should have a cup of tea. She doesn't approve of
cocktails."

The excessively shy monarch thought this over for a few moments,
then observed, "Neither does my mother." They then picked up their
glasses, raised them to one another in an unspoken toast, and quaffed
their martinis.

Dinner proved to be a disaster and a number of family members who
had suffered humiliation at the hand of Sara Delano Roosevelt readily
reported on it. The food was good, but a table loaded with fine china
collapsed, then a butler fell down the stairs, spilling decanters, glasses,
and ice at the feet of the king and queen.

Sara was, of course, humiliated, but her plight certainly did not
arouse any sympathy in Betsey's heart, for over the years she, like
Eleanor, had suffered far too often at the matriarch's hands. Betsey
undoubtedly felt that the incidents were unfortunate, but she surely
must have felt some satisfaction over Sara's social embarrassment. For
once the old tyrant had gotten her comeuppance.

The royal visit proved to be the swan song of Betsey's White House
years. For all practical purposes, her marriage had ended more than a
year earlier, in May of 1938, when Jimmy had asked her for a divorce.

When she refused he insisted on a permanent separation. Around that time he had checked into the Mayo Clinic, in Rochester, Minnesota, with a perforated ulcer. There surgeons had removed two-thirds of his stomach, and during his long period of recuperation, he had managed to fall in love with his nurse, Romelle Schneider.

Jimmy had a considerable amount of time to review his life and bring into focus various aspects of his relationship with Betsey and his newfound sentiment for his attending nurse. He reasoned that Romelle needed his help as Betsey never had. He further reasoned that, being from a blue-collar background, Romelle possibly saw him as a glamorous figure from the world of society and politics, someone who could do a great deal for her. This was certainly a once in a lifetime chance for a girl from smalltown America, and that he was the son of the president of the United States only added to the allure. As the romance progressed in the postoperative period, Jimmy decided to take this attractive young woman with him to California to nurse him back to health.

Jimmy resigned from his White House post and was hired by movie mogul Samuel Goldwyn as a studio vice president, with a starting salary of $25,000 a year. Perhaps he did need a long recuperation and considerable care, but he gave little thought to his wife, Betsey, and even less to his young daughters, Sara and Kate. Surely they must have been in as much need of a father figure as Romelle Schneider was. Betsey had actually followed Jimmy to California, but he had again requested a divorce and sent Betsey packing—this time for good.

Once Jimmy had more or less settled in Hollywood, the fact that he had abandoned his wife and children could no longer be ignored or forgotten in a flurry of activity. The president worried not only about the political fallout but about how to soften the blow of the scandalous affair for his favorite daughter-in-law and his beloved grandchildren. Betsey was eating dinner at the White House just after she had first learned that Jimmy had filed for divorce. As she recalls, Eleanor stared at her throughout the nightmarish meal, waiting for her to cry, but she refused to give in to her emotions.

The family was divided over the divorce. The president was firmly in Betsey's corner, even insisting that his personal attorney and longtime friend, Basil O'Connor, represent her. "Jimmy," FDR commented to William O. Douglas, then chairman of the Securities and Exchange Commission, "what a problem he is!"

Anna and Eleanor, not surprisingly, stood up for Jimmy. They both felt that Betsey had deliberately set out to curry the president's favor and remembered the numerous occasions when Jimmy had been tired and had wanted to go home but Betsey had insisted on waiting until the last minute to have a drink with her father-in-law.

In the midst of this domestic havoc, Betsey was shattered by the news of her father's death on October 7, 1939. Harvey Cushing had died in New Haven from a coronary occlusion, just two years after retiring as the first Sterling Professor of Neurology at Yale University and devoting himself to writing. Although he had never had the least notion of bedside manner, he had been a cool, clear, sure medical giant, always remembered for his great contributions to the field that he had pioneered.

Harvey Cushing had not often been present during his children's formative years, but he had indirectly taught and influenced them by his example, and they had loved and respected him. His death was a devastating loss to them all, particularly to Betsey, whose own family was in the process of falling apart.

News of the Roosevelt divorce first hit *The New York Times* on February 16, 1940. Less than a month later, with her lawyer and her brother in tow for legal and moral support, Betsey shuttled from Manhattan to Los Angeles to have her day in court. She arrived at the courthouse wearing a luxurious mink coat and a broad-brimmed spring hat, seeming almost lighthearted as she managed a wry smile for the hordes of reporters who had gathered outside. Jimmy had sued for divorce on the grounds of desertion, and she had countersued on the grounds of cruelty and desertion. As Betsey testified, she had left Jimmy, but only at his insistence and because she thought it would be best for her children. Her brother, Henry Cushing, testified that "her attitude was one of great mental distress and she initially had no desire for a divorce." That was before the president's personal lawyer and her legal counsel, Basil O'Connor, convinced her that it would be better all around that she agree to go through with the divorce. With that accomplished, on March 3, 1940, Los Angeles superior court judge Thomas C. Gould approved an interlocutory decree for Betsey Cushing Roosevelt. Such a decree did not allow the parties to marry until a property settlement could be worked out between the couple's lawyers. This was done almost immediately in chambers. On the basis of Betsey's cross-complaint and the fact that Jimmy had not contested the divorce nor appeared in court, the judge granted the divorce and approved the terms of an out-of-court settlement.

This settlement gave Betsey custody of the two children, Sara, then seven years old, and Kate, then four. Each girl would receive $167.50 a month until reaching the age of twelve; after that each would receive $250 a month, plus some dividends if Jimmy were to make more than $50,000 a year. Betsey was given an immediate lump sum of $65,000 and an option of either $50,000 more after five years or $5,000 a year until she remarried.

When contacted by the *Chicago Herald American* and told that Betsey had received her divorce, Jimmy told the reporters that he was "not interested" in hearing the terms of the settlement. Nevertheless, to meet these financial obligations, Jimmy had to sell Tory Row, the Framingham property from which he had once considered making a run for the Massachusetts governorship. At the time of the divorce he was president of his own film company, Globe Pictures, and he and Romelle Schneider were an integral part of the Hollywood social scene. The movieland gossip columnists expected the couple to wed in the near future, and, in fact, they did marry in April of 1941.

While the Cushing-Roosevelt divorce action had been hot copy in every newspaper throughout the country, not one word had appeared in Vincent Astor's magazine, *Newsweek*. Obviously, Astor had refused to print the story—whether out of loyalty to his lifelong friends, the Roosevelts, or fear of offending his frequent companion, Minnie Cushing.

Betsey, having dubbed herself Mrs. B. Cushing Roosevelt, returned to New York immediately after the trial, once and for all leaving the social and political merry-go-round of the Roosevelt White House. The choice of Manhattan as a new home base seemed a logical one, for Betsey's sisters were living there, as was their recently widowed mother, Kate (now known as Gogsie, thanks to her granddaughters). Then, too, if

Betsey planned to bag a wealthy second husband, there was no greater hunting ground than the glitzy world of New York café society, with its multitude of millionaire playboys. Given her ex-husband's shaky financial status, her own lack of personal fortune, and her two daughters to provide for, an older and wiser Betsey was setting out to make herself a highly visible presence in the glamorous world of top-drawer New York society. Needless to say, Gogsie was monitoring Betsey's every move.

6

BABE'S TURN

HE summer of 1940—so dramatic in the annals of world history—
was a dull time for the Cushing sisters. For a period of about five
months, between Betsey's divorce and all their future brilliant marriages, not one of them had a husband.

Gogsie was undoubtedly at her wits' end. In all likelihood she had
pinned her highest hopes on Babe, the youngest and unquestionably the
most beautiful of her trio of lovely daughters. Extremely tall and slen-
der, with raven hair and sparkling dark eyes, Babe had the classically
perfect features of a Greek goddess and a warm, sunny, generous nature
that drew people to her.

After graduating from the Westover School in 1933 and making her
debut the following year, Babe seemed a sure candidate for an early and
brilliant marriage. She was a smashing success in her first season, the
cream of the year's crop of Boston debs. She threw herself wholeheartedly into the endless round of coming-out parties not only in Boston but
in New York.

Early in 1934, while riding home with a group of friends from a Long Island party, she was involved in a very serious automobile accident. Her fabulous face was nearly destroyed, smashed almost beyond recognition, and most of her teeth were knocked out. It took months of reconstructive surgery, all strictly monitored by her father by phone, but she emerged as beautiful as she had ever been, despite having to wear false teeth. Looking positively stunning, she made her bow to Washington society at Betsey's tea dance, with only her family and closest friends any the wiser.

Despite her two wildly successful seasons, Babe did not allow any of the charming, social bachelors to snatch her up. Instead she moved to New York and got a job at *Glamour* magazine, later becoming a fashion editor at Condé Nast's *Vogue*. According to Millicent Fenwick, who worked there with Babe in the late 1930s,

> Babe was a wonderfully warm human being, genuinely interested in people, not just family and friends but also coworkers. The most lowly employee at Condé Nast was a recipient of her kindness.
>
> And I myself can cite an example of Babe's kindness. During this period when I was struggling to work and raise my children, I mentioned to her that I had planned a trip to England to visit my sister. Babe inquired if I had a warm coat. When I informed her that I did not, she offered me a lovely gray squirrel jacket, for which I paid one hundred dollars. And keep in mind that this fur jacket was one of her most prized possessions at the time. Gestures like that were so typical of Babe then and throughout her life.
>
> Babe was like a stove, a furnace, she generated so much warmth to everyone she came into contact with. She had such a common touch. And she enriched all our lives—just like a ray of sunshine.

Unfortunately for Gogsie's schemes, Babe, rapidly approaching the ripe old age of twenty-five, appeared to be far more intent on furthering her career as an up-and-coming fashion editor than on snaring a suitably wealthy and aristocratic husband. In fact, Babe was a raving success among the distinguished group of elegant young women at *Vogue*— including Millicent Fenwick, Connie Bradlee (grandniece of the magazine's legendary editor, Frank Crowninshield), Helen Weston, Muriel Maxwell, and Sally Kirkland—and seemed well on her way to being the sole career woman in the Cushing family. In a recent interview, a Burden family member who knew all three sisters well spoke of this same period in Babe's life: "Babe lived at the St. Regis occasionally while working at *Vogue*. Lived with Serge Obolensky quite openly." When asked how the Cushing family permitted it, this individual replied, "Morality is for the middle classes."

In a recent interview Alexander Liberman, current editorial director of Condé Nast, spoke fondly of Babe and the days when they worked together. Nast himself had hired her, as he had her contemporaries, for social standing and glamour rather than her educational credentials. According to Liberman, the Social Register was the great publisher's bible. He hired and allowed to be photographed only those whose blue blood entitled them to appear in that rarefied context. In an era when bright, socially elite young women did not necessarily attend or finish college and did not quite know what to do with themselves before marriage, Condé Nast served as a sort of "finishing school." These beauties worked for almost nothing, perhaps ten dollars a week, for almost all were wealthy and didn't need money.

Babe loved the glamorous world of fashion, with all its magnificent clothing and glittering social functions. She was extremely photogenic and often posed for the fashion photographers, both in her own right, as one of the Cushing sisters, and for *Vogue* layouts. Her reputation as the most beautiful woman in New York was especially gratifying for, as Liberman remembered, "This extraordinary beauty of all times was a miracle of reconstructive surgery. But the face," added Liberman, "had a . . . sort of nobility that came across in such a striking fashion in all those photographic sittings."

Like Fenwick, Liberman remembered her as "charming, generous, and kind, and very popular." Moreover, she was a "very good sport, not at all distant . . . or pretentious." And she also had brains. In short, Babe Cushing was almost too good to be true, and it was inevitable that sooner or later she would make a match of which even her exceedingly ambitious mother would approve.

And so it was that at last, on September 6, 1940, Babe announced her

engagement to Stanley Grafton Mortimer, Jr., a New York and Tuxedo
Park socialite and the grandson of one of the founders of Standard Oil.
He was gorgeously handsome—"absolutely one of the handsomest men
I had ever seen," reminisced Newport socialite Tanya Rhinelander—
and wealthy, from the exclusive enclave of WASP old money, which
turned up its collective nose at the nouveaux riches social climbers who
were making inroads in Newport, Saratoga Springs, and Long Island's
Hamptons. Stanley had attended Harvard and was rapidly rising in the
dynamic, competitive world of advertising, already an executive. His
breeding was impeccable, and among his distinguished ancestors he
counted John Jay, first chief justice of the U.S. Supreme Court. Although
he lacked the coronet that Gogsie had dreamed of, he was otherwise a
nearly ideal match.

The wedding took place on September 21, 1940. Unlike Betsey's
highly public extravaganza, Babe's was a relatively small, private affair.
The noontime ceremony at St. Luke's Protestant Episcopal Church was
performed by the rector, the Reverend William Grainger. Attended only
by her young nieces, Sara and Kate Roosevelt, the glamorous bride wore
a deceptively simple gown of white silk jersey, with long sleeves, a high
V neckline, and a short train. Topping the understated elegance of the
dress was a glittering coronet of rhinestones and a lavish tulle veil. In her
hands Babe carried a crescent-shaped bouquet made up of a variety of
pure white flowers. Henry Cushing, the bride's brother and the only
surviving male member of her immediate family, gave her away in
marriage.

The reception was held at Heather Dune, Gogsie's leased summer
home in East Hampton. Lawrence, maître d' of Vincent Astor's St. Regis
Hotel, personally supervised the catering of the elegant reception feast.
The guests sat at tables on the blue-tented veranda, with its spectacular
view of the ocean.

Not far from Heather Dune the dour head of the American branch of
the Astor family had docked his yacht, the *Nourmahal,* in order to
attend the reception. Vincent Astor's primary reason for coming to East
Hampton that day was of a far more personal nature, for at last he was
able to tell Minnie, by then his longtime mistress, that she could begin
planning for her own wedding. Helen Huntington, Astor's wife of

twenty-five years, had secured a divorce in Cody, Wyoming, on September 4. The split was not yet common knowledge, and even the all-knowing Hearst gossip columnist Cholly Knickerbocker (in reality, Maury Paul) had not caught wind of it until nearly two weeks after it was final; in fact, he had only hinted about it two days before Babe's wedding. For the time being, Minnie's impending marriage would have to remain top secret, since Vincent, always extremely leery of publicity, greatly feared that the viperous New York gossip columnists would get hold of the news that had already been grist for the rumor mill for more than a year.

When Babe tossed her bouquet, Minnie caught it, thus adding fuel to the flame of rampant speculation regarding her relationship with Astor. In any event, had anyone cared to notice, the look of absolute glee in Gogsie's eyes would have betrayed her tremendous sense of triumph. Once again she had orchestrated a brilliant marriage. No sooner had the last guest departed from Babe's reception, than Gogsie was beginning to map out a strategy for her eldest daughter's marital venture—with the biggest catch of all.

And then, too, there was Betsey to consider. Despite certain wartime inconveniences, New York offered an ideal camp from which to launch a strategic campaign. With Babe solidly married to her Tuxedo Park aristocrat and Minnie about to wed the cream of old-guard New York society, Gogsie was already planning to devote her full attention to capturing a new spouse for her middle daughter. This time the ambitious mother was determined to make absolutely certain that Betsey's choice would be uncompromisingly "top drawer," with not only impeccable social credentials but vast wealth to accompany them. At her mother's relentless and vehement urging, Betsey began to sift through the list of eligible candidates. Mr. Right's large personal fortune should not be tied up in trusts or based on expectations of a future inheritance. In fact, Gogsie had not lost sight of her lifelong hope for a coronet for at least one of her daughters.

However, as Gogsie was new to New York, she first had to cultivate at least a few key allies, people with influence who themselves traveled in the highest echelons of New York society. One of these allies was Jerome "Jerry" Zerbe, the premier photographer of both the old guard and the headline-grabbing café society. That Zerbe's brother-in-law was Roy Larsen, right-hand man to publisher Henry Luce, was a real bonus, for the Larsen connection assured the Cushing sisters of more than their fair share of publicity in *Time* and *Life* magazines. Another valued ally was Mrs. Charles Dana Gibson, one of the five famed Langhorne sisters of Virginia and the original model for her husband's immortal illustration, "The Gibson Girl." Yet another of Gogsie's major promotors, another Langhorne sister, was the indomitable Lady Nancy Astor, of the British branch of the Astor family, who was the first woman ever elected to the Parliament. These very influential people opened doors to the Cushings that were closed to ordinary mortals.

At first, during the early days of the 1940s, Betsey would venture out to a few select Manhattan restaurants and war-relief fund-raisers, usually in the company of her married sisters (minus their husbands, of course). However, the sisters were smart enough to realize that if they were going to vie for the attentions of New York's fabulously wealthy playboy "royalty," then they would have to become more visible. After all, there were a limited number of available multimillionaires, and the sisters never lost sight of the fact that they faced competition not only with attractive young society women but glamorous stars of stage and screen. Such legendary bachelors as Jock Whitney, Cornelius Vanderbilt Whitney, Alfred Gwynne Vanderbilt, and Laddie Sanford were as well known for their nocturnal gadding about as for their immense wealth. The sisters' proper Boston upbringing was, quite frankly, cramping their style.

And so it was that, with Gogsie's consent, the Cushing sisters decided to bend their exceedingly strict rules of decorum just a little and to venture out into New York's glittering supper-club scene. And that meant becoming regulars at El Morocco, the most prestigious nightclub of all. As another proper Bostonian, columnist Lucius Beebe, wrote, "It was John Perona [owner of El Morocco], of all the nightclub proprietors of the world, who quickly discovered that the fanciest floor show imaginable to a chic and witty audience of New Yorkers is themselves." And Beebe was right. New York socialites were absolutely fascinated by the opportunity to see and be seen, to slander one another with witty repartee, and to bow to themselves in the mirror—and they were willing to pay fabulous sums to do it. The fame, feuds, occasional loyalties, witticisms, and general after-dark conduct of the celebrities who flocked to Morocco (regulars invariably dropped the *El*) became symbols of top-drawer New York urbanity.

It was against this glitzy backdrop that the Cushing sisters, showing themselves to great advantage, plotted their strategies. Information gleaned in the Morocco powder room—who had just married, who was about to be separated or divorced—was ammunition to add to their family arsenal, to share and catalogue and carefully store for future use.

In a recent conversation, a onetime family member explained this phenomenon:

> The Cushing sisters and their mother were very much like a small family-owned business, where the decisions concerning each of the sisters were put on the table, discussed, debated, and finally put to a vote. . . . Gogsie Cushing, like her daughters, had a voice, a vote, but unlike the three girls, she held veto power.

Meanwhile, Babe was entering the most rarefied social stratum on the eastern seaboard—perhaps in the entire country. The Mortimers, along with their friends and neighbors the Pierre Lorillard family, were the pillars of Tuxedo Park society, where wealth was simply assumed and was deemed to be of secondary importance to old, illustrious family and flawless breeding. Tuxedo Park was a rustic area in the Ramapo Mountains, once home to an Indian tribe and only forty-odd miles from roistering Manhattan. At the end of the nineteenth century it had become the home of New York's most elite, well-bred families, inaccessible to anyone of Jewish or other "immigrant" background—in fact to all but a chosen few. The haughty, horsy, quietly athletic residents greatly valued their rural setting, with its deer, partridge, pheasants, and wild turkeys, and considered it vastly superior to contemporary society.

The centerpiece of Tuxedo Park social life was the Tuxedo Club— open only to Tuxedo Park Association members and their families— particularly its annual Autumn Ball. This must-attend festivity had made history in its very first season, in 1886, when young Griswold Lorillard and a few of his friends had daringly worn tailless dress jackets. Thus was born the tuxedo, the standard formal evening wear for gentlemen ever since.

Babe and Stan Mortimer frequently visited the senior Mortimers at their Tuxedo Park estate, but it was in a triplex apartment at 225 East Fifty-first Street in Manhattan that the newlyweds set up housekeeping, aided by the fifty thousand dollars that Stan's Tilford grandmother had left him from her huge Standard Oil fortune. While this did not make the young Mortimers as fabulously wealthy as Gogsie might have wished, it did allow them a degree of luxury. Cholly Knickerbocker rated them among the distinguished "young marrieds" in his listing of "The Old Guard" and "Café Society." Given Stan's family background, he and Babe were in the former category, which in Cholly's opinion—though clearly not that of the Tuxedo Park residents—was grade B. Given time, the young Mortimers might have made it up to grade A, to join the ranks of the trendsetting socialites of New York's café society, but fate would decree otherwise.

Babe continued her work as a fashion editor at *Vogue* well into the first year of her marriage, only taking temporary leave of her job when she became pregnant with her first child. Shortly after the United States entered World War II, on December 8, 1941, Stan enlisted in the fledgling Navy Air Force and was posted immediately to the Naval Training Center in Pensacola, Florida. This northwestern Florida town, located on an arm of the Gulf of Mexico, was hardly known as a fashionable watering hole. In fact, it was a tawdry seaport town whose sole industry was catering to the baser desires of naval personnel. Babe, pregnant with her first child, accompanied Stan to Pensacola and tried living there for a while. Her next-door neighbors were William and Joan Chapin Hutton. Hutton, an air cadet, was an old Harvard buddy of James Roosevelt's who had served as an usher at the Cushing-Roosevelt wedding. Even with the worthy companionship of the Huttons, Babe simply could not tolerate the seedy serviceman's town, with all its fleshpots and boozing young naval officer candidates. Babe soon took her wounded sensibilities back to New York, where she returned to her job at *Vogue*. Meanwhile, Stan completed his pilot's training in Pensacola and was later stationed in the South Pacific. In 1945, he returned to New York, but was drinking heavily and subject to mood swings.

In 1942 Babe gave birth to a son, whom they named Stanley Grafton Mortimer III but nicknamed Tony. A year later their daughter, Amanda Jay, was born. Although Babe's job and two young children demanded a great deal of her time, she did manage to partake of Manhattan's glamorous social life during Stan's absence. She had a legion of admirers and escorts, invariably from the exclusive ranks of the Social Register. Among these notables were Serge Obolensky, Russian prince, sometime brother-in-law of Vincent Astor, and onetime general manager of Astor's St. Regis Hotel; Tommy Tailor; and occasionally Babe's own brother-in-law, Henry Mortimer. Babe took to the café society scene, dominated by the madcap bicontinental set that gathered around the Duke and Duchess of Windsor and other emigré European royalty.

Even before World War II drew to a close, Babe had to face the fact that her marriage was for all practical purposes at an end, for Stan's long absence had not made her heart grow fonder. The war years had just proved too much for this seemingly golden couple. Babe, like Betsey before her, struggled to decide whether to seek a divorce. Of course the decision was not hers alone to make; it was definitely a matter for the Cushing family council. The idea of a second divorce was not at all to Gogsie's liking, especially since, as had also been the case with Betsey, Babe had no multimillionaire suitor waiting in the wings to make her an offer. In the end, the chairwoman of the Cushing board let maternal concerns override material considerations and so cast her all-powerful vote for the divorce action—or at least, she did not veto it.

Unlike Betsey's divorce six years earlier, Babe's was quite amicable. There were no recriminations between the two parties. Stan allowed Babe to have custody of Tony and Amanda, with a substantial trust fund to meet their needs, and Babe in turn permitted him generous visitation and vacation rights. The divorce was granted in Florida in May of 1946, and Babe returned to New York a free agent.

She appeared quite willing to devote herself to her two children and her career at *Vogue*, which was becoming increasingly important to her, but she had her mother to contend with. Gogsie Cushing had never been in favor of careers for her girls. Now that Babe was divorced, with children to care for, Gogsie was completely determined to find a suitable husband for her youngest daughter. In no time she had Babe studying lists of potential mates. The criteria were every bit as stringent as they had been for Betsey. The man Babe chose would have to have a great deal more than fifty thousand dollars in hand.

Fortunately, husband-hunting was a lot easier once the war was over and the long-absent cream of the crop of eligible bachelors and recently divorced young men had returned to their favorite old Manhattan haunts. In addition, Babe's outstanding looks, remarkable personality, and glamorous but unpretentious flair almost guaranteed her matchmaking mother success in her current mission. A longtime Babe observer, Jinx Falkenburg, once noted, "The difference between Babe and other women who wear beautiful clothes is that Babe does something to them. She even looks good in blue jeans." It was this mysterious quality, coupled with her ethereal beauty, that had already landed her on the best-dressed list and would one day make her a legend in the world of fashion.

7

THE BIG CATCH

ON September 27, 1940, Mary Benedict "Minnie" Cushing reeled in the single biggest matrimonial catch in the United States of America— Vincent Astor. Minnie had hooked him the instant they had met at Betsey's party in Georgetown, but landing him was no easy matter. Vincent and Minnie had been companions ever since that fateful meeting. Although they had never lived together, rumor had it that Astor was contributing to Minnie's living expenses during the time that she shared an apartment with a well-known lesbian, Cleveland-born Kay Halle. Rumors further had it that Minnie was his mistress. Despite his best efforts to keep their relationship from the gossip columnists, it was common knowledge among New York's glitterati. For a while it was anyone's guess as to whether Vincent's wife, Helen, would divorce him, and if she did, whether he would marry Minnie. At last, just when Gogsie Cushing was undoubtedly wringing her hands in utter despair, Helen Huntington Astor obtained a divorce at a Wyoming dude ranch.

Jerry Zerbe, the only photographer permitted at the Cushing-Mortimer wedding, revealed an interesting wrinkle in these Byzantine and highly personal machinations. According to the great society photographer, Gogsie had personally confided her role in bringing Vincent to the point. When she had learned of Lytle Hull's divorce from Gertrude Carroll Hull, which would allow him to wed his longtime friend, Helen Astor—as soon as she had freed herself from Vincent—Gogsie brought subtle but substantial pressure to bear on the real estate tycoon, especially in the weeks just before Babe's marriage to Stanley Mortimer. By her own admission, it was Gogsie who won the day for her daughter. Zerbe and other close Cushing family friends were convinced that left to his own devices, Vincent would never have formalized their long-standing relationship with a marriage ceremony. Yet a scant three weeks after Helen divorced him, Minnie became the second Mrs. Vincent Astor.

Thus Minnie—the apparently unmarriageable Cushing sister, already nearing thirty-five years of age—had fulfilled Gogsie's lifelong ambition. Betsey's and Babe's marriages had been mere dress rehearsals for this great moment of triumph. Unfortunately, Gogsie would have to wait to crow over her success, for Vincent Astor, as secretive as ever, was doing everything in his power to throw the press off his trail.

Immediately after Babe's wedding reception, the 265-foot *Nourmahal* had returned posthaste to Manhattan, where it had spent the early part of the week lying at anchor in the Hudson River off the Seventy-ninth Street Boat Basin, awaiting orders. Late that Thursday afternoon a small party boarded the yacht. With Vincent were his mother, Ava Willing Astor, Lady Ribblesdale; fellow Hudson Valley aristocrat and Manhattan man-about-town William Rhinelander Stewart, Jr., whose friendship with Vincent dated back to their boyhood days; and last but not least, Jepson, Vincent's ever-faithful valet. Once aboard, Astor gave the orders to steam to Montauk, at that time an unostentatious fishing village at the very tip of Long Island, beyond the Hamptons. The ship's officers and crew were totally unaware of their romantic mission; in fact, the notice on the *Nourmahal*'s bulletin board stated that Astor would be spending the weekend near Montauk, playing golf.

To further ensure privacy from the press, Vincent even went so far as to carry his golf clubs with him when he disembarked in Montauk at about 10:30 on Friday morning. With Stewart he entered a waiting car, which carried them to East Hampton. Lady Ribblesdale followed in another car, and they all met up at Heather Dune, where Minnie and Gogsie awaited them. Ironically, Helen Huntington Astor had rented this very villa two seasons earlier—little dreaming that it would be the site of her husband's second wedding.

With Jepson's able assistance, Vincent quickly changed from his informal yachting attire and then joined his bride-to-be in the spacious drawing room, with its magnificent ocean view. There Vincent and Minnie became husband and wife in a simple ceremony that took less than eight minutes. Defying convention, the bride's mother herself presented her eldest daughter in marriage. Although it would have been more proper for Minnie's brother, Henry, to give her away, as he had Babe, the glowing Gogsie preferred to reserve that moment of triumph for herself. William Rhinelander Stewart served as the groom's best man, and the only additional witnesses were Lady Ribblesdale, the bride's sister Betsey, and Betsey's two small daughters, Sara and Kate—grandchildren of Vincent Astor's great friend and neighbor, President Franklin Delano Roosevelt.

The only decorations in the drawing room of the yellow stucco villa were late-summer flowers from Gogsie's garden. The statuesque bride was attired in the same afternoon dress she had worn just six days before, at Babe's wedding. It was an Arthur Falkenstein creation of light wool, with a softly draped plum-colored bodice and a full, pleated skirt the exact shade of an American Beauty rose. On her feet Minnie wore deep plum pumps, and topping off the elegant ensemble was a matching fringed felt Lily Daché hat with a short, wine-red veil. The bridal bouquet was of regal white orchids.

After the brief ceremony, Gogsie released to the press the following formal announcement of the nuptials: "Mrs. Harvey Cushing announces the marriage of her daughter Mary B. Cushing to Vincent Astor at East Hampton, on September 27, 1940." The formal announcement was hardly an indication of the intense joy she was experiencing at that moment.

The ever watchful Maury Paul had scooped the rest of New York's aggressive newshounds for his Cholly Knickerbocker column, having demanded that Gogsie notify him of every detail of the ceremony by telephone. Although there was precious little detail to convey, that very evening in the *New York American* Cholly informed his readers: "Mayfair Society is recovering from the 'surprise' marriage of Vincent Astor and Mary Cushing, daughter of the late Dr. Harvey Cushing. . . ."

And so it was that, on the coattails of this odd, secretive wedding, the Cushing sisters entered the exalted ranks of New York's golden "400." This, the most exclusive inner circle of society, had received its name from Vincent Astor's grandmother, Caroline Astor, for that was the number of people her private ballroom would hold. Thus she had to limit her formal invitations to four hundred of her closest blue-blooded friends, whom she dubbed the 400.

There was no reception following the ceremony. In fact, no sooner had Minnie and Vincent been pronounced man and wife than the tall, gangling multimillionaire and the newly minted Mrs. Astor entered a waiting motor car, which swiftly bore them away to Montauk, where the *Nourmahal*'s tender was waiting to carry them out to the yacht. For ten days they honeymooned at sea, traveling aimlessly aboard the massive oceangoing vessel—Vincent's pride and joy.

He had bought the luxurious diesel yacht some years before, paying for her partly by selling the original, more modest *Nourmahal* and partly by using the $371,000 profit he had realized from his investment in the 1926 film version of *Ben-Hur,* starring Ramon Novarro and Francis X. Bushman. Built in Kiel, Germany, the newer vessel had a cruising speed of sixteen knots, a range of twenty thousand miles, and all the latest nautical equipment. Her accommodations were magnificent: eleven staterooms on three decks, several lounges, a walnut-paneled dining room with seating for eighteen people, a pine-paneled library, and to contend with any emergency, a fully equipped operating room. There were even cabins for the forty-two-man complement of officers and crew. The *Nourmahal*'s yearly operating costs were roughly $125,000.

Despite all his nautical acumen, Vincent did not skipper his own yacht. Rather, he left that job to Captain Klang, a native Swede, and reserved for himself the dual role of admiral and chief entertainment officer.

Minnie Astor was very familiar with the *Nourmahal,* for she had been on board a number of times when Vincent had taken off on various of his pleasure and/or scientific expeditions to the Caribbean and the South Pacific. Typically the real estate magnate would spend nine or ten months out of each year concerning himself with the Astor estate and his many directorships. The remainder of the year he would devote to the open sea. His voyages were his chief joy in life, and he was fully aware that the luxurious escape they offered from his pressure-filled everyday existence were the greatest single advantage of his extraordinary wealth. He was one of the richest men in America, and unlike many men of his socioeconomic class, he knew how to enjoy his money.

Often he would combine science and pleasure, taking marine biologists along so that they could collect specimens of rare tropical fish or other marine life. On other occasions he would set off on a far lighter note, simply to have a good time. Sometimes he and his guests would put on diving suits and descend into the ocean to take a look at all the brightly colored fish in their natural habitat. If the laid-back existence aboard the *Nourmahal* became a little dull, he would order the captain to set his course for some remote, mysterious island. There the yacht would drop anchor, waiting for the islanders to paddle out to her, bearing colorful, exotic gifts of carvings, fruit, and flowers. Then the islanders might climb aboard, chase about, and touch every highly polished object in sight, marveling at the reflections of their own images. The chieftain would deliver a speech of welcome in his own language, and Vincent would reply in English. Then he would give the awed visitors a complete tour of the grand ship.

On his numerous trips, Astor became well acquainted with many of the bizarre expatriated Europeans and Americans who set up fiefdoms on little-known isles. One such character was Mrs. de Wanger, a Viennese-born, self-styled baroness who set herself up as the Empress of the Galapagos Islands. The most celebrated resident of Charles Island, she had mysteriously disappeared, and Vincent was sure that she had been murdered. The sole purpose of his 1937 cruise to that island was to investigate her disappearance. He and his guests on this voyage sought to uncover her remains, but after five hours of toting loaded backpacks and digging with shovels and picks under a scorching sun, Vincent's blue-blooded friends mutinied. To his extreme disappointment, he was forced to abort the search, leaving the mystery of Mrs. de Wanger's disappearance forever unsolved.

On another cruise, this one with Minnie aboard, he embarked upon a treasure hunt on Coco Island, off Costa Rica, long known as a haven for buccaneers in a bygone era. Unfortunately, the Astor party ran afoul of a rival gang of treasure hunters, who set upon them in deadly earnest. The incident might have ended in tragedy if the president of Costa Rica had not sent troops to bring order to an otherwise chaotic situation. If the troops had not arrived, and if the group of latter-day pirates had harmed the multimillionaire friend of President Roosevelt, an international incident might well have ensued.

During the winter preceding their marriage, Vincent and Minnie voyaged to the South Pacific. As the Astor yacht lay off Samoa, they spotted the cruise ship S.S. *Kungsholm* as its passengers were going ashore. Among the celebrated guests on the luxurious Scandinavian vessel were Cole and Linda Porter; mining heir Leonard Hanna and his lover, Cleveland columnist Winsor French; and pianist Roger Stearns. Astor entertained the Porter-Hanna party aboard the *Nourmahal* during the stopover, and Porter reciprocated by playing tunes from his upcoming Broadway show *Panama Hatti* on Astor's shipboard piano. Porter and Astor were already well acquainted, and in fact, it was during a stay at Beechwood, the Astor cottage at Newport, that the great composer had written his famous song "Night and Day," which Fred Astaire had immortalized in the 1932 Broadway show *The Gay Divorcee*.

Also aboard the *Kungsholm* on that Pacific voyage were Mrs. John Murray and her two daughters, Jeanne (who later wed Alfred Gwynne Vanderbilt) and Cathie (who would marry the Marquess Alesandro di Montezemolo). Jeanne Murray Vanderbilt recently reminisced about that trip:

> As we strolled around the main town of the western part of the island, my mother pointed out Vincent Astor and his companion, Minnie Cushing, to me and my sister. As I remember, she was a strikingly handsome young woman, blonde and quite tall. My

mother, in her very strict French Catholic way, let us know that Mr. Astor was still very much married at the time. Looking back on that time, I must add that Vincent Astor and Minnie Cushing gave every appearance of being very happy in one another's company.

Mrs. Vanderbilt had another, far more personal, memory of that tour, for when she had turned twenty-one Porter had composed a song, which he called "Bye, Bye, Samoa," in celebration. In typical Porter fashion, he never used it in a Broadway musical, but it later turned up in the 1949 Katharine Hepburn–Spencer Tracy film *Adam's Rib,* with the title changed to "Farewell, Amanda."

As relaxing, amusing, and oftentimes scientifically educating as Astor's sea voyages might have been before Minnie and Vincent had married, the long trips began to bore the new Mrs. Astor. She would frequently isolate herself in her cabin, reading or indulging in one of her favorite hobbies—needlepoint. The Astors had virtually nothing in common. Their temperaments were remarkably different—and not in a mutually complementary way. The couple was seemingly unaware of these differences during the early part of the long courtship, but they were glaringly apparent to their legion of friends. Vincent's friends, mostly male, mostly long-standing aristocratic cronies who also loved the sea, had a penchant for indulging in intricate practical jokes whenever the opportunity presented itself. Minnie, on the other hand, was deeply committed to her mother and sisters, and enjoyed the companionship of artists and writers. While Vincent was rather sullen and awkward in manner and speech, Minnie was vivacious and witty. To make matters worse, this marriage, like Astor's first, lacked a commitment to having children and providing an heir to the Astor millions. In fact, if there was any truth to the rumors that were circulating at the time, it is doubtful that either of Vincent's marriages was ever even consummated.

Minnie's kind of island was Manhattan, with its socially and artistically glittering ambience. Once she set her feet on its solid pavement, she set about formulating her own agenda among her own set of friends and a varied collection of creative individuals, conceding only an occasional nod to her husband and his dull, traditional social obligations. Theirs soon became an even more disparate union than the one Vincent and Helen had endured for over a quarter of a century.

Not long before photographer Jerry Zerbe's death, in 1988, he summed the situation up in one short sentence: "I don't know how Min put up with that man!"

8

THE MAKING
OF
LADY BOUNTIFUL

*A*CCORDING to author John D. Gates, "Vincent's second marriage was sustained more by his love than by Minnie's. She was fourteen years younger than he and a gay, blithe spirit who must have felt weighed down by Vincent's more somber, serious ways." This was undoubtedly the case. In fact, wedding bells had never been in Minnie's game plan, and it is unlikely that she would even have considered marrying Astor if it had not been for the strenuous urging of her mother and sisters.

While Harvey Cushing was alive, Gogsie kept a relatively low profile, deferring to her husband in most matters. Jerome Zerbe was of the opinion that the doctor did not approve of his wife's grand schemes, especially the idea of marrying solely for money. Although Gogsie made no secret of her ambitions for her daughters, she did not go so far as to veto Betsey's match with Jimmy Roosevelt or to push Minnie or Babe in any particular direction. Upon Harvey's death Gogsie came into her own, taking absolute control over her daughters' lives. It was no coincidence that within a year of their father's demise, both the "career woman" and the "spinster" made splendid matches.

Minnie would have been content to remain Astor's mistress, traveling with him when it pleased her to do so and accepting his largesse in order to live in a style that she would not otherwise have been able to maintain. This sort of arrangement was totally unacceptable to her mother—on moral, social, and financial grounds. Once she had heard the first whisper among her friends that Vincent Astor's interest in her eldest daughter was more than just a passing fancy, Gogsie went into high gear, pressuring Minnie to do whatever it took to get this phenomenal catch to the altar. As *the* Mrs. Astor, Minnie would command great respect and virtually anything her heart desired—except perhaps a loving relationship. Of course, Minnie was not allowed to forget for one moment that such vast financial resources would be a great help to the entire Cushing clan, for Harvey had left a very modest estate. With his death, the family business had turned from medicine to marriages.

Despite the huge differences between Vincent and Minnie—in age, temperament, interests, sociability, and commitment—Betsey and Babe cast their votes with Gogsie. It had been Betsey, after all, who had arranged the auspicious meeting. Minnie, devoted as she was to her mother and sisters, had little choice but to go along with the consensus: that the advantages of such a match far outweighed the minor disadvantage of her relative indifference to her suitor.

In all fairness, Gogsie, Betsey, and Babe undoubtedly felt that marriage to Vincent Astor would be a marvelous coup for Minnie. All they could envision was the immense wealth, power, and undisputed social position that would instantly be hers. In fact, almost immediately after the honeymoon, Minnie became a trustee of the Metropolitan Museum of Art and a member of the board of Astor-owned *Newsweek* magazine as well as the boards of any number of war-related charities. In the early 1940s most entertainments took a back seat to her charity work. She became very active in the Ships Service Committee and also the Henry Street Visiting Nurses campaign. She was so busy with these and myriad other enjoyable activities that—except perhaps on long sea voyages—she barely had time to be bored or even particularly introspective.

According to Jerome Zerbe, it was not at all surprising to see Minnie at five or six benefit parties a night. These events threw Minnie into the company of many great Broadway and Hollywood celebrities. Soon such luminaries as Clark Gable and Carole Lombard, Shirley Booth, Henry Fonda, Cecil Beaton, Vivien Leigh, Chester Morris, Dorothy Parker, Jerome Robbins, Greta Garbo, Constance Bennett, Ethel Merman, and Mary Martin appeared on Minnie's guest lists.

Minnie also became closely involved in the operations of the St. Regis Hotel, redecorating it on a regular basis with her trademark brightly colored chintzes. She was so tied into the running of the hotel that, according to columnist Walter Winchell, when the haughty Duchess of Windsor arrived late at the hotel's Maisonette Rousse Restaurant and found that the maître d' had given away her reserved table, she complained directly and vitriolically to Minnie. Undaunted by the verbal assault, Minnie replied, "My good woman, why don't you act your age?"

As the world spiraled downward into a hell of its own making, celebrity and society marriages and divorces continued unabated; Broadway shows, such as Cole Porter's *Panama Hattie,* opened to rave reviews; and Manhattan's stellar café society kept up its rather frantic nocturnal pace, frequenting the glitzy nightclubs without an apparent care in the world. Jerome Zerbe's camera continued to record the antics of the rich and famous as they partied at El Morocco, capturing intimate shots of the celebrities at play. True, some of the playboy darlings of café society did march off to war, but enough remained in Manhattan to keep things interesting.

Although the war years tore Babe's marriage apart, they had no such effect on Minnie's. To the contrary, both Vincent and Minnie were so caught up in the spirit of the times and in their various different contributions to the war effort that they never really came face to face with the grim reality of how very little they had in common. While Minnie immersed herself in planning and attending benefits, Vincent became increasingly patriotic, underwriting many Allied relief causes and even turning his most treasured possession, the *Nourmahal,* over to the government for convoy duty, to carry war materials to Europe and bring wounded soldiers back home. Captain Vincent Astor relished his role, and from time to time his commander-in-chief and old friend, FDR, would take Vincent into his confidence. Astor was understandably proud of his Navy Commendation Ribbon, which he earned for "meritorious performance . . . initiative, unflagging energy and devotion" to administrative duties with the confidential fishing-vessel lookout, who watched for enemy submarines while fishing along the Atlantic coast.

The world that Minnie entered as the wife of this phenomenally wealthy man seemed to be one long, perpetual fairy tale. At least in the beginning, Minnie was reasonably contented with her highly enviable arrangement; she accepted it, much as European royalty had for centuries accepted their arranged alliances. The Astors were as close as America would ever come to royalty—closer by far than the Roosevelts, who were often perceived in that light. During the years between the world wars, the public viewed Vincent Astor as its own homegrown Prince of Wales. Unlike Jimmy Roosevelt, who was also likened to the prince, Astor had the royal treasury to back up such comparisons. Having inherited more than $69 million and having compounded that amount through astute business dealings and investments, Astor was the sole possessor of a king's ransom. In addition, he prided himself on his beautifully though conservatively tailored wardrobe. With the constant attendance of his skilled valet, Jepson, he was always impeccably turned out. Here, however, the royal resemblance ended.

Astor's appearance and bearing were anything but regal. He stood six feet four inches tall and weighed about 155 pounds, with narrow shoulders and a concave chest. Heredity had bestowed upon him his father's low, sloping forehead and protruding upper lip—"the Astor lip"—but Vincent made no attempt to disguise it, as his father had, with a heavy mustache. The heir to these regrettable features moved in an abrupt and ungainly fashion and was cursed with enormous feet that splayed outward, so that he looked very much like a penguin when he walked. Whether from a wry form of self-mockery or a simple affinity to the creature he so resembled, Astor adopted the penguin as his personal trademark, having it printed on napkins and ship flags, embroidered on linens, and engraved on glassware and ashtrays. His lack of coordination and athletic ability led him to avoid most sports, and he never danced, for he felt that he was not good at it. His speech, too, betrayed a decided awkwardness, for it was rapid and rather indistinct. In his youth, Vincent had acquired the irritating habit of cupping his hand around his right ear to give the impression that he had not heard something for which he was unprepared. Although he would from time to time attend a major heavyweight prizefight, and he did enjoy the camaraderie of drinking, singing, telling tall tales, and indulging in practical jokes, he was not what his contemporaries would have called "a man's man." On his better days he could be kind, amiable, and even a decent conversationalist, but he was more likely to be irritable, antisocial, and taciturn.

When not adventuring on the high seas, Vincent Astor was a creature of habit, and he adhered quite rigidly to his rather dull routines. Beginning his day at seven in the morning, he invariably breakfasted in his room—for which Minnie and any houseguests could be most grateful, since his company in the early morning was not something to be desired. Reaching his office by nine, he would spend the entire morning on his real estate business. Then, after a light lunch, he would take a nap, always awakening in a bad mood. In the afternoon he would attend a directors' meeting. Throughout the day Astor smoked his way through two and a half packs of cigarettes, switching to a corncob pipe after dinner. Every evening at seven, no matter what, he listened to "Amos 'n' Andy" on the radio, even canceling or changing appointments to avoid missing his favorite show. Dinner was served immediately afterward, at 7:20 sharp. More than one friend of Astor's has told the story of calling his residence just after seven and being told that Mr. Astor was out but would be back by 7:20. Vincent's bedtime was generally at eleven o'clock, but on rare occasion he would stay up late drinking, talking about the sea and ships, or playing with his electric trains.

Astor was subject to mercurial mood changes. Often somber and withdrawn, he could sometimes even manage to laugh at himself, although when he was in a laughing mood, his sense of humor more often tended to be at the expense of others. His practical jokes were legendary, and some, especially those he played on women, were truly outrageous. In one instance he targeted a married woman who was having an affair. He hired a writer to pen the story of her infidelity in the style of gossip columnist Dorothy Kilgallen, then paid to have an entire facsimile page of the Sunday newspaper magazine specially printed to include the

sensationalistic account. Next he had this "special edition" delivered to
the woman and the other interested parties at breakfast. It was not long
before the *Nourmahal*'s wireless operator received an angry message
from the woman's husband; a short time later there was an even angrier
one from her lover. Apparently, the style of the prank left little doubt
in anyone's mind as to the identity of the perpetrator.

Despite his rather awkward and sometimes even obnoxious personality, Vincent Astor, unlike many of his millionaire peers, enjoyed a very
benign public image. The press was in general extremely kind to him.
He was popular without ever having made any particular effort to
achieve popularity, and he remained popular throughout his entire life
without the aid of press agents or corporate public relations image-
builders. He achieved goodwill through hard work and numerous philanthropic endeavors. Many of these endeavors, like the Astor Library
(now the New York Public Library), were highly visible, but others
received little or no publicity. One such low-profile project was a retreat
for underprivileged children and their mothers near his Rhinebeck estate. His giving did not begin and end with check-writing. In fact, he
often devoted hours to these children.

Actually, as a philanthropist, Astor was not in a league with other
such well-known Americans as the Rockefellers, Mellons, Whitneys,
and Carnegies, but Vincent was far ahead of his close-fisted forbearers
and successors, who contributed little of their vast wealth to the better-
ment of society. Vincent's father, John Jacob Astor IV, had made only
one sizable public gift, a bequest of $400,000 to found the Astor Library.
Thanks primarily to Vincent Astor and later the Vincent Astor Foundation, now run by his widow, Brooke, the New York Public Library even
today receives no tax dollars but supports itself through philanthropy.
To date Brooke has given more than $10 million.

Vincent's first ventures into public giving were somewhat erratic
bursts of generosity rather than an organized system of philanthropy.
His indigent friends had long known him as a soft touch. He was as
likely to give anonymously to whatever charity struck his fancy as to
make well-planned, highly publicized contributions. He had used his
wealth to build a hospital for his old school, St. George's, in Newport;
to form a club for nurses at New York Hospital, of which he was a

governor; to underwrite all the expenses for a convalescent hospital in Rhinebeck; and to provide summer excursions for inner-city poor children and their mothers. In addition, unlike the majority of his peers, Astor paid pensions to scores of superannuated servants.

A committed Democrat, Vincent Astor supported the New Deal programs put in place by his friend and Hudson Valley neighbor Franklin Delano Roosevelt—even after FDR's "soak the rich" policy began to hit home, to the tune of a 63 percent tax bite. Astor was often seen in the Roosevelt entourage, and he put the president's intimate aide Raymond Moley in charge of *Newsweek,* along with fellow millionaires Averell Harriman and Harriman's sister, Mary Harriman Rumsey.

Despite Vincent's patriotism, generosity, and political dedication, he was anything but selfless. For him, charity always began at home, and he had a decided penchant for living very, very well. He owned and immensely enjoyed any number of expensive "toys"—among them his cherished *Nourmahal,* fast motor cars, an elaborate set of electric trains, and two miniature railways. The first of these railways, at his Hudson Valley estate, Ferncliff, had tracks covering a good half-mile of the extensive grounds and could haul twenty people at once. Actually, railways, whether miniature or life-sized, were Vincent's special love. For a time he was even a director of the Illinois Central Railway. He would ring up friends and invite them to accompany him to Chicago.

"Why on earth would I want to go to Chicago?" asked one of his Chanler cousins. "I don't know a soul there."

"Oh, we won't have to go into the city," replied Vincent cheerfully. "We'll spend the day shunting around the yards and start home at nightfall."

When not in Manhattan or aboard a real train or on the high sea, Vincent would retreat to Ferncliff and his miniature railroad, which he called the Toonerville. He often claimed that, whenever he had to make a particularly difficult decision, he would take a ride on the little railroad. He so enjoyed it that he had the superintendent of Ferncliff, Herbert Pinkham, construct a very similar railroad at Ferry Reach, his estate in Bermuda.

Astor also enjoyed the elaborate comforts of a string of homes from upper New York State to Bermuda, run and perfectly maintained by a virtual army of servants. In addition to the indispensable Jepson, who invariably traveled with Vincent, there were eight in permanent residence at Ferncliff; however, the actual number of employees who worked at the estate was far larger, including a retinue of twenty-odd gardeners, stablemen, and chauffeurs—and an even greater number of household servants. It took a full-time staff of twelve to keep his Manhattan residence in pristine order and five to tend Ferry Reach. At Beechwood, Astor's Newport "cottage," he employed only a single caretaker, for the property was generally leased to others on an annual basis, and the renters provided their own servants. Vincent also paid wages to the forty-two men it took to staff and crew the *Nourmahal* and to his retired former servants. Even in 1940s dollars, Astor's payroll must have been formidable—without including the necessary lawyers and financial advisers.

Had Minnie loved the sea and shuttling from house to house, with only the company of Vincent's old-guard buddies and an occasional practical joke to liven up her existence, she would undoubtedly have been deliriously happy, despite the lack of romantic love. However, these were not the things that she enjoyed—or even tolerated—and a number of her intimates knew the reality behind her apparent fairy-tale life. Minnie had always viewed her relationship as one of convenience. The more she and Vincent went their separate ways, the less convenient it became. One of the very few things the couple had in common was their interest in the war effort, and even this they approached from completely different directions.

At first, while Vincent busied himself with the management of his vast wealth and his naval reconnaissance with his hardy band of fishermen, Minnie launched herself into the challenging task of overhauling their various homes to suit her own taste. However dismayed Vincent may have been about the changes, he gave her free rein and an obviously unlimited budget. For one so artistically inclined as Minnie, this huge creative endeavor was undoubtedly very gratifying. The minute she felt secure enough in her new role, she set out to create not merely decorative schemes but an ambience of ease, comfort, and luxury, coupled with a good, healthy dose of her mother's highly valued utility.

While in Manhattan, the Astors resided in an enormous, sprawling apartment at 120 East End Avenue, in New York's Gracie Square area. John Jacob Astor had purchased the property and left it to his favorite grandson, Charles Astor Bristed. Once a neighborhood of dreary tenements, by 1940 Gracie Square had become a prestigious address. Vincent had begun the trend toward chic, posh living when he took over the property in 1927. He had long since sold his father's grand chateau at 840 Fifth Avenue for $3.5 million to the Jewish Society Temple Emmanu-El. The new owners had put the wrecking ball to the glorious old building and then erected New York's most costly synagogue. At that time Vincent had purchased a simple six-story neo-Georgian townhouse at 130 East Eightieth Street, on Manhattan's Upper East Side. There he had reproduced his father's bedroom suite exactly, with the same furniture, artwork, and even the same bathroom fixtures. Vincent and his first wife, Helen, had spent most of their married life in that townhouse, but as they drifted farther and farther apart, the large house became unnecessary. Astor donated it to the Junior League for its New York headquarters.

Thus it was to the East End Avenue apartment that the new Mrs. Astor first turned her creative attentions, completely making over the rather dull, gloomy town residence, converting it, with the aid of New York's top decorator, George G. Stacey, into a cheery, livable home. Lively floral wallpaper transformed the front hall into a warm, welcoming entryway. Forest-green walls and bright red, pink, and white chintz window treatments provided the inviting backdrop for a homey, almost cluttered living space, lovingly accessorized by Minnie's artistic hand. There were books and magazines in every room, a jigsaw puzzle on a table here, an elegant objet d'art there, and great masses of fresh white flowers everywhere.

One room departed sharply from the vibrant color scheme of the rest of the apartment. This was Minnie's very own library, her personal refuge in the enormous apartment, a cool blue-gray room overlooking the East River. She would begin each day there, seated at her antique desk with its sculpted bust of her father. To her left, on the wall, was a John Singer Sargent sketch of the doctor. In effect, Minnie had created a nearly sacred memorial to her beloved father, and the memory of the great man burned brightly in her thoughts each and every day of her life.

Elsewhere, scattered throughout the apartment, a great assortment of memorabilia attested to the widely varying hobbies, interests, and tastes of both inhabitants. On display were a small silver replica of the engine that pulled the Ferry Reach miniature railroad, a painting of the beautiful *Nourmahal*, a set of electric trains in the library, and a liberal sprinkling of Minnie's collection of miniatures, including tiny models of paneled English drawing rooms, lovely little enameled Battersea boxes, and small bird-cage music boxes. Above the mantel in the library, dominating the entire room, was a painting of William Astor and his family: Mrs. James Van Allen, William Astor, Mrs. Roosevelt Roosevelt, John Jacob Astor, Mrs. William Astor, and Mrs. Orme Wilson. And tying everything together was Minnie's superb taste and real talent for creating wonderfully comfortable surroundings for her husband and guests. Minnie was a highly creative and gracious hostess—a talent her somewhat misanthropic husband never really appreciated. In fact, he rarely bothered to grace her social gatherings with his presence.

In a recent conversation, longtime family friend William Hutton recalled a New Year's Eve celebration at the Astor apartment in Manhattan: "The midnight hour was fast approaching, and I happened to ask Minnie, 'Where is Vincent?' and she replied that he was in the library, playing with his train set."

Although Minnie spread loving care throughout the Manhattan apartment, she made no secret of her intense dislike for Ferncliff, the 2,800-acre Hudson Valley estate in Rhinebeck, New York, which is now a Carmelite home for aged nuns. Minnie wasted none of her energy and flair in decorating or in making the estate more comfortable. In fact, the first thing she did was consign the enormous main house to oblivion by having it torn down.

Built in 1874 by William Backhouse Astor, Jr., and greatly expanded by both his son John Jacob IV and grandson Vincent, this huge Victorian Gothic pile had quite possibly been Vincent's favorite land-based property. He loved the great, rambling, high-ceilinged house that stood proudly above the Hudson River. As its inhabitants had never decorated purely for the sake of decorating, it was a most interesting amalgam of old and not-quite-new, with a definite feeling of being lived in and an old-fashioned cachet that would have been impossible to buy. Each room held old furniture—some quite grand, some rather shabby—and innumerable relics of times past. The long strips of damask that decorated the drawing room walls had seen nearly a half-century of Astor living. That Vincent Astor let Minnie demolish this beloved old house spoke volumes for his feelings toward her.

In addition to the main residence, Ferncliff contained a massive casino-playhouse, which Vincent's father had commissioned Stanford White to design and build. Inside this structure were a tennis court and a swimming pool (the latter frequented by FDR for his therapeutic swims). Also occupying the vast acreage were a series of barns with marble floors; wide, green lawns sloping down to the riverbanks; magnificent, world-renowned gardens brought to their full glory by Helen Huntington Astor Hull during her reign as the first Mrs. Vincent Astor; a teahouse; English-designed greenhouses; and an antique-filled Early American guest house.

It is hard to understand why Minnie so detested the grand property, why she should not have enjoyed the enormous challenge of converting the monstrous old main house into a warm, inviting country home. Perhaps it was simply her love of city life and dislike of out-of-the-way places that drove her to raze the house. Or perhaps she found its size unmanageable, its architecture too unsuitable for the sort of cozy atmosphere she was so successful at creating. Even when Minnie turned the casino-playhouse into much more manageable living quarters, she lavished none of her affection or taste on it. It remained a rather unattractive, not particularly comfortable setting for her unavoidable country entertaining. And while this vastly scaled-down version of the original Ferncliff was easier to maintain, it still required dozens of servants and staff. Minnie left all the other structures intact, if not charmingly decorated, and in fact took great pleasure from the flowers grown on the grounds and in the hothouses, regularly bringing them into New York City to decorate the Gracie Square apartment.

Minnie's arrival as chatelaine of Ferncliff spelled vast changes in the social life at the estate as well. It was out with the old-guard, patrician families who were so much a part of Vincent's heritage and youth, and in with a whole new cast of café society and show-business characters. The blue-blooded Morgans, Goelets, and Rhinelanders gave way to an eclectic group including photographer Jerry Zerbe, Nedda and Joshua Logan, socialite-heiress Vivian Woolley-Hart, Salvador Dali, Fred Astaire and his sister Adele, Beatrice Lillie (Lady Peel), Noël Coward, Thelma Chrysler Foy, Moss and Kitty Carlisle Hart, Elsa Maxwell, and actress Ina Claire.

Soon Vincent was making as few appearances in Minnie's company as he had in Helen's. He acutely disliked the sort of parties and carefully planned get-togethers that Minnie excelled in giving and relished attending. Quite frankly, they bored him, as did her arty guests themselves. They simply were not his kind of people, any more than his friends were hers. Vincent's idea of a good time was the easy camaraderie aboard the *Nourmahal* with his yachting buddies. He hated bridge but would occasionally indulge in a game of backgammon, and in his later years he developed a passion for croquet, which he played both at Ferncliff and Ferry Reach. Croquet was just about the only interest other than the war effort that the couple shared. Minnie was actually quite an accomplished player. Kitty Carlisle Hart, in her biography, *Kitty,* commented on the Hollywood version of purdah, according to which women were invited to play croquet only in extremis. "Only two were really welcome," Hart reminisced, "Dorothy Rodgers and Minnie Astor, and they played better than the men." But it would take a lot more than money and croquet to hold the Astor marriage together.

In truth, Minnie found her wealthy husband to be a dead bore. Her major interest was in the arts. While she was extremely intelligent, with an impressive knowledge of science, she was most comfortable in the world of artists, writers, and actors. Unless she was entertaining at home, she could usually be found in the company of her sisters or among her collection of arty friends in the glittering world of café society. But never with Vincent. Her crowd—including such celebrities as Jerry Zerbe, actress Ina Claire, international hostess Elsa Maxwell, composer Cole Porter, Broadway's Moss and Kitty Carlisle Hart, and playwright Noël Coward—was totally alien to Vincent's staid lifestyle. For solace he would often retreat to the Hudson River estate of his ex-wife, Helen Huntington Astor Hull, where he would spend hours in comfortable conversation. Ironically, after more than a quarter-century of distant, unsuccessful marriage, they had become friends, their relationship almost seeming to evolve into that of a mother and son.

Meanwhile, with the Astor millions behind her, Minnie began early in her marriage to fashion herself into a patron of the arts. Her greatest ambition was to establish a grand salon in Manhattan, to put herself at the hub of all New York artistic circles, as a sort of latter-day Marquise Marie de Sévigné. Of course, Minnie could not and did not pretend to the literary brilliance of that seventeenth-century French aristocrat and writer, but she desperately wanted to surround herself with artistic talent.

In a recent interview, a family member confided that Minnie truly saw herself as a major figure in the New York art scene. And not entirely without reason. In fact, many great artists, writers, and actors attended her soirees, which ran like clockwork. According to the relative,

To be invited for five o'clock tea or cocktails meant just that: one was expected to leave promptly by six o'clock. If your invitation read six o'clock, you would be ushered out at seven. And those who were expected at seven would be expected to leave shortly before eight o'clock, so as to accommodate those invited for dinner.

It went on like that for years, to the great consternation of many of the guests, who found the assembly-line style of entertaining somewhat unnerving and unflattering. Certainly, it was an unorthodox departure from the gracious style that Gogsie had inculcated in her daughters from their earliest days. However, few people dared to decline Minnie's invitations. To do so might have spelled social ruin, as offending Minnie might well have meant being ostracized by her sisters, Betsey and Babe. The Cushing sisters were a major force to be reckoned with in the New York social scene.

Babe, already a fashion icon, would soon top the Best Dressed list and eventually be inducted into the Fashion Hall of Fame. Women in all walks of life did their very best to emulate not only her clothing but her bearing. Minnie, however, was content to dress in the quiet elegance that went hand in hand with old money. She felt no need to make a fashion statement each time she stepped out into society. Her favorite designer was the Russian-born Valentina, wife of businessman George Schlee, who was actress Greta Garbo's intimate friend and financial

adviser. It was no secret that the designer and the actress barely tolerated each other, observing only the absolute minimum of mutual courtesy—and that only because of their great respect for Schlee.

Among Valentina's customers, besides Minnie Astor, were some of
the most elegant women in the United States; she had designed the
costumes for Katharine Hepburn in *The Philadelphia Story* and had also
dressed actresses Lynn Fontanne and Vera Zorina, as well as Standard
Oil heiress Millicent Rogers. In addition to her genius for fashion,
Valentina had considerable talent as a hostess, with a reputation for
giving some of the best parties in Manhattan. Her Russian Easter celebrations were legendary, the invitations much sought after among New
York's elite.

Valentina's New York brownstone was so lavishly furnished that
Vogue was moved to rhapsodize even on its "scarlet stools . . . like
exclamation points." It was here each year that Valentina and her
husband, the shadowy Schlee, brought together a group of guests that
every New York Social Register hostess would have killed for. Among
this exalted company were society columnist Lucius Beebe; theatrical
producer John Wilson and his wife, Princess Natalie Paley, of Imperial
Russia; opera star Gladys Swarthout; movie legend Greta Garbo; vapid
society beauty Mrs. William Rhinelander Stewart; author John Gun-
ther; international hostess Elsa Maxwell; famed decorator Lady Mendl;
Mrs. Harry Hopkins, once the steady girlfriend of Jock Whitney; Mrs.
Harvey Cushing; Minnie Astor; and Babe and Bill Paley, after Babe had
divorced Stanley Mortimer and entered into her second marriage. Needless to say, Vincent Astor seldom, if ever, accompanied Minnie to such
"frivolous" social activities.

As World War II drew to a close, even the most obtuse of observers
became aware that the winds of change were circling the globe. Gone
were both the blithe frivolity and the abject poverty of the thirties, swept
away by blood and guns and bombs. Vincent Astor sensed the change
and, with the wise counsel of his brilliant manager, Alan Betts, began
to liquidate his real estate holdings and to invest his profits in the stock
market, a rather daring move at the time. Their instincts paid off in
spades, and within five years in the mid-fifties, Astor had nearly doubled
the original stake that he had inherited from his father. He did, however,
draw the line at divesting himself of a few prime items. Although Betts

described the St. Regis Hotel as "lusterless," Vincent refused to sell it, insisting that he liked "to lunch there." And none of his staff, not even Betts, dared to suggest that he part with his prodigy *Newsweek,* which was at that time run by Astor's close friend Raymond Moley and had Minnie as a board member.

The radical changes in Vincent Astor's business tactics were but a preamble to those in his personal life. In a series of conversations shortly before Jerry Zerbe's death, in 1988, the socialite photographer spoke often of Minnie's relationship with her mother. While Gogsie had managed to push Minnie to the altar, she had never been able to convince her eldest daughter to produce an Astor heir. Zerbe voiced the opinion that Minnie's marriage had never even been consummated— before or after the vows. And while Zerbe would never say outright that Minnie may have had lesbian tendencies, he let it be known that she often preferred the company of gay men and women—especially if they were talented or had celebrity status—to that of heterosexual couples. While both Babe and Betsey committed themselves to having children, Minnie remained childless year after year. Vincent's sister Alice had produced three children, and his estranged half-brother, John Jacob Astor V, had added three Astors to the family genealogical chart.

As the decade of the forties neared its end, the Astor marriage became more and more strained. Minnie and Vincent spent less time than ever together. Vincent frequently retreated to his clubs or to Ferncliff or to cry on his ex-wife's shoulder, and Minnie held court with her many youthful companions over luncheon at the Colony, Le Pavillon, and Voisin or in one of the elegant restaurants in the St. Regis. At night she could frequently be found at 21 or at some benefit party in one of the big ballrooms of Manhattan's grandest hotels. But almost never with her husband!

In 1948 Vincent Astor, convinced that he would be the last of his line to control his huge personal fortune, created the Vincent Astor Foundation, which was to receive half of his estate outright. This caused his half-brother, John Jacob, who had long been bitter over his relatively small ($3 million) share of their father's wealth, to remark rather petulantly, "Not the way my great-great-grandfather would have wanted it."

In the beginning the foundation, sweepingly dedicated to "the allevia-

tion of human misery," contributed mainly to the children's home in
Rhinebeck. At the time the home did not seem to be very well run, and
Vincent felt that perhaps good Catholic management could shape it up.
According to an Astor observer of the time,

> Legend has it that he let it be known at the Brook Club one day
> that he would like to meet Cardinal Spellman, and good connec-
> tions being what they are, a luncheon was arranged for the follow-
> ing day. At any rate, Spellman agreed to take over administration
> of the home, and he and Astor became good friends.

Another keen observer of the New York social scene was Igor Cassini, who served for a time as columnist Cholly Knickerbocker for the
Hearst newspapers. Cassini had this to say about Gogsie Cushing:

> There is no question that Mrs. Harvey Cushing orchestrated the
> lives of her daughters. She told them early on that beauty fades and
> that only money and the power it brings is the ultimate goal. She
> maneuvered them into those marriages with three of the richest
> and most powerful men in America.

9

BETSEY'S COUP

*A*FTER successfully marrying off her eldest and youngest daughters within six days of each other, Gogsie Cushing might well have been expected to relax and bask in her success for a least a little while. Instead she immediately turned her full attention to recently divorced Betsey in an effort to secure her future. Nothing but the best—the wealthiest and most socially prominent—of suitors would do. After all, Vincent Astor was a hard act to follow, and Gogsie wanted nothing less for her middle daughter. Fortunately for Betsey, Gogsie was not the only matchmaker in town. In fact, the mother of the groom-to-be ultimately sealed the fate of the only remaining single Cushing sister.

On September 24, 1930, not long after Betsey had married Jimmy Roosevelt, multimillionaire playboy John Hay Whitney, known to friends, family, and the nation's tabloid readers as Jock, married Philadelphia debutante Mary Elizabeth "Liz" Altemus. Coincidentally, the Reverend Dr. Endicott Peabody, of Groton (Jock's prep school) performed the ceremony, as he had Betsey and Jimmy Roosevelt's.

Jock's mother, Helen Hay (Mrs. Payne) Whitney, the daughter of President Theodore Roosevelt's secretary of state, was not overly pleased with her son's choice of a bride. Liz's mother, Mrs. Nedom A. Eastman, was overjoyed by her daughter's alliance with the scion of one of America's richest families. Maury "Cholly Knickerbocker" Paul, who knew both the bride and groom well, had this to say of the marriage:

> When the sun goes down late this afternoon on the banks of Philadelphia's Schuylkill River, the tall, modish, and decidedly astute Mrs. Bessie Eastman will be in a position to calmly fold her hands and rest on her laurels—content in the knowledge that her only daughter is safely married to one of the richest young men in all America [with an estimated fortune of $200 million in 1930 dollars].
>
> It would be utter nonsense to say Liz is not making THE match of the season. And no one appreciates that fact more than her mama. Society has known for four years past that Bessie Bobson Altemus Eastman's chief ambition in life was to see Liz the bride of Jock Whitney. She had seen to it that Liz had been on view wherever Jock happened to be. If the Whitney heir sailed to England to attend the Grand National, Liz was on the next boat; if he journeyed to California to indulge in polo at Pebble Beach, Liz found an obliging hostess to invite her to the Pacific slope.

It should be noted that when Jock made known his intention to marry the dark-haired, dark-eyed, olive-skinned Philadelphia beauty, his mother insisted that he promise to wait two years. He complied with her wishes and kept his promise. Once he had fulfilled that obligation, the wedding took place as scheduled, with Jock's boon companion and great friend, the legendary humorist and writer Robert C. Benchley, serving as best man. Also in attendance at the splendid ceremony were many of Jock's other illustrious intimates, including Fred Astaire, author Donald Ogden Stewart, polo great Thomas Hitchcock, Jr., Charles Payson, Whitney's brother-in-law, and fellow Yalemen James J. Wadsworth and W. Stuart Symington, Wadsworth's brother-in-law.

Jock's rather spectacular prenuptial gifts to his bride were a check for $1 million and a two-thousand-acre estate, Llangollen, in Upperville, Virginia, in the foothills of the Blue Ridge Mountains. Liz spent most of the summer prior to the wedding—and three-quarters of the check—furnishing and decorating the place with priceless antiques. The entire complex, geared to the tastes of its highly athletic chatelaine, was complete with a gymnasium, a swimming pool, enormous stables, and more than two hundred horses. The charming old house itself could boast of the fact that both George Washington and the Marquis de Lafayette had slept there.

The young couple also had a suite set aside for their use at the Payne Whitney townhouse on Fifth Avenue, and a year after their marriage they acquired a 130-acre, $350,000 summer home at Saratoga. It had only ten rooms but came with a mile-long private racetrack and stables that accommodated sixty horses. Jock's August 17 birthday parties were the highlight of the racing season in those days. He always brought in first-rate talent from New York to entertain his guests. And one of his great favorites was comedian Joe E. Lewis, who used these occasions to test out the new jokes that he was planning to deliver in the nightclubs the following season. If the jokes made Jock roar with laughter, they stayed in the act; if not, they got the ax.

Jock loved the outdoors and animals, and like many another café society multimillionaire playboy, he was a polo player, albeit a rather mediocre one, with a six-goal rating (out of a possible ten). In truth, although his mother, Helen Hay Whitney, reigned supreme as "the first lady of American racing," Jock was not a particularly talented horseman, and his association with the horsy set was relatively superficial. Probably his greatest love was Broadway, and along with his older sister, Joan Whitney Payson, and occasionally his first cousin, Cornelius Vanderbilt "Sonny" Whitney, he was one of Broadway's biggest "angels." His great friend Robert C. Benchley often served as Jock's adviser on Broadway investments, and it was to Benchley whom Jock generally turned for insight into the merits or flaws of a proposed show. Once, after Jock received a manuscript from a Broadway producer and sent it on to Benchley for a recommendation, the humorist immediately replied, "I could smell this alleged comedy you want to back before the mailman got it up to the door. I can't see a thing in it. If you don't want to lose your shirt, lay off." But Jock was famous for asking advice from experts and then disregarding it. Nevertheless, most of his investments paid off, keeping him in shirts—and almost anything else his heart desired.

Liz, on the other hand, cared little for the bright lights and big city. She was obsessed with animals, horses and dogs in particular. This obsession, coupled with her absolute refusal to have children, would ultimately bring her marriage to an end.

Whether at Llangollen or at Saratoga, Liz always surrounded herself with animals. At one point in her ten-year marriage to Jock Whitney, she had more than 250 thoroughbreds in her stables. Her houses were invariably overrun with dogs. Once Liz even brought a horse into the drawing room at Llangollen during a cocktail party.

An upper-crust, blue-blooded Englishwoman who was a frequent guest at the Whitney homes remembers one particular visit to the Saratoga place. When she arrived at the door, she was greeted by an extremely harried butler, who was attempting to disentangle himself from the pack of six large, howling dogs who were determined to greet the visitor in their own exuberant fashion. "I thought for an instant I had descended into Hades and was being welcomed by Cerberus," she commented.

Visitors to Llangollen sometimes found it exceedingly difficult to find a place to sit down, for there seemed to be a dog occupying every chair and sofa. The same Englishwoman, who had spent numerous weekends at the country estates of many eccentric, animal-loving peers of the realm, found the atmosphere at Llangollen extreme even by those standards. "You'd walk into your bedroom and find a bitch whelping puppies all over the place," she reminisced.

Even Jock's mother, a woman devoted to animals, found Liz's obsession a bit much—especially when, on a visit to the Whitney plantation at Thomasville, Georgia, Liz entered Mrs. Payne Whitney's spotless drawing room with a pair of pet goats in tow. This led E. J. Kahn, Jr., to comment that Jock's marriage to Liz "was . . . made, if not in Hades, considerably short of heaven; and it did not fare well on earth."

The sad truth was that this seemingly golden alliance had almost

nothing going for it. While Jock and his family had long been connected
with the breeding and racing of fine horseflesh, this was for him only one
relatively minor facet of his magical life. Liz was totally alien to the
other facets, especially to the smell of greasepaint and roar of the
Broadway crowd, to the gala openings and huge investments that drew
Jock like a magnet. Her obsessions had long since gone well beyond
what was pleasing to her husband and his family and friends. Little
wonder that this ill-fated marriage came to an early end, in May of 1940,
at the same time that Jock decided to give up polo, never having become
a star player, and to revel in the enormous success of his investment in
the 1939 blockbuster film *Gone With the Wind*. Coincidentally, this was
just after Betsey had finalized her divorce from Jimmy Roosevelt. Even
before Betsey and Jock had become acquainted, their lives seemed to be
running on parallel tracks, almost as if fate were lending a hand to the
ambitious Cushing mother and daughter. Jock would take one major
detour before winding up with Betsey.

For Liz Altemus Whitney the ten years of her marriage to Jock
Whitney had been extremely profitable ones—at least in financial terms.
Jock, a most humane and generous man in all aspects of his life, provided handsomely for the beautiful but headstrong woman who had
often put her horses before her marriage. The final balance sheet showed
that Liz would continue to live at her beloved Upperville estate, Llangollen, and would also retain the modest twelve-acre Santa Monica ranch,
with its magnificent views of the Pacific, which she had purchased with
Whitney money. She planned to reside there for at least six months a
year. In addition, she would receive $3 million—a tidy sum, though far
less than she had hoped for.

Ironically, after steering clear of Jock's show-business interests for so
long, Liz had recently developed a strong desire to carve out a Hollywood film career for herself. She had been bitten by the bug when she
had tested for the role of Scarlett O'Hara in *Gone With the Wind*. Her
$3 million divorce settlement would certainly allow her to indulge this
and every other whim, despite her disappointment over the amount.

According to close friends of the couple, Jock had first sought the
divorce in 1937, at about the time when his pal Robert Benchley had
introduced him to Louise Macy. Liz kept on holding out for more

money. The behind-the-scenes legal wrangling over the exact dollar figure dragged on for around three years. Once Jock began to be seen publicly escorting Louise around New York's hot spots and their romance became almost daily grist for the gossip-column mills, the negotiations speeded up considerably. At last the long-rumored news that Liz and Jock's marriage was on the rocks hit the front pages of New York's tabloids, and Liz went off to Reno, Nevada, to secure a divorce. With the signing of the divorce decree, she left behind her seemingly enviable existence among the Whitneys. She never did make it in Hollywood, but she reached nearly legendary status as one of the most brilliant luminaries of café society, marrying twice again, first to Dr. John Person, who left her a widow, and then to Colonel Cloyce Tippet, whom she met on a Peruvian fishing trip.

Like Liz, Louise Macy had more family lineage than money. She was one of three daughters of the late Mr. and Mrs. Lloyd R. Macy, of Pasadena, California. Louise and her sisters, Gertrude and Mary, received an elite and expensive education at Miss Madeira's School, in Washington, D.C., and then went on to the prestigious Smith College. After they graduated, their maternal grandparents, General and Mrs. John Gill, of Baltimore, took the three orphaned Macy sisters under their wing. So lofty was Mrs. Gill's position in Baltimore society that she was known as "Mighty Lou" Gill, but the three independent young women almost immediately struck out on their own. Gertrude became a secretary and later the business manager for actress Katherine Cornell, finally becoming a Broadway producer. Mary married socialite Nicholas Ludington, of Philadelphia, who later went on to wed Gwladys Hopkins. Gwladys, Jock Whitney's cousin by marriage to Sonny Whitney, would in time play a pivotal matchmaking role in Jock's romance with Betsey Cushing Roosevelt.

Louise had wed broker Clyde Brown, Jr., in 1932—only to divorce him just ten months later in Reno. The beautiful divorcée had risen to the exalted post of Paris editor of *Harper's Bazaar*. It was during her sixteen-month sojourn in Paris that she gained her well-earned reputation as an elegant and inventive hostess. Unlike her French counterparts, who entertained almost exclusively at dinner dances in fashionable Parisian restaurants, Louise entertained the cream of American and

European society in her leased eighteenth-century house on the Place des Vosges. When the outbreak of World War II forced her to return to New York, she continued to host small, elegant dinner parties, for eight or ten friends, at least once a week. Among her guests were Jock Whitney, Bob Benchley, and many celebrities, including Bette Davis, Fred Astaire, Bernard Baruch, David and Irene Mayer Selznick, and always a visiting diplomat or foreign businessman. Louise justifiably prided herself on successfully combining an eclectic mix of personalities.

After his divorce, Jock returned with a vengeance to his former bachelor existence, with Louise as his steady date. He played hard, but he worked hard, too. For as much as he enjoyed his social life, he was an astute businessman, with a Midas touch when it came to investing. He truly derived as much pleasure from earning as he did from spending. Most of his business ventures—aviation, mining, film production, publishing, and theatrical investment—were successful. Jock's love for the theater dated back to his theatrical pursuits at Yale under the ample guidance of Monty Woolley (star of *The Man Who Came to Dinner*) and close friend Cole Porter. Of all his businesses the Broadway ventures were his great love, and a list of the productions that he backed resembles a history of great American theater during the mid-1930s and early 1940s: Cole Porter's *Gay Divorcee,* starring Jock's personal friend Fred Astaire; *Kind Lady; Whistling in the Dark; Charley's Aunt;* the long-forgotten *Broken Dishes,* far more noteworthy for having launched Bette Davis's career than for any intrinsic value; *On Borrowed Time; Dark Victory,* for which he had coaxed his onetime girlfriend Tallulah Bankhead to return from London to play the starring role; his biggest money-maker *Life with Father;* and Tennessee Williams's immortal *Streetcar Named Desire.* Jock's brilliant attorney, John Wharton, whose knowledge of the theater matched his expertise in the law and who also happened to be Cole Porter's lawyer, closely monitored Jock's theater and movie investments. Wharton once said of Jock, "Actually, he is prouder of giving New York stage debuts to such stars as Bette Davis and Frances Langford than he is of the biggest money-making hit he's ever had."

Jock and his cousin Sonny Whitney financed the development of Technicolor and were also the money men behind friend David O.

Selznick's Selznick International, which gave the world the blockbuster film version of Margaret Mitchell's *Gone With the Wind*. Jock's investment in this movie was $100,000, half the sum the author received for the rights to her book. But after the film's great success, Jock—gentleman that he was—chipped in another $50,000 of his own money for Mitchell.

Whenever he was in New York, Jock continued to be seen with Louise Macy, but after more than two years of steady dating, the couple was no closer to the altar than before. Not that either Jock or Louise lacked the interest or the desire for commitment; they cared deeply for each other. The stumbling block to their marriage was none other than Jock's mother, Helen Hay Whitney, by then, at the dawning of the 1940s, one of the five wealthiest people in America.

Jock, by that time a financially independent—in fact stupendously wealthy—young man in his early thirties, actually lived with his mother, maintaining his own suite in the cavernous Whitney mansion on New York's Fifth Avenue. He also stayed at his mother's home, Greentree Farms, in Manhasset, Long Island. So in a sense he had never really gone and established a home of his own, not even during his ten-year marriage to Liz. Llangollen was really *her* home, and he felt like a visitor there—a feeling that Liz never exerted herself to help him overcome. In effect, Jock was still tied to his mother's proverbial apron strings; he was even closer to her than was his sister, Joan, who was married to Charles Payson and had a growing family to look after. Jock didn't need to be told that his mother would never countenance a match with Louise Macy. Helen Hay Whitney openly disapproved of Louise's career-girl image and the worldly air that she displayed both in public and in private. More specifically, Jock's mother strenuously objected to the fact that Louise had known too many men and had been on her own far too long. This image, which would play so well in post–World War II America, was not yet socially acceptable in the highest strata of early 1940s society. In short, Louise was simply not a "proper" wife for the only son and heir to the vast Whitney wealth and power. The matriarch was determined to find Jock a mate worthy of the highly impressive Whitney name.

As Franklin Roosevelt prepared the nation for the inevitability of its entering the war, Jock, a devout Democrat, championed the president's cause. His brother-in-law, Charles Payson, was vehemently isolationist, even going so far as to contribute great sums of money to a neo-Nazi publication. Not surprisingly, these diametrically opposed politics made for many a lively discussion.

Jock had also turned his attention away from polo and to the acquisition of early American portraits by such artists as Francis Alexander, Matthew Jouett, Gilbert Stuart, and Thomas Sully. When friends of the Whitney family founded the Museum of Modern Art, Jock would become a trustee. This involvement led to his assembling a first-rate collection of postimpressionist art—Van Goghs, Derains, Matisses, Toulouse-Lautrecs—a collection that soon rivaled that of many major museums. Onetime Museum of Modern Art director Rene d' Harnoncourt once told Jock's biographer, E. J. Kahn, Jr.:

I'm simply amazed by [Jock's] general knowledge of art. You mention somebody to him whose name you wouldn't suspect he even knew and he'll not only be familiar with the name but what work the person is currently doing. Jock's an extremely well-informed amateur.

When it came to art, Jock was no dilettante, and he would become even more knowledgeable and acquisitive as time went on. The prestige in the art world lent a certain cachet to a man who was already considered the biggest catch in town, if not the entire country. In addition to being fabulously wealthy and well-rounded in his interests, he was extremely tall and attractive, standing six feet one inches tall and weighing about two hundred pounds. Finding him a suitable mate should not have been at all difficult. In fact, his mother began in a very subtle way to cast about for just the sort of daughter-in-law who would meet her exacting standards.

Jock made Helen's task still easier by being a rather diffident young man; from the time he was at Yale, he would always bring his girlfriends home to meet his mother. She had already at least tacitly turned her thumbs down on Louise Macy; so Jock obligingly brought a new candidate—none other than Betsey Cushing Roosevelt, whom he had met at a dinner party hosted by his not-yet-alienated cousin, Sonny Whitney, and his wife at that time, Gwladys, affectionately known as Gee. Gee was the actual matchmaker, for she felt that she owed Jock a favor for his having introduced her to Sonny. From the beginning Sonny had doubts about the evening she had planned with the expressed purpose of finding "the perfect mate" for Jock. In fact, Sonny even told Gee point-blank, "You've got the completely wrong girl for Jock." But the headstrong Gee was undeterred.

Certainly, Jock and Betsey were two very different people. If their friends had made book on the likelihood of their making a match of it, the nays would have been in the vast majority. But Jock seemed almost immediately smitten with Betsey. The fact that she remained the favorite daughter-in-law of President Roosevelt—even after she had divorced Jimmy and left the Roosevelt fold—made an especially favorable impression on the young man, and on the entire Democratic branch of the Whitney family. Jock lost no time in bringing Betsey home to meet his mother. This first visit to the Whitney mansion went so well that Helen issued a follow-up invitation for the comely ex-Mrs. Roosevelt to spend the night. For Betsey, this second visit proved rather unsettling, for after escorting her son's new friend to a guest bedroom, the matriarch casually commented, "This is the perfect room for you. It's the one in which Jock's grandmother died."

Betsey hung in, possibly even finding Helen's brand of maternal possessiveness a relief after so many years of dealing with such old dragons as Sara and Eleanor Roosevelt. After a number of subsequent visits, the spirited but not vicious Whitney dowager stunned Betsey by saying in the usual straightforward manner for which she was notorious, "I'd like you to marry my son." This blunt imperative was all the more disconcerting as it was issued long before Jock had even gotten around to asking Betsey to be his wife. With a little nudging from his mother, things moved ahead rather rapidly. At last he came through with a proposal.

The New York gossip columnists had a field day for weeks, predicting when the marriage would take place or if in fact it would take place at all. Being the gentleman that he was, Jock felt great qualms over so publicly jilting Louise Macy. He confided to Betsey that he would like to help Louise save face by letting her announce her engagement to him and then almost immediately break it off with a public announcement. Then he would be free to formalize his engagement to Betsey. Jock had taken it into his head that a formal recognition of his almost two-year relationship with Louise would not only leave her with her dignity intact but would help her in an impending business venture; after all, the Whitney name had considerable weight in New York.

Betsey was furious over this unusual proposal. She sent Jock a highly emotional letter, telling him in no uncertain terms that if he went through with this incredibly bizarre scheme, he had seen the last of her. It worked. Jock went to Betsey to ask her to marry him—and she readily accepted. Betsey's ire, however understandable under the circumstances, and Jock's instant capitulation set the pattern that would prevail throughout their marriage. In the years ahead, Betsey would transform Jock's lifestyle and even his thoughts and his personality, seeing to it that his show-business and literary friends were largely dispersed, his political views changed, and that he became far more staid than he had been in his earlier days.

The wedding, far less spectacular than either the bride's or the groom's first trip to the altar more than a decade earlier, took place on March 1, 1942. The ceremony was a simple one, held in the drawing room of Gogsie Cushing's East Eighty-sixth Street apartment, with only immediate family members and a few close friends in attendance. The bride, unaccompanied by bridesmaids, wore an elegantly tailored slate-blue suit with a matching hat and a simple white blouse. Instead of carrying a bouquet, Betsey chose to wear a corsage of white flowers at her shoulder. Jock's best man this time around was William Harding Jackson, whom he had met playing polo in the late 1920s. Although a Tennessean by birth, Jackson was well known in New York legal circles.

Guarding the apartment were United States Secret Service agents, sent to ensure the safety of the president's granddaughters, Sara and Kate Roosevelt, who were of course present at their mother's wedding. After the ceremony, the few guests joined a far larger crowd at a reception given by Minnie and Vincent Astor in their Manhattan home. Among the guests were the gleefully triumphant Gogsie Cushing and the smug

Helen Hay Whitney; Joan and Charles Shipman Payson, sister and brother-in-law of the groom; Babe Mortimer; Sonny Whitney and his wife, Gee; Mr. and Mrs. Henry K. Cushing, brother and sister-in-law of the bride; Misses Lorinda and Payne Payson, Joan's daughters; Nelson Rockefeller, Jock's political mentor; Clarence d'Hommedieu; Major Thomas Hitchcock, Jr.; and Major Louis A. Beard, who had served almost as a surrogate father to Jock since the death of his father. It was with Beard that Jock had lunched at the Racquet and Tennis Club the day before the wedding, rather than indulging in a traditional raucous bachelor dinner. Notably absent were Robert Benchley, who had been Jock's best man at his first wedding, David O. Selznick, and John McClain, all unable to get to New York at least in part because of the inclement weather.

Immediately after the reception, the newlyweds departed for Greenwood Plantation, the Whitney estate in Thomasville, Georgia. From there they planned to proceed to Florida. Within two weeks of the wedding, the young couple was back in Washington, D.C., where Jock was serving under Nelson Rockefeller as director of the motion picture division of the Office of the Coordinator of Inter-American Affairs. Betsey and Jock established their residence in the leased mansion of Admiral Cary Grayson, on the beautiful and exclusive Foxhall Road. One of their first visitors was President Roosevelt, who was still extremely fond of his former daughter-in-law. FDR would continue to stop by the Whitneys' home throughout their stay in Washington, much to Jock's delight. He was a great admirer of the president and was overjoyed to meet the great man on such intimate terms. Despite Jock's great wealth and exposure to the worlds of society, the arts, and politics, he had managed to maintain an engaging innocence and was still in many ways an impressionable young man. He was awed by the president, and these familylike gatherings with FDR were the high point of Jock's life during this period. Jock felt very lucky indeed to have chosen a bride with such a unique and warm relationship with the nation's chief executive.

Better yet, the president frequently reciprocated by inviting the Whitneys to the White House for intimate dinners, generally with only one or two other guests and invariably when Eleanor was away on one of her many missions for her husband. FDR's secretary, Grace Tully, always acted as hostess on these occasions.

More than once Jock attempted to conduct some business concerning his agency, trying to discover whether it would remain independent or would, as rumored, be taken over by General William "Wild Bill" Donovan and his newly created Office of Strategic Services. The president, however, was far too astute to let these strictly social evenings serve anyone's political interests other than his own. He sincerely wanted to enjoy the company of his adored former daughter-in-law; yet he was aware that Betsey's new husband, with his astronomical family fortune and his well-earned Democratic credentials, could prove useful to the party and its candidates in the future. And far be it from FDR to pass up any possible political opportunity.

Other than their evenings with the president, the Whitneys held their entertaining to a minimum, largely due to the increasing seriousness of the war in Europe. Jock was getting restless, consumed by a desire to serve his country in active duty. His boss, Nelson Rockefeller, did everything in his power to persuade Jock to remain with Inter-American Affairs, but Whitney was adamant; he wanted to be in the thick of things in Europe, even if it meant enlisting in the British Armed Forces. Betsey was in complete agreement with her husband, unconditionally supporting his wish to serve. On May 22, 1942, Jock received his commission— as captain in the army. On June 18 he began his military tour of duty. Jock's enlistment marked the beginning of great change for both Betsey and himself. They had barely been married for three months, barely become accustomed to their new marriage, when he went off to war. During their long separation, Jock would mature immeasurably, and Betsey, on her own once again, would develop even greater strengths than she had during her Roosevelt years.

While Jock was off serving his country, his mother took Betsey under her wing, determined to teach her new daughter-in-law about the vast Whitney wealth. Helen Hay had come from a socioeconomic background very similar to Betsey's, with little preparation for dealing with such a huge fortune. When Payne Whitney died, leaving Helen a widow with children who had not yet attained their majority, it was up to her to educate herself—and quickly, at that—on the management of the enormous Whitney patrimony. She had passed on all her knowledge of its intricacies—and attendant obligations—to her son and daughter, and now made Betsey's education her chief mission in life. Helen was a masterful teacher, and to her delight, she found a very apt pupil in Betsey. The matriarch's creed, almost from the day she had inherited the Whitney millions, was that while it was her duty to be an ever-vigilant conservator of the fortune, she must also do as much good with it as humanly possible. The years ahead would show just how well Betsey could adhere to her mother-in-law's dictates.

10

FAREWELL
TO
BROADWAY AND HOLLYWOOD

*W*ITH Betsey's marriage to Jock Whitney, Gogsie Cushing had reached the pinnacle of her ambitions. Although not one of her daughters could boast of a coronet, all three had captivated and captured not only the bluest of America's blue blood but very nearly the richest of the nation's rich, eligible men. The three attractive young women had laid seige to New York and married it into submission within less than eighteen months' time—a feat never before or since duplicated by three siblings. Babe had bewitched a handsome, debonair Tuxedo Park aristocrat; Minnie had married the grandson of the doyenne of New York's lofty 400 and the possessor of one of America's most legendary fortunes; and Betsey had secured the scion of one of the few families that surpassed the Astors in wealth, a man who numbered among the all-time great capitalist movers and shakers. And Betsey had gone her sisters one better by maintaining a warm, loving relationship with the president of the United States.

But Betsey's marriage to Jock Whitney was far more than a feather in her mother's or even her own cap; it was a relationship based on mutual love and respect, despite great personal differences. Rather than merely making her husband's life gracious and comfortable, as her mother had decreed, Betsey began to mold Jock into her own personal ideal of a mate for life. In the end, Betsey's strong will and Jock's malleability made for a more harmonious relationship than her mother and sisters had enjoyed.

Almost all Whitney's intimates agreed that his second marriage had a marked effect on his life and lifestyle. Betsey Cushing Roosevelt brought to the marriage an inclination toward liberal thinking and a practical sort of intellectualism, which she owed at least in part to her years of favored status within the Roosevelt family circle. One close friend of the Whitneys at the time of their marriage has summed up Betsey's influence on her husband:

> Betsey brought a whole new set of values into Jock's life. Some of these she had inherited from her father, who was the essence of an oriented man, and some from her close association with President Roosevelt and the brilliant and innovative men who made his era. I don't think Betsey transformed Jock, but I'm sure that to him she represented awareness of a larger world in which he wanted to play a part.

In addition Betsey brought her two young daughters into Jock's household and his life, instantly making him a paterfamilias—quite a change from his role as Helen's "baby." In time, he would legally adopt Sara and Kate Roosevelt.

Without a doubt, Jock and Betsey had their differences. Until this point in his life he had been a high-living, strenuous sportsman and a two-fisted drinker. According to Earl Blackwell, founder of Celebrity International, in a recent conversation: "Jock Whitney had quite a torrid romance with Tallulah Bankhead. And it went on for some time."

Betsey, on the other hand, had never forgotten her prim and proper upbringing. Yet even as she subtly began to mold her new husband into her ideal, her primary concern was ensuring his health, safety, and happiness—a monumental task for a woman married to such a multi-faceted man.

Jock's friend Shipwreck Kelly, onetime All American and husband of the nation's number-one debutante, Brenda Frazier, often recounted an incident that took place at a World Series game at Ebbets Field, in Brooklyn. Jock had given the tickets to his season box at the field to Betsey and her daughters and their friends. At the last minute, he decided to go to the game himself and invited Kelly to come along. There were of course no seats left by the time they arrived, at the top of the third inning, but Jock had clout. He encountered a team official, who arranged for a couple of folding chairs to be set up on the roof of the stadium—near the edge, which had no guard rail. Cheering wildly, greatly animated by liberal infusions of bourbon, the two rooftop spectators soon attracted the attention of some of the fans below, including Betsey. In no time she had climbed to the roof and, according to Shipwreck, insisted that Jock, who generally had an aversion to heights, watch the rest of the game lying on his belly, while she remained on the roof-top, quite literally clinging assiduously to his coattails.

Paradoxically, Betsey made no attempt to dissuade Jock from enlisting; in fact she wholeheartedly supported his decision, even in the face of Rockefeller's legitimate opposition. Early July 1942 found Whitney at his first duty station, an army air corps intelligence school in Harrisburg, Pennsylvania, where he took a six-week advance-training course. Betsey accompanied him to Harrisburg, and they rented what was, by their standards, an apartment of exceedingly modest size, with only four or five rooms, and hired only one part-time servant to see to their needs.

From time to time shades of their civilian life surfaced. At one cocktail party the Whitneys gave during their stay in Harrisburg, the wife of a fellow junior officer timidly introduced herself to an older gentleman in a well-tailored dark blue suit, thinking that he was some distinguished Whitney family member; he was in fact the butler from Greentree, dispatched to the "outback" by Jock's mother to ensure the comfort and general well-being of her only son and his new bride.

The Whitneys were greatly pleased by the arrival in Harrisburg of Second Lieutenant C. Tracey Barnes and his wife, Janet. Barnes was in fact a Whitney relative, Jock's second cousin, the son of the late Payne Whitney's first cousin. Many years before, the senior Whitney had built a summer home for Tracy's parents on the grounds of Greentree. Since Tracy was six years younger than Jock, and had not even entered Yale

until two years after Jock had graduated, the two men were only casually acquainted before their chance meeting in Harrisburg.

Whitney's biographer, E. J. Kahn, Jr., recounts an incident from
those days in Harrisburg, as Janet Barnes had told it to him:

> One evening during the scorching summer of 1942, a bat flew into
> our apartment [in the same building as Jock and Betsey's] and
> began buzzing over our bed. Tracy tried unsuccessfully to rout the
> intruder with a tennis racquet and appealed for reinforcements to
> Captain Whitney, who, putting bravely behind him his apprehen-
> sions about the winged creatures, took to the field in shorts and a
> shower cap of Betsey's, armed with a second racquet. In time the
> two fledgling intelligence officers destroyed the bat.

. . . and in the bargain, according to Janet Barnes, managed also to
demolish much of the furniture in the rented apartment.

The atmosphere in Harrisburg at that time was reminiscent of the
carefree undergraduate days at Yale, with long weekday stints of classes
and late-night homework, followed by serious Saturday-night partying
and lazy Sunday picnics. As the six weeks drew to an end, Jock, a newly
appointed air corps captain, awaited his transfer as an intelligence
officer with the American Eagle Squadron, based in Watford, just outside London. Of course, Jock was no ordinary GI, who could simply
pick up his duffel and ship out. First he set up three different bank
accounts in London: a sterling area account, a free sterling account, and
a registered sterling one. Then he had to arrange for his New York office
to deposit among these accounts a thousand pounds a month, enough
money so that he would not have to scrape by on his army pay. He also
turned over his custom yacht, *Aphrodite,* to the Coast Guard, which
then deployed it to escort the trains that carried President Roosevelt
along the east bank of the Hudson River between New York and his
residence at Hyde Park. The Coast Guard also used the magnificent
yacht to shuttle foreign diplomats and other visitors up the river to
spend the weekend at Hyde Park with FDR.

Jock was not required to live on the air base. On arriving in London,
he leased a large flat on prestigious Grosvenor Square, which he shared

with ten-goal polo player and longtime friend Tommy Hitchcock. There, in these London digs, the two gave parties that attained legendary status for their great liveliness and good cheer, their liberal offerings of libations, and the steady stream of beautiful, glamorous women who paraded through the stately portals. In fact, Jock and Tommy's parties were among the most spectacular ever seen in wartime London. The male guests were primarily fellow officers, especially those at the command level (Jock's superiors at the time, as he did not receive his major's oak leaves until December of 1942). The attractive female guests included titled Englishwomen, exotic foreign adventuresses, and American and British actresses, eager to do their bit for the "boys" in uniform. On any given weekend the guests might include Lady Edwina Mountbatten, Pamela Churchill, Vivien Leigh, Michael Tree, Oliver Messel, and English airman Lord Kinross. It was an extremely lively set, and Jock was often seen around London in those days with a beautiful woman on his arm. The Blitzkrieg was a minor inconvenience for the beauties and their British and American uniformed escorts, who were almost too wrapped up in their endless social life to notice the buzzing German planes and exploding bombs. Almost desperately they clung to their memories of the café society era that was so much a part of their younger, more carefree days. And no doubt this almost frenetic atmosphere allowed Jock to sew a few remaining wild oats before returning home to his future public image of a devoted husband and great American statesman.

The photographer and set designer Cecil Beaton, who was well acquainted with the American and British branches of the Whitney family, recalls that giddy period and the men who, like Jock and Tommy, made up the American Eagle Squadron:

> It is the spirit of adventure that has inspired these young men to join the Eagle Squadron and to come here in search of excitement. They are fighting for the fun of it. . . . They want to know about English history; they are enthusiastic to see Nelson's Column and the interior of Windsor Castle. They complain a certain amount about England: the climate, the lack of heating and the draughts. They bemoan the monotony of English wartime food, and except

for Lady Mountbatten, they do not always admire English women. They cannot tolerate or appreciate the charm of the slowness of England, and they become maddened by the delays on the telephone. Yet in general they take everything as a matter of course, accepting easily our strange ways. Oddly enough, they don't complain about the BBC programmes or the London dance bands. They listen eagerly to Bob Hope, they like "Elmer's Tune" and "Daddy You Wanna Get the Best for Me." They read a lot, but seldom trash. They like Shakespeare, Dickens, Kipling. And they like, of course, to see American magazines. . . . Their friendliness to all and sundry is genuinely warmhearted. They think for themselves more than most young Englishmen do. They do not accept unchallenged certain orders or pronouncements. But, once it is kindled, their admiration is sincere.

Betsey had planned to join Jock there, to be with him when he received his major's rank and possibly also to become an American Red Cross aide or a volunteer with some other agency. With this in mind, she arranged a meeting with the president, hoping that he would secure all the necessary clearance for her to be with her husband in England, at least until he was reassigned to another duty station. But FDR refused Betsey's request. If Betsey went abroad, she would not be available for their occasional pleasurable visits. Or he may have been worried about his former daughter-in-law's safety.

Betsey was disappointed, but she was a practical, mature young woman. She threw herself into war-related volunteer work on the home front, giving many hours and much hard work to the American Red Cross, Minnie's National War Fund, and the American Relief for France. In addition, Betsey constantly looked in on Jock's mother, who had slipped into a chronic state of ill health since her only son had gone off to war. Her illnesses were at least in part the result of her alcoholism, one of the Whitneys' worst-kept secrets. It was hard to accept the fact that this active, dynamic woman had taken to her bed and gradually become a confirmed recluse. She still divided her time between her Manhattan mansion at 972 Fifth Avenue and her stately antebellum-style home at Greentree Farms. Once settled, she rarely ventured out or received anyone other than her daughter, Joan; her Payson grandchildren, Sandra, Payne, Lorinda, Daniel, and John; and Betsey and her two daughters, Sara and Kate, whom the matriarch treated courteously but not quite as family members.

In her day, Helen Hay Whitney, the daughter of a man who served as secretary of state during the administrations of Presidents McKinley and Theodore Roosevelt, had been a remarkable woman, a force to be reckoned with in literary, racing, gardening, and art circles. She had produced some worthy poems, generally about her children, and had for many years enjoyed the status of "first lady of the American turf." In an era when few, if any, women were actively involved in horse breeding and racing, she bred some of the most magnificent thoroughbreds in the country. The famous cherry and black Whitney colors commanded unanimous respect, for Helen had turned out, among numerous successful colts, two Kentucky Derby winners—the all-time great Twenty Grand, who captured the roses in 1931, and Shut Out, who won in 1942. The excellence and professionalism of her endeavors paved the way for an entire generation of women, her daughter among them, who would breed and race out of their own stables and in their own names.

Helen also tended her own spectacular gardens at Greentree Farms and won numerous national and international awards for her prized flowers. Art collecting was another of her great passions, one that she passed on to both her children. As time went on, her huge inheritance from her husband became more of a burden than a source of pleasure. Payne Whitney's estate, divided among his widow and two children, was appraised in May of 1927 at $178,893,655, earning the distinction of being the largest estate ever presented for probate in New York State.

Helen's strong humanitarian philosophy led her to contribute great sums toward educational grants, especially for those disenfranchised by the establishment. In this and in her indifference to race, creed, and color, she was definitely ahead of her time. Early on she imparted these values to her children. Jock once recounted an incident that had left a lasting impression on him:

I think it must have been something Joan and I absorbed when we were very young. I remember, when we were kids, the grown-ups were discussing a guest who was coming for the weekend and someone asked if he was Jewish. My mother looked astounded and asked: "How could anyone know or care?" So we were very young when it came to us that a person's race or religion or position had no bearing on whether he was attractive or right to be a friend. If you start like that, it's natural for your feelings to broaden as you grow older. I think there's a lot of truth in that song that you've got to be taught to hate.

That philosophy remained with Helen Hay Whitney to the very end, which was drawing near. Her health suffered another severe blow when she received the shocking news that Jock had been taken prisoner by the Germans while he was on a secret reconnaissance mission in France. Landing in Provence shortly after the establishment of the beachhead in southern France, Jock was to make a first-hand study of the operation of the OSS, which coordinated French Underground activities.

Not long before this perilous venture, Jock had struck up a friendship with a public relations officer and fellow Yaleman assigned to the Eighth Air Force, John Regan McCrary, affectionately known as Tex. The two men remained lifelong friends. Years later, Jock introduced Tex to Jinx Falkenburg, a ranking tennis player, whom Jock had met when she caddied for him and his Minute Maid orange-juice partner, Bing Crosby, in California. Tex and Jinx immediately hit it off, later gaining fame as a radio team.

Tex recommended Jock to the commander of the Eighth Air Force, General Ira Eaker. The general lost little time naming Jock his public relations officer and promoting him to the rank of lieutenant colonel. Naturally, Jock saw to it that his newfound friend, Tex, became his top aide. The two men traveled to Italy, where they met with Wild Bill Donovan, chief of the OSS. After much badgering from Jock, Donovan assigned the newly minted lieutenant colonel to a field operation in southern France.

On August 21, 1944, once he had managed to get inside occupied France, Jock received his orders for his top-secret mission. The orders came from none other than the legendary "M. Henri," the French-raised American lawyer Henry Hyde, who had, from his base in Algiers, organized all OSS operations in southern France.

From an air base near the newly freed St. Tropez, Whitney rode north up the Rhone Valley with two French civilian agents and a driver whose OSS identification was PFC Moretti. The agents were to get as close to the retreating enemy as possible, but Jock's party made the terrible mistake of driving too far up the wrong road. The sudden chatter of machine-gun fire told the group immediately that they had stumbled into an ambush. To quote in brief from Whitney's official report:

> Moretti stopped the vehicle and fired a burst from his machine gun. I jumped from the weapons carrier, taking a position by the right wheel, and fired with a carbine. The position which I had assumed quickly became untenable, however, since the vehicle rolled backwards down the hill, leaving me exposed. Weapons carrier, agents, Moretti and I all arrived together in a small gutter beside the road.

Jock and his small band crawled along the ditch, still under fire, and took refuge in a nearby house, which had recently been evacuated. Whitney covered one of the agents while the man reconnoitered the rear of the house. He soon returned to report that there was an enemy tank just to the rear of the grounds. Jock wanted to know how many soldiers the agent had seen, but he ran into the house too quickly to answer. Just then Jock saw through a high hedge the legs of appearing enemy soldiers. Moretti shouted to him to hold his fire and come back into the house, which Jock readily admitted, he 'gladly dis.' Unable to defend themselves, the agents, Moretti, and Whitney were all captured. The enemy separated the prisoners during the subsequent interrogations, and they never saw one another again. Soon Jock found himself in the back of a German half-track armed with a Howitzer, in a convoy traveling up the Rhone Valley. In a *Saturday Evening Post* profile of the millionaire art patron, he stated some of what happened next:

> About midnight on a heavily wooded road, we were ambushed by French Resistance forces. The firing was intense from our convoy, which was being crisscrossed by machine-gun tracers and rifle fire. I climbed out of my place in the half-track to jump, but the gun loader caught me by the seat of the pants.

During the night Whitney managed to dispose of several incriminating documents, among them his orders to report to the OSS. Strafing attacks by American fighter planes often interrupted the following day's journey. That night Jock and three other captured GIs were held in a granary. Jock managed to get the ear of the Frenchman who owned the granary, giving him the names of the other prisoners and telling him that a note would be left hidden in the straw after their departure. Whitney had written and addressed the note to Tex McCrary, public relations officer at M.A.A.F., located in the former summer palace of the king of Italy, at Caserta. In the note Jock asked Tex to inform Betsey of his capture but to assure her that he was in good shape.

At that moment McCrary was prowling around behind the German lines in France, and he did not return to Caserta until three days later. When he got back, the message was waiting for him on his desk. A wire-service correspondent happened to get wind of the note, and putting two and two together, linked it with Jock's unexplained absence. He sent a report of the capture to his London office, with the usual "withhold-for-notification-of-next-of-kin" warning. Unfortunately, the report somehow got out through the regular news channels, and that afternoon the public address system at Belmont Park interrupted the race commentary to announce to the crowd in the grandstands that an especially esteemed member of the Jockey Club, Mr. John Hay Whitney, was in enemy hands.

Betsey, who was at Greentree Farms with her daughters, received the shattering news from a friend who had gone to the races that day. Kate, then only eight years old, crawled under a bed. "I remember thinking," she recalled years later, "Good Lord, we've just got ourselves a new father and now it seems we've lost him again." Kate's grandfather, FDR, had already gotten word of Jock's capture, and Harry Hopkins phoned Betsey from the White House and asked her not to mention the fact to anyone, lest the Germans discover that they had captured not only a high-ranking intelligence officer but the scion of one of America's wealthiest and most prominent families. This knowledge might create incalculable repercussions for both Jock and his country. Nevertheless, the news was out, and it spread like wildfire. The news hit the stands just ten days before the subject of the article would gain his freedom.

As the boxcar carrying Jock and a large group of other prisoners rattled through the Haute-Saone Department toward the German border, eleven of the forty-five men, including Jock, decided to make a break for freedom. The door of the boxcar opened, revealing a countryside bathed in bright moonlight. Jock remembered that night well:

Finally I heard someone say, "Go ahead, jump." I hit the stones of the track side, going too far for my legs to keep up, but before the ground could smack me in the face it ran out and I was rolling down the bank.

The following day the six men who had managed to escape were moving carefully along the edge of a dirt road when they met a small boy, who warned them that there was a party of fifty Germans just down the road. Whitney asked the boy to find them some food and clothing. For three hours they waited. Then, at last, a group of Maquis led by the young boy arrived, bearing baskets of sausage and bread— and even a demijohn of champagne to wash the food down. Jock spent three days with the Maquis, dressed in French-peasant blue. Then on September 11, he had the great pleasure of introducing himself to advance units of the 143rd Regiment of the 36th Division.

Betsey was in New York on September 10, when she received a visit from two officers on General Eaker's staff, who asked in a most delicate manner just what she wanted them to do with Jock's effects. The two men were with her when she got a call from Washington, on instructions from the White House, informing her that the Pentagon had just learned that Colonel Whitney had returned to duty; confirmation, the caller assured her, would reach her hands within the hour. When that confirmation did come through, Betsey immediately telephoned Jock's mother, who at that point was seriously ill, and then his sister. As soon as Betsey hung up, in her typical and inimitable manner, she invited the two officers to lunch at 21. They all got thoroughly drunk and joked and laughed uproariously. Some of the other patrons lunching at the exclusive restaurant knew Betsey and, not being aware that Jock had won his freedom, frowned on what they took to be her unseemly behavior. But Betsey felt sure that Jock would have approved of her little celebration.

It was not long before Jock arrived home on a well-earned leave, but he was not in time to see his mother, who died on September 24. While mourning her death, he learned of syndicated columnist Drew Pearson's snide suggestions regarding the manner in which Jock had gained his freedom. According to Pearson's column, Whitney had not escaped but had instead bought his freedom. All in all, a most disheartening home-coming!

Several years after the war ended, Jock and Betsey and the two girls went to Europe. Starting at Aix en Provence, they retraced the route of his capture, his long journey as a prisoner, and his escape. Along the way they sought out the many French civilians who had been kind and helpful to him as a prisoner and as an escapee.

During his captivity one of the few things Jock had been able to do was contemplate the future. He had spoken at length with the other prisoners and was appalled by their lack of understanding of the issues involved in the war. As he later explained:

> During long conversations with my fellow prisoners I rarely en-countered a GI who was able or willing to say what he was fighting for. I never heard one of the boys throw it back to the Nazis and say he was fighting for freedom or for a moral reason. I don't think this was through any fault of theirs. It seemed to me that it repre-sented a fundamental fault in our democratic educational system. I decided that when I got back—if I got back—I'd try to do something about that.

For Jock those late summer weeks of 1944 had been eventful in other ways. On August 17, his fortieth birthday and just six days before his capture, he had assumed control of a $20 million trust fund, which his father had established for him. And with his mother's death, he received another $20 million and various real estate holdings, including the Fifth Avenue Whitney mansion, Greentree Farms on Long Island, and the family plantation in Thomasville, Georgia.

Back in civilian life he began the task of setting up the John Hay Whitney Foundation, which he had envisioned during those long days and nights when he had been a prisoner of war. With the help of

William H. Jackson, a Whitney family attorney and former OSS officer, and Sydney Spivack, a close friend of the Cushing family—in fact, almost like an adopted son to Gogsie and Harvey—Jock settled on a plan that provided for educational philanthropy, a business organization that would encourage small enterprises, and a personal reserve of his fortune for meeting his obligations and continuing his private gifts.

With his foundation set up and his business affairs taking shape in a new and different postwar world, Jock and Betsey began to think about the future of her two Roosevelt daughters. They reached the decision that Jock would legally adopt Sara and Kate, although not immediately. Out of respect for the girls' grandfather, Betsey and Jock felt that they should wait a bit longer before actually setting the legal action into motion. For the present, there was little they could do without causing FDR great suffering, for he was very fond of his young granddaughters.

Both girls attended his fourth inauguration, on January 20, 1945. The man who had led his nation out of the Depression and through a world war to victory had now received yet another vote of confidence; the public fully expected him to reap the fruits of peace for America. But fate would deny him that final opportunity, for on April 12, 1945, he died at his Warm Springs, Georgia, retreat.

Betsey and the president's children and other in-laws decided not to attempt to bring any of FDR's thirteen grandchildren either to the funeral in Washington or to the burial at Hyde Park. The children had all been with him on inauguration day, and their parents decided that it would be better for them to remember their grandfather as he had been then.

During those memorable days surrounding the sudden death of the president of the United States, friends reported, Betsey spent part of the time in seclusion; perhaps she was reminiscing about all the heady moments she had been a part of during her Washington years, about the closeness she had shared with her father-in-law, or the kindness he had showered on her. The great man had truly been her friend, and his friendship had helped her during some very difficult times.

Now that Jock was home, busy with his foundation and his venture capital business and an occasional foray into politics, the Whitneys sold off the Fifth Avenue mansion that Helen had bequeathed to her son, along with most of the furnishings. Then Betsey set about brightening up the main residence at Greentree, which had fallen into a sad state of repair during Helen's final illness, despite the horde of servants who should have been keeping the place up. Here Betsey proceeded with caution. After all, this had been Jock's boyhood home, and few grown men would tolerate any radical changes in their lifestyle. Jock Whitney was no exception. Once, for instance, Betsey diffidently asked him if it would be all right for her to dispose of some of the hundreds of photographs that were cluttering the vast drawing room. Jock gave the matter careful thought and finally consented to the displacement of only those photographs in which he could not identify the people; all the others had to remain. With the help of the grande dame of American interior decorating, Sister Parish, Betsey was able to turn the residence into quite an attractive and livable home for Jock, Sara, and Kate. Lively chintzes, combined with wonderfully comfortable furniture, created a perfect setting for Jock's collection of Matisses, Toulouse-Lautrecs, and Picassos. Sister Parish (Mrs. Henry Parish II) was a member of old-guard New York society. She had turned to decorating as a young matron and is still going strong today at more than eighty years of age, one of the best-known and most exclusive decorators in the history of this century. She is on retainer to Betsey and has decorated and continues to decorate all of her homes, with the exception of the London residence.

The one thing that Jock and Betsey did not intend to do was to join the fast-living New York café-society-turned-jet-set. Shortly after the war, Jock received a routine letter from the Social Register, asking him to verify the family listing and append their summer residence. Jock, after discussing the matter with Betsey, wrote to request that his name be dropped from the register. As he explained at the time and later to a writer from *The Saturday Evening Post*,

> I think some people believe that this was a kind of snobbism in reverse. Actually, the Social Register is a handy reference for people who want names and addresses. We weren't trying to lead any parade; it was simply that Betsey and the kids and I felt it was anti-American mainstream."

Abdication from the lofty Social Register did not in and of itself qualify Jock and Betsey as champions of tolerance and social equality, but in the quietly persistent way it illustrated the trend of their concerns—away from social positions and toward human conditions in postwar America.

11

———

SEEKING
A
LATTER-DAY CROESUS

$\mathcal{A}$LTHOUGH Gogsie Cushing had been incredibly successful in marrying her daughters off, *keeping* them married was another matter altogether. For a brief time in 1944, when Jock Whitney fell into enemy hands, she had feared that Betsey would have to begin husband-hunting all over again. After Jock and Stan Mortimer were safely back home, Babe had dropped her bombshell—she wanted to divorce Stan.

It was not unreasonable to hope that Babe might do even better the second time around—perhaps even bag the coronet Gogsie had long envisioned. Stan, for all his blue blood and Standard Oil heritage, had relatively little ready cash. The Mortimers, while not in a league with the Astors or Whitneys, were enormously rich, but much of that wealth was held in perpetual trusts, which meted out just enough money to provide comfortable living standards for the past, present, and future heirs of the family fortune but did not allow for an extravagant lifestyle. In short, the Mortimers were really second rung rather than top drawer. While Babe could hardly be considered a spendthrift, she did love the good life and all the fine trappings that money could buy.

Even with her limited budget and the impossibility of spending huge amounts on an extravagant high-fashion wardrobe, she had managed to top the Best Dressed List for two consecutive years (1945 and 1946), nosing out such distinguished contenders as Chrysler heiress Mrs. Byron Foy, Standard Oil heiress Mrs. Millicent Rogers, and Louise Macy Hopkins, wife of Harry Hopkins and the woman who had lost Jock Whitney to Babe's sister Betsey. Babe's fashion status was all the more amazing. With the exception of Louise, the other women Babe beat out had unlimited funds to spend on their clothes—and for that matter on anything else they might happen to fancy.

That Babe managed to dress so well on a relative shoestring was a great tribute to her ingenuity, her glamour, and her taste. She invariably chose quality over quantity, perhaps only buying two evening gowns a year in the early days. Yet she was able to acquire a spectacular eclectic mix of coutourier creations—from Charlie James to Balenciaga to Molyneux—because her position at *Vogue* entitled her to enormous discounts, denied by top designers to ordinary mortals, if, in fact, she paid at all. Her elegant beauty and natural grace led many of the great designers to vie for the privilege of seeing Babe Cushing Mortimer in their creations. She had merely to appear in an ensemble for the designer to gain instant recognition and indeed celebrity in the highest echelons of fashion and society, and to garner continued acclaim in the fashion press. Such "advertising" would be well worth the relatively small cost of adding an item or two to the wardrobe of the famed beauty and reigning queen of fashion.

It was no secret that Babe and Stan's marriage was on the rocks. Gogsie wanted desperately to make sure that Babe had an even bigger catch waiting in the wings before divorcing Stan. Gogsie, as the mother-in-law of both Vincent Astor and Jock Whitney, had immediate entrée into the most prestigious and elegant social events. She made the most of these opportunities, doing some serious scouting for her soon-to-be-divorced daughter.

For a while it looked as if this relentlessly ambitious mother might realize her fondest wish. When Babe became estranged from Stan, she found a willing escort in Prince Serge Obolensky, the former husband of Alice Astor. But the relationship came to naught. When Babe finally got her divorce in May of 1946, she had not yet lined up a second husband.

Even so, neither she nor her mother had any cause for alarm, for Babe was still an extremely marriageable young woman, as glamorous as she was beautiful, and with the quintessential patina of old-guard class, bestowed on her by her ill-fated marriage to Stan Mortimer. In addition, Babe was highly visible in the New York fashion and social scene. Her photograph appeared everywhere, and she attended all the right parties and benefits, was seen at all the right places. Her flair for fashion served her in good stead, and her "Best Dressed" title came at a strategic time for her. Having conquered the worlds of fashion and old-guard society, Babe fully intended to blaze new frontiers, to attain celebrity status and all the perks that it would accord. She made no bones about thriving on all the glamour and press adulation generally reserved for stars of stage and screen or visiting royalty. Undoubtedly with some urging from Gogsie, Babe made a calculated decision to seek as much publicity as possible, to pursue the status of a cult figure among Manhattan's glitterati.

Babe received her uncontested divorce in Miami in May of 1946. She, like her sister Betsey, came out of her first marriage without any substantial monetary compensation. Babe had to undertake her husband hunt in deadly earnest. With the responsibility of rearing Amanda and Tony on only a modest divorce settlement and barely adequate child support—and with a demanding, time-consuming job that paid off more in celebrity than in hard cash—time was of the essence. She moved into her mother's apartment, to ensure a stable home life for her young children during her numerous absences as she pursued the dual careers of *Vogue* fashion editor and husband-shopping divorcée.

The return of glamour to postwar New York society made Babe's job a lot easier than it would have been during the war. New York, a larger-than-life reflection of the hopes and aspirations of the rest of the nation, was a city full of optimism and a great desire to move beyond the tragic toll in human life that World War II and Nazi tyranny had taken. And the press was all too happy to accommodate this new spirit. Harry Truman, the plain Missourian who succeeded to the presidency on the death of President Roosevelt, was gaining tremendous popularity throughout the country. The antics of movie stars were as noteworthy as politics; so when actress June Haver insured her lovely legs for $500,000 with Lloyds of London, almost everyone in the nation knew all the details. And in New York, husband-and-wife radio teams held amusing morning chats over the breakfast table to help their fans start their day with a smile. Ed and Pegeen Fitzgerald were the pioneers in this light morning format. Broadway columnist Dorothy Kilgallen and her husband, Dick Kollmar, followed. And as previously noted, ex-model, actress, and tennis player Jinx Falkenburg McCrary and husband, Tex, entertained New Yorkers with their early-morning "Hi-Jinx" show. Still great friends of Jock Whitney, they later moved into a house on the grounds of Greentree Farms. Although Jinx and Tex opted to broadcast from a Radio City studio, rather than from their home breakfast table, they delivered the same kind of sparkling chatter and gossip as their forerunners.

At the same time, American art was moving away from its former complacency and provincialism. New York's Whitney Museum high-lighted the trend by presenting a daring show entitled "Pioneers in Modern Art in America," featuring for the rather skeptical public the then-radical work of such artists as Joseph Stella, Charles Burchfield, and Georgia O'Keeffe—all of course recognized as masters today. During this same period of rapid change Laurence Olivier was the stage and movie actor of the moment, with his famed performance in the magnificent production of *Henry V*—truly a rare work of cinematic art.

Café society climbed aboard planes and became known as the jet set, with another fashion presence, the Duchess of Windsor, soaring off toward a postwar summer on the French Riviera, her enormous trunk full of top-dollar Hermes creations—beach pajamas, coats, dresses, playsuits, and the most stylish of swimsuits. Also among the trendsetting Riviera habitués was the great author Somerset Maugham, who, in a supreme gesture of Anglo–American friendship, put his much-sought-after manuscript *Of Human Bondage* beyond the reach of the dealers by donating it to the U.S. Library of Congress.

Marriages and divorces of the rich and famous were not restricted to the seamier tabloids but were in fact hot items for the established press. The divorce action of Jacob L. "Jakie" Webb, the errant great-great grandson of the original Commodore Cornelius Vanderbilt, and the former showgirl and café character Lenore Lemon was especially juicy news, as it took place after only ten days of actual married life, followed by a four-and-a-half-year separation. On a happier note, the world rejoiced at the news of the marriage of John Robert Manners, tenth Duke of Rutland and nephew of the glamorous Lady Diana Cooper, to Mayfair model Anne Bell, who was known as "the girl with the most perfect figure." Rutland had inherited, along with various stately homes, a fortune of more than $2 million.

Even as press baron William Randolph Hearst celebrated his eighty-third birthday atop his mountain, the two-thousand-foot Enchanted Hill, at San Simeon, he continued to exercise complete control of his far-flung press empire. His publications included seventeen newspapers, nine magazines, and the nation's biggest news syndicate, and his influence was immeasurable. Needless to say, the birthday dinner—attended by his five sons and their families and hosted by his longtime intimate friend, former movie queen Marion Davies—received more than adequate news coverage.

Meanwhile, back in Manhattan, William de Rham, dance master to generations of Vanderbilts, Whitneys, and Astors, continued to instruct the heirs and heiresses of these gilded families in the proper art of ballroom dancing. Some things never changed, even in a rapidly changing world.

In the period during and after the war, the United States prospered. The old fortunes grew even larger and new ones emerged, all seeming to beckon to Babe Cushing Mortimer. While she had no intention of surrendering any of the old-guard luster that she had acquired during her marriage to Stan, unlimited wealth was the primary focus of her ambitions; she had definitely set her sights on money.

In the meantime her career was going beautifully, and this was unquestionably a wonderfully happy period in her life. She enjoyed her work and had developed a close camaraderie with her fellow workers—from Condé Nast himself to the lowliest employee.

Nast, along with his longtime editor, Edna Woolman Chase, had developed an innovative working environment. His unique hiring policy not only kept his staff happy and productive but made *Vogue* the leading fashion magazine on both sides of the Atlantic. He had consistently and without hesitation hired women for the most important editorial positions on the magazine, at a time when his fellow publishers in the field of women's magazines refused to consider women for top positions. Certainly they would not think of granting full editorial control to any woman, no matter how capable. But Nast had an unshakable respect for women, and he considered them the proper editors and writers for other women. He was famous for a speech he made early in his career to a group of businesswomen. "Nothing," he said vehemently, "is too clever for you. Nothing we can print is too advanced for you. Making a magazine for you is like perpetually playing [to] a first-night audience of an astute and responsive character."

For all that, Condé Nast still had his detractors. Critics accused him of providing an agreeable finishing school to young ladies of good breeding and private means—at the lowest salaries in town. There was no disputing that this accusation was at least partly justified. Actually, Nast cleverly divided his women employees into two distinct categories: the professionals and the socialites. Among the pros were Edna Woolman Chase, Carmel Snow, Jessica Daves, Margaret Case Harriman, Francesca Van Der Kley, and Allene Talmey—whose responsibilities included putting the magazine together and seeing it through every stage from initial concept to delivering it to the printer. All these women received decent salaries. The socialites, who lent the magazine instant chic and, through their contacts, provided the necesary entrée into the most important drawing rooms, the right clubs, and the couturier salons, were by mutual consent unreliable and ephemeral. Nast allowed his socialite staff members great freedom of movement so that they could make the social scene in London, Paris, Biarritz, Palm Beach, and Newport. They made contributions to the magazine on their own time schedules, when work would not unduly interfere with their social calendars. Among these glittering young women were Ellin Mackay (who later married Irving Berlin), Caroline Duer, Millicent Fenwick, and of course Barbara "Babe" Cushing Mortimer—all of whom worked for a pittance.

From time to time these attractive young socialites appeared as models in the pages of *Vogue,* photographed by the most celebrated photographers of the day, including the likes of Edward Steichen, Cecil Beaton (until his anti-Semitic stance got him ousted), Baron George Hoyningen-Huene, Toni Frissell, Jerome Zerbe, and Horst P. Horst. These and other internationally known photographers helped create the legend of Babe Cushing Mortimer (soon to add "Paley" to the string of names), which persists even to this day.

Condé Nast may have known nothing about fashion, but he was a true connoisseur of women, and his respect for them as colleagues was only surpassed by his appreciation of them as romantic inspirations. Helen Brown Norden Lawrenson, Nast's editor at *Vanity Fair* and a great favorite of his, explained this aspect of her boss's nature some time ago in the Nast biography, *The Man Who Was Vogue*:

> Certainly, I've never known a man who savored sex more raptly. It was his primary interest in life and he pursued it with wholehearted, shockproof, uninhibited enthusiasm. That he appeared to be exactly the opposite probably lent a picquancy to an affair with him, because it was all so unexpected. It really didn't matter to him if women were duchesses or call girls, socialites, actresses, models, waitresses, salesclerks, manicurists, or what, as long as they were good-looking. Of course, being Condé Nast, he could just about have his pick. The models and the society women always hoped to be photographed for *Vogue,* the actresses for *Vanity Fair*. He was aware of this, but he never traded on it. At one point rumors flew around the office of *Vogue* that he and Babe Cushing Mortimer, one of his most beautiful editors, were linked romantically, but nothing has ever been substantiated, despite the fact that at the time Babe was having a rough go in her own marriage to Stanley Mortimer and that Condé Nast [had recently divorced] his second wife, Leslie Foster, a young *Vogue* employee . . . the same age as his daughter Natica [Mrs. Gerald Warburg] and was at the height of Babe's career at *Vogue* . . . casting about for someone to share his huge apartment at 1040 Park Avenue and play hostess at his constant round of parties. But Babe saw Condé Nast as a caring employer and a kindly father figure and sought no more than the glamorous limelight afforded her by her position at *Vogue*.

Nast provided yet another perk for his glamorous staff—invitations to his fabulously sumptuous parties, which he gave on an almost non-stop basis at his forty-room Park Avenue penthouse. The vast apartment with its equally large terrace was the unique creation of Nast's long-standing friend and legendary decorator, Elsie de Wolfe. Under her direction he had amassed a collection of painted and antiqued furniture that dazzled the eye. De Wolfe then installed an incomparable collection of Watteaus and Schalls, Savonnerie rugs, and Louis XV and Louis XVI furniture, all set against a backdrop of Chinese wallpaper that had been found in the attic of Welbeck Abbey, in England. The publisher was so taken with the results of de Wolfe's deft hand and infallible eye that he never changed a single thing in the seventeen years he lived in the apartment.

Nast's guest lists were as eclectic as the apartment itself, including at any given time such diverse and glamorous characters as Lord Birkenhead, Mary Pickford, Grace Moore (the great love of Condé Nast's life), Loretta Young, Millicent Hearst (the estranged wife of William Randolph Hearst), Beatrice Lillie, and Paul Robeson. These and other equally prestigious soirees that abounded during the heyday of café society helped to fine-tune Babe's graceful entrance into the exalted upper echelons of society. The old guard was reluctantly making room for the nabobs who were beginning to control new and often far greater fortunes than what remained of the millions once in the hands of the Vanderbilts and Du Ponts. This phenomenon presented a unique and highly practical education for Babe, always a quick study and always ready to seek out new experiences and new people—especially if they happened to be in possession of multimillion-dollar fortunes. This open-mindedness and willingness to depart from the conservative social standards of many of her set would prove to be a great asset—as well as a great liability—in her post-Mortimer years.

Babe's career at *Vogue* also honed her professional skills. She took her work seriously and became totally professional in the art of supervising the work of photographers, making sure that they enhanced the best qualities of their subjects and thus produced the very finest possible shots for *Vogue,* making it the finest international fashion magazine of the era. Babe also honed her own modeling skills, becoming increasingly aware of how best to present herself to the camera.

Vogue editor Edna Woolman Chase, who worked for the magazine for sixty-two years, has provided in her autobiography, *Always in Vogue,* an excellent view of what went on there, especially highlighting the years of Babe's tenure:

One of the most incredible aspects of the whole incredible state of the world between 1939 and 1945 was the contrast between the areas of peace and those of war. The atrocities and the starvation, the freezing cold and the desperate, straining economics in the war zones and the booming business—or what would have been booming were it not for the crippling restrictions—and the continuing elegance of the continental U.S.

People so often asked us who selected the clothes shown in *Vogue* that I got the idea of turning our studio cameras on the fashion editors. We decided to show eight of our ladies [Babe included] in the clothes they themselves preferred and to have them write brief articles on their personal fashion philosophies. I had thought my idea modestly inspired; before the issue got on the newsstands I was beginning to wish I could put it back in my head.

At the prospect of themselves in print and pictures my cohesive worldly staff fell apart. It usually took them two weeks to pull a number together. This one took eight. Nothing was good enough; nothing was too good for the great occasion—and that included themselves. They spent hours in steam baths and at the hairdressers'. Should I need to speak to one of them about some infinitely more lowly feature, she was never available. Her colleagues would look at me with reproach. "But Mrs. Chase, she's getting ready for the editors' issue."

The preparations were bad enough; the actual sittings were chaos. Each lovely creature, either having been a model, as was our Muriel Maxwell, or having worked with them at sittings, as had the others, was *experienced.* They knew *what was what.* They cajoled and browbeat Rawlings and other photographers, Joffe and Mili, into changing the lighting, softening the angle, retouching the prints, and in other ways prostituting stark art in order that they might appear as melting beauties in *Vogue*'s pages.

To tell the truth, they were enchanting. They were both elegant and pretty, and there was not a hard-boiled, brittle Lady-in-the-Dark character among them, although I would not go so far as to say that they were unsophisticated.

Our Babs Rawlings was not naive. Babs's flair was for pajamas and sarongs and shorts, and highly keyed color. On the other hand, there was long-legged, coltish Sally Kirkland, your true American girl in inexpensive, easy-to-wear sports clothes. And we had our ingenue, Connie Bradlee, in frocks befitting her twenty years.

There was our Famous Face, Muriel Maxwell, of the blunt beautiful profile, who liked conservative, impeccably tailored interchangeable jackets and skirts. And there was our lovely Barbara Mortimer, one of the three famous Cushing sisters of Boston, who has since become Mrs. William Paley and who so enhanced the elegant and traditional fashions of her choice.

Because of human rivalries or jealousies or incompatible temperaments we were not always a happy family on *Vogue,* but we were always a family curiously united, and during the war the adventures and fate of any of our wanderers were passionately followed by every member of our home staff. [Sally Kirkland and Mary Jean Kempner served as *Vogue* correspondents in the Pacific theater. Photographer Lee Miller covered the landing in France and the Liberation of Paris.]

Edna Woolman Chase set the fashion and editorial tone at *Vogue,* and each of her "girls" was expected to follow it to the letter, adding only her own distinctive flair for fashion. And among those who learned that lesson best was Babe Mortimer.

When Babe had obtained her divorce and had very nearly perfected her editorial and fashion expertise at *Vogue,* she began to feel restless. With the brilliant examples of her sisters' multimillion-dollar marriages to goad her, Babe became determined to step up her efforts to find a second husband. The recipient of her attentions would have to be in actual possession—no more trusts for Babe, thank you—of a fortune equal to or greater than those of her brothers-in-law, Vincent Astor and Jock Whitney. In any event, Babe continued to work for *Vogue* and to hunt for the ideal mate, and within a short time after her divorce from Stan Mortimer, she zeroed in on an exceptionally worthy contender.

It is interesting to note that at this juncture of her life, Babe did not attract or pursue any of the scions of America's top-drawer monied aristocracy, such as the Phipps, Goelets, Guests, Vanderbilts, and the newly "arrived" Rockefellers. Perhaps she unconsciously feared that she might fail in direct competition with her sisters, and thus felt more secure striking out in a different, somewhat more daring direction. In all probability, she quite consciously calculated that she would stand a better chance with mega-money somewhat outside the mainstream; after all, to the scions of the top-drawer families, who had everything they could possibly want, even her beauty and celebrity would seem relatively commonplace. But if she could find a Croesus-rich mate, for she had a lot to offer someone—her great beauty, her celebrity status in the world of fashion and design, her sterling old-guard social credentials, and last but not least, her relationship by marriage to the glittering, solid-gold Astors and Whitneys, whose names and great fortunes represented the ultimate in social prominence and great wealth—she would almost certainly be able to snag him. After all, new money was as spendable as old. A newly elevated mogul, bereft of social credentials and hungering for acceptance by top-drawer WASP society, would undoubtedly be impressed by Babe Cushing Mortimer. Babe may also have wanted the edge that a trade-off would give her in marriage. After years of pursuing and succeeding in her career, she may well have been loath to surrender her independence, which would undoubtedly have been the case had she married a completely self-satisfied scion.

Or maybe—just maybe—she really fell for William Samuel Paley, the son of a Russian Jewish immigrant who had built a modest cigar-manufacturing business into a thriving concern. William had attended the Wharton School of Finance and Commerce at the University of Pennsylvania, then gone into the family business. His father had acquired a little radio network, and William most reluctantly became involved with it. Paley's wealth was not entirely brand-nouveau, and he was no Johnny Raw fresh off Ellis Island. True, his bloodlines were hardly blue—not even acceptable in the lofty circles Babe traveled in— but he was a man of great personal charm and extraordinary business talent. At the age of twenty-seven he had taken over the "pipsqueak" radio network, United Independent Broadcasters, and within ten short years had parlayed it into the fantastically successful Columbia Broadcasting System, which was challenging megalithic NBC for dominance of the airwaves. In short, his fortune was of a size to dazzle even a Cushing sister.

That he was Jewish seemed not to bother Babe at all. There was, however, one rather significant stumbling block—and that was his fourteen-year marriage to Dorothy Hart Hearst, former wife of John Randolph Hearst. The Paleys had adopted two children, Jeffrey and Hilary, and Dorothy herself had set about refurbishing many of the studios at CBS headquarters in New York. She was also instrumental in providing Bill with an art education.

During the war, from early in 1943, Paley had served as deputy chief of the Psychological Warfare Division, on the staff of General Eisenhower in London. It was there in London that he was reunited with Edward R. Murrow and Charles Collingwood. One London gossip touted this trio as three of the handsomest men in the city at that time. And Murrow, with his elegant ways, saw to it that Paley met all the right people, including the members of the various governments in exile. Throughout his tour of duty, Bill lived in regal splendor at Claridge's Hotel.

The strain of the war years, coupled with Paley's penchant for extramarital affairs, had already sapped the strength of his marriage. Dorothy Hart Hearst Paley was a woman of monumental resolve, and she had more than once endured casual brushes with her husband's lady friends. One especially scandalous liaison, which hit the nation's headlines, was virtually impossible to ignore. On March 8, 1940, a twenty-eight-year-old woman, clad only in a costly gray satin ensemble and a new silver fox cape, leaped to her death from a seventeenth-floor suite of Detroit's Book-Cadillac Hotel. When newsmen arrived at the scene, they found two Burns detectives looking through the woman's effects. The detectives refused to identify their employer for the newsmen. The woman was registered under an assumed name, Mrs. J. Stoddard, of New York City. She had taken oil paint and a brush and written the names of a number of prominent Detroit automobile executives on the mirror. Also on that list was the name William S. Paley. At the bottom, the woman, an aspiring but unsuccessful actress, wrote the famous show-business line "Exit laughing."

Scattered throughout the suite were expensive gowns and other apparel, along with two hundred dollars in cash and several letters, including one addressed to Bill Paley. The reporters dutifully copied the letters and took the embarrassing messages back to their newsrooms.

It turned out that Johanna Stoddard had begun life as Geraldine Kenyon in Battle Creek, Michigan. Roughly seven years before her leap she had deserted her husband, Dan Bourque, a Pontiac, Michigan, auto worker, and their infant daughter, to seek a glamorous life in New York. It was there that she met Bill Paley and numerous other men. When interviewed by reporters, her estranged husband said that he had not seen her since the day she left him.

Johanna's letter to Paley, properly addressed but not stamped, and dated December 8, read:

Dearest Bill,

I just wanted to thank you for your kindness. You know how things were with me. I may have said things in desperation that I didn't mean. I hope you do not hate me, and I mean, I'm sorry. I know you will understand and forgive me. I'm not well. My lungs are in a precarious state, where I have to be careful.

I still love you, but I guess you were right. I only fought so hard because my heart hurt so. You've been very white about everything. I can only hope to emulate you and try to do something good with my life. I am very tired.

Goodbye darling,
Johanna

While CBS rocked with this news, a rumor spread that Dorothy Paley would be asked to put out a statement to the press. But ultimately the rather lame explanation came from Bill himself. He stated,

I met Miss Stoddard about a year ago in a restaurant with a group of people. Although I had seen her only once, she wrote letters to me six months later asking for help on the grounds that she had tuberculosis. She told me she was an entertainer but she had no talent and, so far as I could find out, no experience that would justify putting her on the air.

Mrs. Paley and I both talked to her several times, trying to straighten her out but she became more mentally disturbed all the time. Finally she began to write letters to me declaring that she had developed an emotional attachment for me.

She had spoken of some relatives in Michigan and through my lawyers we tried to locate those relatives in the hope that they could take care of her and induce her to come home. No relatives could be found, and meanwhile she kept writing and telephoning me that her health was getting worse and that she wanted to go out to Arizona. She refused to accept medical attention here and all my efforts to convince her that an association with her was impossible.

A few days ago I was informed that she was going to Michigan and then to Arizona. That was the last I heard from her.

Unfortunately, this was not the last time that Bill Paley would get involved with "another woman." His philandering would continue up until the end of his first marriage. The first Paley marriage limped along, with Dorothy and Bill going their own separate ways. Dorothy continued her interest in the art world and in education as a board member of New York's New School. Bill just kept on building CBS into a broadcasting giant, all the while coming into contact with some of the most glamorous women in the world. In fact, he had long had his eye on one particularly beautiful woman—Babe Cushing Mortimer, *Vogue* editor, youngest of the famed Cushing sisters, a legend in the world of fashion, and wife of the grandson of a cofounder of Standard Oil.

According to Alexander Liberman in a recent interview,

Bill was a friend of Frank Crowninshield. I first met Bill Paley at one of our lunches . . . A "French lunch," perhaps, but I know Bill came to lunch and I remember meeting him for the first time, long before he married. And maybe this is how he met Babe because she would be present at the lunches. It's quite possible!

Paley, in his somewhat-less-than-honest autobiography, *As It Happened,* tells a different version of how he met the stunning Babe Mortimer:

> One night, at a small dinner party in New York given by Betsey and Jock Whitney, possibly for the benefactors of the Museum of Modern Art, about a year after my separation from Dorothy, I became aware of a slender, beautiful woman introduced to me as Barbara Cushing Mortimer—"Babe" to all her friends. If our paths had crossed before, I was unaware of it at the time, which was strange, because sister Betsey was married to Jock Whitney, an old friend and neighbor at Kiluna Farm. But that night at that dinner party, we talked for some time and, struck by her extraordinary beauty, character and personality, I invited her out to dinner the following week.

Of course, the fact that Paley had purchased a Long Island estate that abutted Greentree Farms didn't hurt his cause. Although there had never been a road between the two estates and it took ten circuitous minutes by car to get from one farm to the other, it would be easy enough to level a hedge and construct a road between the properties. This was in fact what Jock and Bill would do, once Babe and Betsey became country neighbors. The road, only 125 feet long, would be known by the somewhat grandiose name of Baragwanath Boulevard, in honor of the renowned mining engineer John Baragwanath, who with his artist wife, Neysa McMein, was a regular party guest at both estates.

After "that first meeting" Paley, according to his *As It Happened,* could often be heard saying,

> Ah, how can I describe this marvelous woman whom I loved . . . ? It was obvious that Babe was one of the loveliest women in the world. Men and women, too, stopped and stared when passing her on a walk on the avenues of New York. Anyone who knew her well came to realize also what an unusual woman she really was, as beautiful in her inner being as in her outer appearance. Tall and thin, sculpted by the maker with a sort of (Greco-) Roman nose,

poised, shy and yet very direct in her dealings with people. She had deep brown, often flashing eyes that saw right into you.

However and whenever he met Babe, Paley became determined to end his marriage to Dorothy in order to wed this ravishing young woman and make her his alone.

Babe, despite her resolve to marry, did not immediately fall into Bill Paley's arms. When assigned a trip to Europe in the summer of 1946 to cover the fall collections, she jumped at the chance. Strange but true, this cult figure among Manhattan's glitzy fashion and design professionals had a well-hidden provincial side. She had never before been abroad. One of her coworkers at *Vogue* accompanied Babe on her first trip to Europe. They stayed in Paris, at the Ritz, and according to this coworker, who requested anonymity during a recent interview, it was a fairy-tale experience for Babe. She gloried in meeting the newly emerging postwar designers, including Christian Dior and Jacques Fath, and also witnessing the rebirth of the indomitable Coco Chanel, who had somehow clung to her celebrity all during the Nazi occupation of Paris and could at last emerge, to rise to even greater heights in the years after the war.

A fellow editor at *Vogue* and traveling companion remembers that Babe dated furiously, picking and choosing among a legion of European bachelors who were completely entranced by the ravishing American beauty who was taking Paris by storm. Soon no party, whether on the Right Bank or the Left, was complete unless it was graced by Barbara Cushing Mortimer. *Le toute* Paris, from the Baron Guy de Rothschild to the dashing Count Jimmy de Pourtales (son-in-law of the great American heiress Anna Gould, Duchess de Tallyrand), vied for the privilege of having Babe attend one of their sumptuous soirees.

Babe's fellow editor had ample opportunity to observe her stellar colleague during this "working" trip to Paris, as well as during the many years they worked the New York fashion market for Condé Nast. According to her,

Babe had a way of being a presence. She liked money. Had charming manners, very quick, very gentle, and a great sense of humor.

Lively energy, lively talk, and an infectious giggle. You don't want somebody morose hanging around. She had a way of making you laugh. And she flirted around a good deal.

Upon her return from the European junket, this fellow editor remembers, Bill contributed to Babe's support and set her up in an apartment on East Fifty-second Street, the same apartment where Aristotle Onassis would keep his friend Ingse Dedichen in later years.

These circumstances could not have been pleasing to the ever proper Gogsie Cushing. And furthermore, she was distinctly unhappy about Bill's immigrant Jewish origins and none too pleased that his money was so new and largely self-made. In short, Gogsie was not favorably impressed with her youngest daughter's illicit situation or with her choice of a suitor. However, once Minnie and Betsey clued their mother in on the extent of Bill's wealth, she soon began to accept him. Throughout the courtship, she kept her council, for in the larger scheme of things, Gogsie's appreciation of such phenomenal wealth overrode such relatively minor considerations as social propriety and bloodlines. Once assured that Babe would soon be joining her sisters at the pinnacle of American wealth, as the consort of a Croesus-rich mate, Gogsie set aside her qualms.

Paley, although still legally married to Dorothy, was clearly devoted to Babe. When she suddenly fell ill with phlebitis and had to be rushed to a hospital, where she remained for a month, Bill was constantly at her bedside. In his own words from his autobiography,

Each night during that month, I went to one or another of my favorite restaurants in the city and had the chef prepare a special dinner for two. The menu would be discussed in great detail— something I was rather good at and practice to this day, and each time something new and different would be tried. I would then take our dinner, packed in a warming container, to her room in the hospital. We both enjoyed her delightful wonder and wild guesses at what the dinner surprise would be. Although she was ill, she admitted to no pain. Babe took illness always with great fortitude, spirit, and undiminished wit.

Those evenings together in the hospital gave us a unique opportunity to come to know one another extremely well. We talked privately night after night, with no one interrupting or distracting us, and we came to feel even more strongly than before that we belonged and wanted to be together. The decision came easily. We would get married as soon as my divorce came through.

On July 23, 1947, the New York *Daily News* headlined this story from Reno:

This rough and ready divorce capital gasped tonight when it learned that William S. Paley, president of Columbia Broadcasting System, had given his wife a check for $1,500,000 as a settlement in the divorce she obtained today. Verification of the payment, the largest ever made in this Mecca for parting couples, came from those who saw photostatic copies of the check. . . . Mrs. Paley, so far as is known, has no further matrimonial plans, but the CBS president is reportedly planning to marry Mrs. Barbara (Babe) Mortimer, willowy socialite eyeful from Boston.

And sure enough, the society scribes were right on the money with this news, for five days later, on July 28, 1947, Babe and Bill's wedding took place at the home of the bride's mother on the Greentree Farms estate of brother-in-law Jock Whitney.

The old Cushing family friend, society potographer Jerome Zerbe, was there to record the wedding for the family, as well as for the media. The wedding and the reception that followed were strictly a family affair, with Minnie and Vincent Astor and Betsey and Jock Whitney looking on with great pride as the youngest Cushing sister joined the exclusive ranks of the very, very rich. Bill's parents, Sam and Goldie, and his sister, Blanche, attended the afternoon ceremony, performed by New York Supreme Court justice J. Edward Lumbard, Jr. The other few guests included Babe's nieces, Kate and Sara Roosevelt; Babe's children, Amanda Jay and Stanley "Tony" Mortimer III; and Babe's brother, Henry, and his wife, down from Boston to witness the tying of yet another multimillion-dollar knot.

Bill ruffled quite a few feathers at CBS by inviting none of the men who had helped him build the broadcasting empire. To make matters worse, he had borrowed some extremely valuable movie cameras from CBS president, Frank Stanton, an avid photographer, bluntly saying that he hoped Stanton wouldn't feel slighted by not having been invited to the wedding. Then Bill even returned with the film, asking Stanton to edit it. There, in the film of the brief ceremony, was proof positive that Bill had made a single exception to his family-only rule; CBS vice president Edward R. Murrow was clearly visible.

That Bill and Babe were a very devoted couple was evident to all who knew them. In the words of "CBS Talks" director Helen Sioussat,

At first he looked on her as a child. She was a lot younger than he. She'd sit on his lap and he would treat her just as a little girl. She and her two sisters were beautifully brought up and very attractive. They all had lots of charm and knew how to please a man. Babe was a little shyer—quieter than the other two. . . . Bill was very proud of Babe and she was crazy about him.

Shortly after the wedding, Babe gave up her job at *Vogue*. After honeymooning in the South of France, Italy, and Switzerland, the couple settled down to life in and around New York, commuting between Kiluna Farm and an apartment at the St. Regis Hotel, owned by brother-in-law Vincent Astor. It was Kiluna Farm, which Paley had purchased in 1936 from publishing magnate Ralph Pulitzer, that Babe and Bill and ultimately their children, William Cushing Paley and Kate Paley, would call home.

The old main house remained very much as it had always been, with no major changes other than extending the terrace and the garden, which Babe would come to love. The eighty-plus-acre grounds had ample guest cottages, barns, indoor tennis courts (for day or night playing), and even a new swimming pool, in addition to the original rustic one, deep in the woods. Babe had finally arrived.

12

TAKING STOCK

*W*ITH Babe's marriage to William Paley, Gogsie Cushing had achieved her lifelong goal. By hook or by crook she had married off all three of her lovely daughters to fabulously wealthy and powerful husbands.

True, Paley's bloodlines were not what Gogsie would have wished for; as the son of a Jewish immigrant, with a newly minted, largely self-made fortune, he was not of the lofty social stratum that Gogsie considered the proper milieu for her girls. Nevertheless, Babe's glamour, her Cushing-Mortimer credentials, and her Astor and Whitney connections, coupled with the Paley millions, opened all but the most steadfastly closed doors. Even the socially ambitious Gogsie could not quite harden her heart against all that Paley money and success. In any event, Betsey had very nearly surpassed her mother's fondest dreams by capturing the debonair John Hay Whitney. And Minnie, over whom Gogsie had very nearly despaired, had acquitted herself most admirably when she finally snared Vincent Astor. At last all three Cushing sisters seemed to have settled into the lifestyle their mother had groomed them for. Each had reached the pinnacle of success in the one career their mother had charted for them: marriage to a prime catch. Only Babe had even tried another career, but left her job at *Vogue* without so much as a backward glance once she wedded Bill Paley. It was just as New York and Palm Beach socialite Helen Bernstein recently said: "Marriage was a business for the Cushing sisters."

Shortly before his death, Jerome Zerbe confided that

> . . . from the moment Betsey married into the aristocratic Roosevelt family, Kate doubled her efforts on behalf of Minnie and Babe. While not born into upper-crust society, Kate had always been a keen observer of America's social elite. And once she had a foot in the door, as a result of the Roosevelt alliance, she was determined to engineer glittering marriages for Minnie and Babe. It was a driving ambition . . . Quite honestly it was Kate's life work.

According to Tex McCrary, "Mrs. Cushing was clearly a wise and forceful part of New England's intellectual 'royalty.'. . . She had a large measure of what the English call 'a touch of class.' And she raised her daughters to the same summit standards."

Every time one of the captivating Cushing sisters stepped out in public, she was met by the glare of flashbulbs and the crush of press photographers, on hand to capture her every move for the glamour-starved public. Babe welcomed the publicity and nurtured her relations with the press, especially the fashion press, which ultimately made her their high priestess of American style. In the word of decorator Billy Baldwin, "Those girls had a kind of monopoly on taste." In the face of this idolatry, their ever-vigilant mother and guru suppressed her ingrained Victorian notions of propriety, knowing that such image-building could only aid her cause.

Publicity was not the only area in which Gogsie had to reevaluate her moral ideals. Given her upbringing, she was undoubtedly governed by a strict moral code. At critical times she shrewdly chose to put it aside in the interest of furthering her goals for her daughters. One such case was when Minnie took off for New York, seeking a career in the arts.

The career never materialized, but her relationship with Vincent Astor did. For all intents and purposes Minnie became the mistress of the real estate magnate. However repugnant this arrangement must have been to Gogsie, she did not exercise her power of veto. Later, when Babe took up residence in an apartment on East Fifty-second Street and Bill Paley paid the rent, Gogsie again put aside her scruples. It simply was not in her interest to interfere.

Gogsie's shrewd instincts paid off. In the end, she could hardly have been disappointed with her daughters' choices of mates. The Whitney and Astor families were the closest thing this country had to royalty, and the Paley fortune was quite literally a king's ransom. Furthermore, by the time each of the sisters had married her multimillionaire, she was already in her thirties—not exactly the prime of life for a single woman in that era. But Kate Cushing had succeeded in her ambitions for her children's marriages. All three daughters called her several times a day, visiting her or receiving her visits on a daily basis, or as often as their busy schedules permitted.

There was no doubt that Gogsie continued to reign supreme with her daughters. No area was too minute or too personal to discuss with her and with one another, whether concerning their marriages, their children, or intimate details regarding their husbands. Everything was put on the table, talked about, weighed, and ultimately decided by Gogsie. All three young women remained deeply dependent on their mother, looking to her for guidance and answers to their questions and problems. According to Jerry Zerbe, they never openly challenged her once she had rendered a decision. Rather, they uncompromisingly committed themselves to whatever course of action she decreed.

But what had Kate Cushing wrought with her ambitions, strategies, and controlling ways? In all the years she had devoted herself to making brilliant and highly profitable matches for her daughters, to guiding their every step in society, she had never really focused on the psychological toll such marriages might take. Although Betsey, with ten years' head start on her sisters, fared quite well in her second marriage, both Minnie and Babe would have a far less agreeable time with their egotistical and difficult spouses. Gogsie's late-Victorian mentality, undoubtedly influenced by the incredible effort it had taken for her to land Harvey

Cushing, dictated that marriage was an end in itself, and that, once married, a woman could create her own happiness by seeing to her husband's comfort and raising their children. Gogsie's own marriage, while certainly falling short of any romantic notion of wedded bliss, had been satisfying to her. She must simply have assumed that the same would hold true for her daughters, especially with unlimited funds at their disposal.

Gogsie was certainly not averse to the changes her daughters' marriages made in her own life. Although as the wife of an eminently successful doctor she had always lived quite well, the Depression had wiped out most of Harvey Cushing's life savings. But for the indulgence of her three fantastically wealthy sons-in-law, she would never have been able to lead the comfortably grand life that she enjoyed in her later years. Like one of the less affluent members of the British royal family to whom the sovereign grants life tenancy to a grace-and-favor cottage on a royal estate, Gogsie had not only the spacious cottage on the grounds of Greentree but a Manhattan apartment on East Eighty-sixth Street, in a building rumored to be owned by son-in-law Vincent Astor. Once Babe married Bill Paley, Gogsie had ready access to the abundant flowers and produce of Kiluna Farms. At her beck and call was the limousine fleet of all three sons-in-law. Perhaps even more important, the Cushing matriarch, as the mother-in-law of three of the richest men in America (whose combined fortunes *Life* magazine in 1947 conservatively estimated at $125 million), was assured of a secure position in New York's upper-crust WASP society. Gogsie Cushing rarely failed to put in an appearance at any of the myriad charity and/or cultural events her daughters were involved in.

If Gogsie had a favorite son-in-law, it was Jock Whitney. Not only did he give her financial support but he provided her with her own home on the grounds of his spectacularly beautiful estate, Greentree. In addition, she felt most comfortable with Betsey and Jock and her first two grandchildren, Sara and Kate Roosevelt. Gogsie realized early on that Betsey and Jock had achieved a real partnership in their marriage—an impossibility in the marriages of Minnie and Babe, given the intransigent nature of their respective mates.

Bill Paley, on the other hand, was undoubtedly Gogsie's least favorite son-in-law. When she first heard the rumors that Babe was seriously contemplating marriage to the communications magnate, Gogsie was horrified—not only because he was married, for after all, Astor had been married, too, but because, quite simply, she was a social snob and Paley was a Jew, so patently self-made. He was also a very brash man, with a personality that Gogsie neither understood nor accepted. Jerry Zerbe once confided that, just before Babe married Paley, Gogsie had told him, "He may well love Babe, but her Whitney and Astor connections are very much a part of his strategy." Jerry also spoke candidly about "the underlying current of anti-Semitism in the upper reaches of New York old-guard clubs . . . such as the Racquet and Tennis and the Knickerbocker, [which] were strictly WASP clubs." Since appearances and a public display of family harmony meant everything to Kate Cushing, she was always cordial to Bill, even though she could never manage to shower him with the love she did Jock Whitney.

As for son-in-law Vincent Astor, Gogsie was duly impressed with his name if not his personality. The Astor name and the wealth and power it stood for—both in America and in England, where it had been ennobled by the Crown—was enough to win her approval, but she privately disapproved of Vincent's excessive drinking and his taciturn manner. He was not an easy man to like. When rumors reached her ear that Minnie and Vincent were married in name only, Gogsie was totally unable to comprehend the situation. There was the problem of securing the Astor millions; this would be difficult, if not impossible, without an heir.

One astute observer of the Manhattan social and cultural scene, Kitty Carlisle Hart, remembers meeting Kate Cushing at Mainbocher's East Fifty-seventh Street showroom. "She had a very matronly figure but was warm, outgoing, full of life, and a great charmer. The girls fussed over her and adored her. She seemed not to take it seriously."

Mrs. Hart, currently serving as New York State's cultural commissioner, remembers many famous people and lots of good times from that era, when her husband, Moss Hart, was the toast of Broadway. "Society, theater, and the movie crowd were more mixed up in those days," she reminisces. "The demarcation between them was not very strong. It was fun then."

It was during the years just after World War II that the Cushing sisters were enhancing the image they had attained during the mid-thirties and early forties, consolidating the material gains that came to them through their various marriages and, more important, continuing to polish that image of style and class that had made them the most glittering stars on the New York social scene. To the very end, Gogsie Cushing unabashedly let her daughters know that they were "wonderful."

In the early spring of 1949, Kate Cushing was hospitalized for various ailments, major among them a heart condition. According to Jerome Zerbe, one of the few nonfamily members permitted to visit Gogsie during her final weeks, Betsey, Minnie, and Babe kept an almost constant, around-the-clock vigil at their mother's bedside for the entire time, looking only to one another for solace.

The end came quietly, in a pristine white room in New York Hospital, after an illness of six weeks. Nowhere in sight were the trappings of wealth and privilege that Gogsie had grown accustomed to during her reign as mother-in-law to three of the richest men in America. She died of a severe heart condition on May 8, 1949, with all three of her daughters at her bedside. She was seventy-eight years of age. After a simple service at New York's prestigious Holy Trinity Church, Kate Crowell Cushing was laid to rest beside her husband in a quiet New Haven cemetery.

Each of the Cushing sisters kept her immense grief to herself, at least publicly, and each felt the loss in her distinct way. Minnie had throughout the years accepted the role divined for her by her mother. During Kate Cushing's lifetime, Minnie never openly challenged her mother's dictums, but now it was time for Minnie to begin planning for the future—a future tailored to her own needs and aspirations. Betsey, the daughter most closely aligned with her mother, quite possibly felt the loss of her beloved mother the most. She, unlike her sisters, could share her grief with husband and be comforted. For Jock was as fond of Gogsie as she was of him. Babe, who was her father's favorite child and who from time to time had exhibited a degree of contrariness in some of her dealings with her mother, was given little time to devote to her mother's memory, for Bill Paley saw to it that she continued her highly publicized role as Babe Paley.

With each of her daughters retaining her own memories of her mother, it is interesting to note that Kate Crowell Cushing may well have had the last word in the manner in which she directed the disposal of her estate. That estate, totaling nearly $230,000 and acquired through the generosity of her daughters and their husbands, was left to Barbara Cushing Paley and her brother Henry Kirk Cushing. In her will, it was cited that both Betsey and Minnie had asked her to dispose of her property for the benefit of their sister and brother. All personal property and the contents of her East Eighty-sixth Street apartment and her cottage at Greentree were divided among her four children.

With Gogsie gone, each of the sisters resumed her role as a premier social presence among New York's top-drawer society. Minnie continued to serve on the board of the Vincent Astor Foundation and attempted to steer its benefits toward the arts. While Babe had inherited her father's bone structure and Betsey his single-mindedness, Minnie was favored with his intellect and his great humanitarian ways. She may not have offered her husband a great deal of companionship, but during her years as his wife, she helped to give far greater direction and selectivity to his philanthropic endeavors. This was no mean feat, especially considering Vincent's rather haphazard generosity at the time and his family's history of tightfistedness. On a more personal level, Minnie began the long process of liberating herself from what she considered a stifling marriage. She had married Vincent Astor at Gogsie's insistence and had remained married to him, despite their almost total estrangement, for much the same reason. While Gogsie had reluctantly countenanced both Betsey's and Babe's divorces, she would never during her lifetime have allowed Minnie to throw away her phenomenal catch. With Gogsie laid to rest, Minnie began in earnest to lay the groundwork for her final break with Vincent. Her strategy, according to Jerry Zerbe, would have put any of Napoleon's marshals to shame, for she was well aware that freeing herself from her husband would prove to be far more difficult than snaring him in the first place. Astor's first divorce, from Helen, had been traumatic for him, involving as it had a radical departure from his personal philosophy, and he was adamantly opposed to a second divorce. Minnie knew that her only chance was to find a malleable man for herself from among her court of admirers, and finding an attractive woman for husband Vincent Astor proved a real stumbling block. In fact this part of her plan had her stymied for quite some time, actually delaying her freedom for several years.

As she waited, refining her strategy from time to time, Minnie continued to pursue her numerous social and charitable activities. Always the most avant garde of the Cushing sisters, Minnie bucked tradition by beginning to promote interracial cooperation while enlarging the Sydenham Hospital in Harlem. One of Manhattan's oldest hospitals, Sydenham had long been supported by Astor money. Minnie's management of the Sydenham Institution Fellowship and her sincere commitment to racial equality went a long way toward bringing about a policy change both at the hospital and in society.

Even as she continued to play the role of Mrs. Vincent Astor, Minnie kept agitating for a divorce, and Vincent kept denying her her freedom. Never one to talk about his private life, he once confided to a friend, over drinks at the Brook Club, how incredulous he had been when Minnie first mentioned her desire to end the marriage. "She must be mad," he commented. He found it incomprensible that any woman should not wish to be Mrs. Vincent Astor.

At last, however, long after a less determined woman would have given up, fate lent Minnie a hand—and she was quick to grasp the once-in-a-lifetime opportunity. On one of the rare occasions when the Astors went out together, they attended a dinner party in the home of their longtime friends Jim and Ellen Bruce. Jim had succeeded Charles "Buddie" Marshall as president of the Brook Club, after Buddie's death six months earlier. (Buddie had been Cole Porter's Yale classmate and friend.) The Bruces had also invited Buddie's widow Brooke. Although she was still in mourning for her beloved second husband, Brooke Marshall decided to accept the invitation. The events of that evening and their far-reaching consequences are best told in Brooke's own words as set down in her autobiography, *Footprints*:

> I decided to go to that dinner. It was a decision that changed my life.
> When I went to dine with the Bruces, I wore my very best dress. I

Brain surgeon Dr. Harvey Cushing, father of Mary, Betsey, and Barbara.

Mother and children: Katherine Cushing (second from left) with her four children, before Babe's birth (from left) Betsey, Henry, Bill, and Mary.

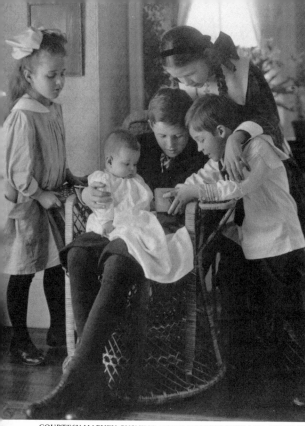

The Cushing children (from left): Betsey, Barbara (Babe), William, Mary, Henry.

Dr. Harvey Cushing with young daughter Betsey.

Mary (Minnie) Cushing Astor, September 27, 1940.

Betsey Cushing, March 1, 1942.

Barbara (Babe) Cushing, February 11, 1937.

Betsey Cushing marrying James Roosevelt. Brookline, Massachusetts, June 4, 1930.

Betsey Cushing Roosevelt, Minnie Cushing, and Rose Kennedy on the patio of the Kennedy estate in Palm Beach, February 5, 1933.

The Roosevelt/Cushing family (from left): Eleanor Roosevelt, Katherine Cushing, FDR, Betsey Cushing, James Roosevelt. Albany, New York, 1929.

President Franklin D. Roosevelt with daughter-in-law Betsey Cushing Roosevelt and wife Eleanor in the presidential motorcade, Washington, D.C.

Babe and Betsey Cushing, bonded in spirit and style.

Babe marrying Stanley Grafton Mortimer, Jr., September 21, 1940.

Babe in her working-girl days at Vogue *magazine.*

The son of the president, James Roosevelt, with sister-in-law Babe Cushing at the Harvard-Army football game, October 19, 1935.

Minnie Cushing Astor and Vincent Astor embark on their honeymoon to Bermuda aboard Vincent Astor's private yacht, September 27, 1940.

Minnie Cushing Astor and café society luminary Bertrand Taylor at the New York National War Fund Benefit at the St. Regis Hotel, November 1945.

Betsey and Jock Whitney on their wedding day, March 1, 1942.

Betsey and Franklin D. Roosevelt, Jr., at FDR's birthday ball at the Waldorf-Astoria, New York City, January 31, 1941.

Babe and Bill Paley's wedding day, July 28, 1947. From left, standing: Mr. and Mrs. Henry Cushing, Minnie and Vincent Astor, Bill and Babe Paley, Jock and Betsey Whitney. Sitting: Kate Roosevelt, Tony Mortimer, Katherine Cushing (in chair), Amanda Mortimer, Sara Roosevelt.

Minnie and Jim Fosburgh's wedding day, October 23, 1953: Minnie and Jim (standing, rear center), Jock Whitney (behind), Betsey (left of Minnie, obstructed), Babe (kneeling), Henry Cushing (kneeling right).

Betsey Cushing Whitney
(center) with daughters Kate
Roosevelt (left) and Sarah
di Bonaventura (right), and
grandchildren Christopher
(behind) and Andrea di
Bonaventura at Winfield
House, the Whitneys' am-
bassadorial residence in
London.

Babe, 1949, voted one of the
world's ten best-dressed
women.

Babe Paley at home.

Betsey and Jock Whitney, U.S. ambassador to Great Britain.

Fashion icon Babe Paley and her husband, CBS chief Bill Paley, December 19, 1957.

Truman Capote arrives at his legendary Black and White Ball with his guest of honor, Katharine Graham, November 1966.

Babe Paley with Boaz Mazor, New York man about town, at the Paleys' home in the Bahamas.

Babe and Stanley Mortimer's daughter Amanda weds Carter Burden. Roslyn, Long Island, June 14, 1964.

Babe in the sanctuary of her stunning garden at Kiluna Farm, 1964.

remember it well. It was a black tulle with a large skirt over many petticoats—the "new look" by Dior—off the shoulders with a ruffled tulle fichu that tied in front . . . I wanted to look my best for Buddie's friends . . . I knew them all well except for the Jack McCloys and the Vincent Astors. I had known Vincent for years, because when he was married to Helen, he had come to Bernardsville [New Jersey] and Helen's younger sister was Buddie's [first] wife. We knew a lot of the same people, and I also saw them in New York, but Vincent had his own little clique who went off for six months at a time with him on his yacht, *Nourmahal,* all over the world. I had known Helen, and she had sent telegrams of congratulations to us when Buddie and I sailed to Europe on our wedding trip.

Minnie, Vincent's second wife, I hardly knew at all, but she was always very sweet and most responsive when we saw one another . . . There were sixteen of us, and we sat at two tables of eight. I sat between Jim Bruce and Eustis Paine. Vincent sat opposite me, and every time I looked across the table, I found him looking at me in an intense way. I could not understand why he was concentrating on me. What had I done to him? I wondered what was wrong with him. However, I did not really give it much thought, as I was having a very happy time with Jim and Eustis who were singing Buddie's praises and telling me the latest news of the Brook Club. It was a charming conventional evening, with a feeling of good will pervading, and no passions aroused.

The ladies went into the drawing room, leaving the men to smoke and chat in the dining room, and I had just started talking to Ellen Bruce when I heard a gruff voice behind me saying, "I must humbly apologize to you. I did not write you when Buddie died. I was out in Arizona, but I should have written you."

"That's all right," I answered. "I got over fifteen hundred letters."

"If we were alone, I would kneel at your feet," said Vincent. "Tell me about yourself and Buddie."

From the opposite end of the large room, Minnie must have been nearly beside herself with glee as she watched her husband making a positive fool of himself over this casual acquaintance.

"I thought him very melodramatic," Brooke remembered. In a recent interview, she said she felt that "Vincent must have been very much in love with Minnie prior to their marriage and on into the early years of that marriage."

The Astors dropped Brooke off after the party and during that ride insisted that she join them for the Memorial Day weekend at Rhinebeck. She was most reluctant but after numerous calls from both Astors, she gave in and on the appointed day Brooke arrived at Ferncliff in the Astor limousine. (They broke the rule for Brooke, for they never sent the car into town on weekends.)

It was a typical Astor weekend at Ferncliff that Brooke was introduced to, with a goodly mix of Vincent's and Minnie's friends. There was jewelry designer Fulco di Verdura, Hudson River neighbor Olin Dows, Billy McCann, and Kate and Bill Osborn, a couple that were among Vincent's closest friends. In this beautiful setting along the Hudson River, events would unfold that would take Brooke totally by surprise. As she recounted in her autobiography:

> During lunch Vincent announced that he was going to take me for a drive after lunch. The assembled guests all laughed at that, and Kate Osborn bent across to whisper in my ear that nothing, absolutely nothing, could change the routine of Vincent's afternoon nap. The Osborns left soon after lunch and the others went off to play canasta in the teahouse . . . Vincent appeared from a hall that led to the bedrooms. "All set?" he asked. "Ready for a drive?"
>
> "Yes." I answered. "I'm all set." He then backed the Mercedes out at a rapid pace . . . But we didn't go very far. We stopped abruptly under a tree, halfway between the main house and the teahouse . . .
>
> Vincent turned off the engine, then turned to me. "Minnie wants to leave me," he said, "and up to now, I refused to give her a divorce, but now that I have met you, I will give her a divorce if you will marry me."
>
> I couldn't believe my ears. "But you hardly know me," I said. "We really don't know each other at all."
>
> "I know a lot about you," Vincent answered, "and I have never

known anyone to have more friends and to be more loved and admired than you. And I can swear on the Bible that, if you marry me, I will do anything I possibly can to take care of you and make you happy—and earn your love."

Brooke certainly saw a side of Vincent Astor few people, including Minnie, ever got to see. In a recent interview, a distinguished American actor and Burden family member who knew Vincent and the Cushing sisters well had this to say about him: "Vincent was difficult. His natural manner was very detached and overbearing."

Then Brooke and Vincent drove up and down the Hudson River Valley, and Vincent told her tales of the great houses along the river and the people who lived in them or had lived in them.

When they returned from the drive at teatime, all the others were still playing canasta. Brooke and Vincent had their tea alone together, then went separately to their rooms for a rest before dinner. Throughout the meal Brooke wondered if Minnie had any inkling of what had happened during the drive. In fact, although Vincent and Minnie did not have a very intimate relationship and his complicated personality had infuriated her from the very first days of their life together, they had always spoken very openly to each other. Since the question of divorce had been eating at both of them for a long, long time, it is almost certain that he had already told Minnie the gist, if not the details, of his earlier conversation with Brooke.

On her return to New York, Minnie told Babe all about the strange weekend and began to make plans to obtain a divorce as soon as she returned from her planned trip to Europe. All the interested parties agreed that everything would remain the same until then. As for Brooke, she took leave of her job at *House & Garden* to spend the summer at her place in the Berkshires. It would be a time of contentment and review for her.

As summer ended, things began to happen very quickly. In September of 1953, on her return from Europe, Minnie spent several weeks on a dude ranch in Pocatello, Idaho, obtaining a divorce. Thus ended her thirteen-year marriage with the scion of the Astor dynasty. Her divorce settlement was modest considering the fact that Vincent's holdings totaled nearly $200 million. Minnie received a little over $2 million—and not even the Gracie Square apartment.

But upon her return from Idaho, Minnie felt like a young filly breaking out of the starting gate in her first big race. The past thirteen years had been so stifling for her! True, she had enjoyed the name and the great wealth, and compared with many marriages, hers had allowed her a great deal of latitude. But none of that had been enough. Many people have wondered over her decision, especially in view of the man she chose to replace Vincent Astor a month later. He was James Whitney Fosburgh, a Manhattan artist and World War II army glider pilot—and a member of New York's budding gay community.

Vincent and Brooke were married at Bar Harbor, Maine, at the home of their friends Joseph and Elizabeth Pulitzer. The St. Louis *Post-Dispatch* scooped all the New York dailies.

From start to finish, this strange episode in the lives of Minnie, Vincent, and Brooke seemed more like one of Noël Coward's more inspired moments in the theater than a real-life tabloid headline-grabber. This was, in fact, drawing-room comedy at its best.

13

BABE AND BILL: THE EARLY YEARS

*M*R. and Mrs. William Samuel Paley honeymooned in Europe for three and a half weeks, then returned home to New York aboard the *Queen Elizabeth*. If ever there was a couple who had it all, it was Babe and Bill. For her part, Babe had landed a mate whose fortune and power, if not his pedigree, were at least equal to the standard set by Vincent Astor and Jock Whitney. Babe was no longer a poor relation. And Bill had gained what he most wanted out of life, the one thing that all his money couldn't buy: unassailable WASP credentials and connections, coupled with the ultimate in glamour and chic. Babe Cushing Mortimer Paley was, in effect, Bill's ticket into the social stratum that had always been just beyond his grasp. That she enjoyed the reputation of being one of the great beauties of twentieth-century America was icing on the cake. The newlyweds appeared well satisfied with their union.

Almost at once the Paleys set up their household at Bill's magnificent eighty-acre estate in Manhasset, on Long Island's "Gold Coast." It was here, at Kiluna Farm, that Babe and Bill would spend most of their time. Paley and his first wife, Dorothy Hart Hearst, had rented the property from newspaper heir Ralph Pulitzer. Almost from the beginning Bill had desperately wanted to own it, because the area was an old-guard enclave, populated with a goodly number of Bakers, Vanderbilts, and Whitneys. Paley had eventually managed to purchase the beautiful estate, which included a large, rambling wooden house, completely hidden from the highway by tall trees, exquisite gardens which would become even more beautiful during Babe's tenure as chatelaine of Kiluna, guest cottages, stables, a pool, and an all-weather, glassed-in tennis court for year-round play.

When social commitments or personal whims dictated, Babe and Bill would head into Manhattan, where they kept a small but elegant pied-à-terre at Vincent Astor's St. Regis Hotel. Although largely furnished with hotel furniture, the three-room apartment was a tribute to Babe's ingenuity and taste. Using yard upon yard of Indian cotton, in slipcovers and gathered in tent fashion on the pictureless walls, Babe transformed the space into an exotic fantasy. On the drawing-room floor she placed her own needlepoint carpet, and in the center of the room she hung a whimsical chandelier. The effect was like stepping into an opulent Oriental tent.

The St. Regis pied-à-terre was far too small for entertaining even the immediate family, and larger-scale parties were out of the question. This presented no problem, since Babe and Bill could always take over one or more of the public rooms of the grand St. Regis—at vastly reduced rates, of course, courtesy of the Astor connection.

The famed international interior designer Billy Baldwin worked with Babe on the St. Regis apartment. Baldwin, like so many others who crossed Babe's path, was charmed by her glamour and sweetness. Describing her at this new juncture in her life, Baldwin rhapsodized,

> She might have been painted by Boldini or by Picasso during his Rose Period. So great is her beauty that no matter how often I see her, each time is the first time.
>
> She is the essence of the chic and sophisticated woman; yet inside is a delightful little girl who every so often bubbles to the

surface—she can become giddy with excitement over the planting of a new garden. . . . In dreams, I see Barbara in a lofty white contemporary room, with soft furniture in white, blue, brown. Kabuki!

Both Bill and Babe lavished the majority of their attention on Kiluna Farm. Bill loved the role of country squire, greatly enjoying the new-found friends he had acquired through the Cushing alliance. Perhaps one of his proudest moments was when the fence between Kiluna and Greentree came down. Before he had married Babe, the adjoining Whitney estate had been so near but yet so far, a ten-minute, circuitous car ride and a social eternity away. When Babe became Betsey and Jock Whitney's neighbor and "Baragwanath Boulevard" was built between the two main houses, Paley felt that all real and imagined barriers had been removed.

No expense was too great for Paley's homes. Bill might count pennies when it came to Babe's hiring staff and making small, everyday expenditures—even canceling magazine subscriptions for the house if they were among the supply Bill could bring home from the office. But when it came to display, everything had to be the very best—and Bill was ready to pay top dollar. Shortly after he married Babe, he ordered a total overhaul of the estate, although without making extensive structural changes on the main house. He extended the terraces, and had Babe completely redecorate the interior. Under Babe's exacting eye, Kiluna Farm became a showplace, filled with the finest antiques and most beautiful fabrics. Corps of internationally renowned interior designers paraded their priceless, unique wares through the farm for years. Among the stellar cast of characters were Syrie Maugham, Stephane Boudin, Billy Baldwin, Sister Parish, and Natalie Davenport. It fell to Babe to coordinate the efforts and soothe the ruffled feathers of these highly charged, temperamental artists, while dealing with the mercurial moods of her second husband. Rather like a latter-day Cosimo de' Medici, Bill Paley would settle for nothing short of perfection in any setting he deemed worthy of his presence.

Babe did not let him down, although she found that pleasing him was a physically and emotionally exhausting task. She too was a perfectionist, and the house was indeed magnificent. But it was to her exquisite gardens that Babe turned the major portion of her time, attention, and hard work. She had discovered a talent and indeed a passion for gardening, and Kiluna became a magical kingdom of glorious flowers, impeccably pruned shrubs, and manicured lawns. Soon gardening began to take on a new meaning for Babe. As Bill's mood swings began to weigh on her spirits, her gardens became a refuge from her increasingly troubled marriage, indeed a sort of initial therapy. In later years even her love of gardening would not suffice, and she would embrace psychotherapy and take mild tranquilizers, in an attempt to cope with a marriage that grew less and less ideal.

In the meantime, when Babe was not up to her elbows in soil and seeds or sitting back and watching Bill's meteoric financial and social ascendency, she was concentrating on maintaining her position as the ultimate fashion and social icon of New York's dazzling scene. While she adored the media attention, it too placed a certain stress on her day-to-day existence. The image Babe had created for herself was perfection, and nearly every moment of every day was devoted to upholding that image—for both her husband and the general public. Her name was a household word, her face recognizable to all but the most determined of recluses, and her every move was the fashion and social pulse for millions of American women. Babe was hot copy for not only *Vogue* but *Women's Wear Daily* and *W,* and whatever Babe wore triggered a domino effect throughout the entire nation's fashion consciousness. Once, as she emerged from a fashionable Manhattan restaurant and discovered that the weather had turned warmer, she removed the scarf from around her neck and unthinkingly tied it to her handbag. Naturally, the media flashbulbs were awaiting her, and soon this "innovative fashion statement" was transmitted via the fashion press to the nethermost regions of the country. In no time, women throughout America were tying scarves to their handbags. So great was Babe Paley's charisma that women of all ages and from every walk of life would do nearly anything to emulate her. They wanted not only to look like her but be like her.

Babe's style, however, was so personally and uniquely her own that it simply could not be duplicated. In fact, it was undoubtedly this highly individual flare that catapulted her to the top of the heap. One of the few other American woman to reach such an exalted level of social and fashion influence was Jackie Kennedy Onassis, who followed Babe by a generation and who may well have looked to her as a role model. In any event, Babe had paved the way for latter-day fashionable trendsetters by showing them the critical importance of the right blend of originality and taste.

Babe's public image grew by leaps and bounds, as did Bill's business and his social acceptability. This seemingly perfect couple had everything they could have wished for, including an heir. Their first-born son, William Cushing Paley, was born on March 30, 1948, a scant eight months after the wedding. There is nothing on the record as to Gogsie Cushing's comment at the time regarding this early arrival. Her grandson's birth so close on the heels of Babe's wedding could only have added to the discomfort and strain that existed in her relationship with her newest son-in-law and that tenseness remained right up to the time of her death.

By the time Bill and Babe's second child, Kate, was born, in 1950, family and a handful of close friends could detect the first signs of strain on the marriage. Bill was a very demanding man, and however hard Babe tried to please him, he managed to find something that needed redoing or rearranging. A example of this was recently cited in an interview with author/journalist Michael Thomas: "Babe was famous for her lists. I remember her being constantly surrounded by yellow legal pads." Even at grand gala events, Babe had a miniature legal pad framed in gold so as not to forget something that Bill might want done.

While in his own peculiar way he loved all his children (two by his first marriage, who lived with their mother most of the time, Babe's two Mortimer children, and two young Paleys), he was not a demonstrative or approachable father, never one to roughhouse or pitch baseballs. His aloof behavior isolated the children early on, and this isolation would affect their development and ultimately their adjustment as adults.

Bill's aloofness even extended to the unusual living arrangements that he devised for the family. No matter how much time Babe and Bill spent in Manhattan, the children almost invariably remained at Kiluna—in their own separate five-bedroom cottage. The cottage had all the comforts: its own living room, kitchen, and lavish playroom. The playroom was in the attic, adjoining the servants' rooms. The children had their own live-in cook, as well as a nanny, who oversaw all their activities. Even when Babe and Bill were at Kiluna, they spent little time at the cottage with the children; in fact, more often than not these incredibly remote parents were too busy with their own houseguests. Perhaps Babe would have wished to take a more nurturing role, but Bill and his constant demands had to come first.

Paley wrote in his autobiography, *As It Happened,* "I do not like the idea of depending on others. When I find myself becoming dependent on one particular person I start to worry about what would happen if he or she were no longer there . . ." He apparently equated closeness with dependency, and this attitude extended in quite an extreme way to every relationship in his life—whether with business associates, whom he would dismiss at the snap of his highly manicured fingertips, or family. In effect, Bill Paley had built an unscalable wall between himself and others, including his parents, his first and second wives, and all his children.

Early in life Bill had determined that he would center his life around material things, rather than people. Things, at least, would be less likely to disappoint or leave him, and they were usually replaceable. Babe, for all her vitality and her earnest efforts to please her second husband, was never able to change him in this regard. In fact, she was really more a possession to him than a wife or companion—and worse yet, not even his most prized possession. It was upon CBS, the network he had built with the assistance of some brilliant people like Frank Stanton, Arthur Taylor, and Edward R. Murrow, that Bill Paley lavished incredible amounts of love and attention. CBS was his baby, and he ruled it in the manner of a Roman emperor. All other relationships took a back seat to his business. True, he would occasionally summon Babe to accompany him on business junkets or to broadcasting conventions around the country, but he required her presence not for its own sake but as an adornment, a trophy to show off, in a calculated move to impress his peers. And impress them she did.

Of course, Babe was quick to understand his motives. Just before the birth of their daughter, Kate, she determined that this would be her last child. She was well aware that, as little better than a purchased possession, she was to be on constant display in order to gratify her rich and powerful mate and thus to retain her value to him. So Babe, hiding her growing discontent, indulged Bill's every whim and played her public role with total dedication and aplomb. After all, this was what she had been raised to do. Of course, what went on behind the scenes never made the gossip columns, and only a few intimates had any idea of the disheartening truth: that the marriage had dissolved into a business arrangement and that Bill had already begun to stray. Not that this was the way Babe had wanted things, but this was what she got—and settled for.

One of the few people who knew the truth about the Paleys' seemingly ideal marriage was Babe's sister Betsey. Once the wall had come down between their properties, Babe would frequently hike over to Greentree, often in tears, and Betsey would console her. Unlike her husband, Jock, Betsey had never really managed to become a fan of Bill Paley. Having herself been the victim of a callous mate, Betsey gave succor to her baby sister. Still, we can only speculate that she, having learned so well the lessons that Gogsie had taught all three sisters, counseled Babe to endure the occasional pain that went with marriage to a tycoon with a definitely roving eye.

Actually, Babe managed to cope quite nicely, finding satisfaction in seeing to the raising and educating of her children (albeit from a distance), in gardening, needlepoint, sketching, and garnering attention from the press. She took great pleasure from the fact that her fashion-star image rivaled that of her husband's as a communications-industry giant. In fact, at both public and private social gatherings, whether in Manhattan or Capri, it was Babe who people came to see and be seen with.

As one of Paley's CBS colleagues once commented, "He didn't pick the programs. He picked the stars. He didn't make Jack Benny a star, but he knew he was one. He didn't make Babe Cushing the best of the beautiful women, but he knew she was."

Babe played the wifely role as Bill expected her to play it, but she also went ahead with her own design for living, devoting a great deal of time to her hobbies. Her passion for gardening evolved into a real art form.

She began to have large-scale plans and drawings of her gardens laid out in detail during the winter months, paving the way for the profusion of both flowers and vegetables that would come forth to delight the eye and palate during the spring, summer, and fall. Over the years, under her expert eye, the grounds of Kiluna became more and more magnificent, but always with a simple beauty that belied the intensive work and artistry that had created it. Close to the main house was an extraordinary wooded hollow of wildflowers, bordering an oval lily pond. Cascading down the hill into the hollow were trees and bushes of various heights and subtly varying colors. The appearance of this pastoral scene was completely natural, the design completely Babe's. She also laid out paths upon which her family and guests could stroll to gaze down at the serene but sumptuous beauty of what nature and Babe Cushing Paley had created. This particular spot must have given a great deal of pleasure to a great many people—but to none so much as to its creator. For Babe the planning, hard work, and serene enjoyment provided many hours of contentment and escape from the numerous stresses of her life.

Babe's genius, taste, sensitivity, and perfectionism did not begin and end with her wardrobe or her garden. These qualities extended to all areas of her life—and to all the homes she shared with Bill Paley. No matter how many talented decorators she employed, every room in every home had her distinctive stamp on it. And no meal reached the table without Babe's having scrutinized the harmony and variety of colors on the plate.

From early childhood, growing up in Chicago in a caring Jewish household, Bill Paley had always had more than a layman's interest in food. Babe literally and figuratively catered to this almost obsessive interest, making sure that he would have whatever he wanted to eat, whenever he wanted it. She personally oversaw preparation and service of his food and always discussed the day's menu with him in advance. When they went out, they constantly experimented with new restaurants. At home at Kiluna, Babe's kitchen was well stocked for any kind of meal at any hour. She even created and stocked a kitchen directly adjoining Paley's bedroom suite, for one of his greatest pleasures was to be able to fix himself late-night snacks, especially scrambled eggs and any type of German sausage. Of course, Babe also had to concern herself with his great love of food at all the other Paley homes and during any travels they undertook. In their travels, especially on business trips, she and Bill would insist on being chauffeured directly to a favorite restaurant rather than to their hotel to unpack.

Paley, in turn, took care of Babe in the only way he knew how—by lavishing on her a king's ransom in furs and jewels, thus of course priming her to better enhance his own image. In winter Babe was swathed in full-length Russian crown sable, and at any point in time she was sure to be wearing some part of her million-plus-dollar jewel collection, which clearly rivaled those of Betsey and Minnie.

As her material possessions increased, Babe's private life began to spiral downward. With Tony and Amanda almost fully grown and Billie and Kate nearing adolescence, she became more and more interested in charting a separate course for herself. She reasoned that if in fact her great beauty and style, along with her first-class social credentials, had won the day with Bill Paley, then these three great assets, coupled with the power of the Paley name, should enable her to achieve anything she wanted. In this way she could gradually become her own woman—within the confines of her marriage, of course. Having learned to live with her marital situation as it was, at this late date she had no intention of sacrificing the wealth and security it provided. Although Babe never became as successful as her husband, he had never really played by the rules. Babe could not really play without them. For her, carving her own independent niche was a gradual learning process, with many hits and many misses. The new course she was charting for herself and the new friends and acquaintances she would bring into her widening circle would occupy reams of copy in both the highbrow and lowbrow press, as well as the glossy fashion and social magazines. Babe's world became a triumph of "hip."

14

"JOCK, JOCK, JOCK"

WHILE Babe gloried in the constant adulation of the press and public, and was at her very best in the glare of the media limelight, Betsey Cushing Roosevelt Whitney avoided all publicity, with a truly old-guard, old-money aversion to any intrusion into her privacy. In all fairness, this profound dislike of media attention may well have had more to do with the pain it had caused her during her fishbowl existence in Washington than with inherently snobbish convictions. Betsey was at last totally satisfied with her life, precisely the sort of life for which her mother had groomed her. She adored being the wife of multimillionaire John Hay Whitney and the mistress of their seven-hundred-acre Long Island estate, with its staff of eighty-five.

Greentree abounded with stables, paddocks, pastures, dairy facilities, a chicken house, kennels, and accommodations for about half the people who staffed the estate. It also had its gardens and greenhouses, but unlike her sister Babe, Betsey left the actual planning and work to her staff of gardeners, who provided her with an ample supply of flowers for her decorating needs.

The main house was a veritable art museum, as Jock had long been involved in the collecting of fine paintings. Clearly he was a man of great taste and one with the fortune to indulge his passion for the best. He had served as a trustee of the Museum of Modern Art since 1930, and at the time of his marriage to Betsey, he had one of the greatest private collections of Impressionist and postimpressionist paintings in the world. The walls of the enormous house were filled with Manets, Pissarros, Utrillos, Seurats, Rousseaus, Gauguins, Renoirs, Vuillards, and many other equally impressive works.

If there was any cloud on Betsey's horizon, it was the fact that she had suffered two miscarriages, and having passed the age of forty, she felt she had to face the fact that she would not be able to produce a Whitney heir. The next best thing, she reasoned, would be to convert her Roosevelt daughters into Whitneys, which meant that Jock would have to adopt them. With Greentree once again a family home, one where both Sara and Kate felt very comfortable, adoption seemed a reasonable step for Jock to take. This was especially true since Sara was already sixteen and Kate twelve, and both girls were more than willing to be adopted. Jimmy Roosevelt, remarried and raising a new family, had never paid them the least bit of attention—not even remembering their existence on their birthdays or at Christmas.

When Jock confided his plans to close friends, family, and business associates, they all warned him about the difficulties that might arise from adopting children whose natural father was still alive. To make matters even more awkward, these particular children happened to be granddaughters of the president of the United States, and they had always enjoyed the privileges that went along with that status, including full Secret Service protection. When they were youngsters, a Secret Service agent had always driven them to school. Whenever they offered one of their classmates a ride, the child would inevitably mistake the agent for the Roosevelt girls' father. In any event, Franklin Delano Roosevelt was especially fond of his grandchildren and would have been deeply grieved had Jock adopted them. Betsey, although anxious to sever her daughters' remaining ties to their father, had no desire to cause her former father-in-law such pain or to draw massive media attention to herself and her children.

The death of FDR, on April 12, 1945, removed the sole obstacle to

Betsey's ambition. Jimmy Roosevelt did not in any way contest the adoption. In fact, he readily furnished the requisite papers. On March 30, 1949, seven years after Sara and Kate had come to live at Greentree, a Mineola, Long Island, judge formalized the adoption. The following year Jimmy sent Jock Whitney a heartfelt, plaintive handwritten note, asking permission to see his daughters sometimes and suggesting that the Whitneys could arrange such reunions through the girls' grandmother, Eleanor Roosevelt. He did not specify any date or time, and the former First Lady never did have to play the role of go-between, for Jimmy did not get around to seeking out his first two children. Their meetings with their natural father were fleeting and for the most part accidental. James Roosevelt did not even attend their weddings. Once when their half-brother James Roosevelt, Jr., the son of Jimmy and Romelle Schneider, asked his father who Sara and Kate were, Jimmy replied, "Oh, just two people I know."

Prior to the adoption, Sara and Kate had referred to Jimmy as Papa or Dad and to Jock Whitney as Boss. Afterward, their natural father became "Jimmy," and their adoptive father became "Dad." While Sara and Kate could never inherit their new father's genes or come naturally by his remarkable human qualities, they certainly could profit from his example and the fathering he gave them. Moreover, as his legal daughters, they stood a good chance of inheriting a goodly portion of his $300 million fortune. Betsey had in effect pulled a coup that neither of her sisters would ever match; she had secured the Whitney legacy for her children. Like her mother, Betsey had a farsighted, dynastic sense of family, and also like her mother, she had very great ambitions for her girls. That Jock Whitney had so easily acceded to her strategy only illustrated how very well Betsey had assimilated Gogsie Cushing's master plan.

Becoming a father and withdrawing from the Social Register were but two of the changes that marrying Betsey had wrought in the life of bon vivant Jock Whitney. As time went by, most of his boon companions from his café society days fell by the wayside. No longer on the Greentree guest list were such well-known personages as Donald Ogden Stewart, Fred Astaire, and Robert Benchley, best man at Jock's first wedding and for many years a resident of a grace-and-favor cottage on the estate grounds. It was no secret that Betsey had never been very comfortable in the company of theatrical and literary types, and like her mother and Babe, Betsey was quite masterful at dropping old friends and acquiring new ones to suit her needs.

How Jock felt about the loss of his old buddies we will never know, for apparently he did not discuss the problem with anyone. He had always been most reticent about airing personal and family matters, anyway, and it is possible that Betsey was so subtle in her manipulation of their friendships that Jock never knew what hit him. A longtime Cushing watcher once characterized Betsey as "by far the smartest of the three sisters, the most formidable." She was, this acquaintance observed, "very controlling in a low-key way—'the iron hand in the velvet glove.' "

In any event, the man who, along with his sister, Joan Whitney Payson, had been known as a number-one Broadway angel, was becoming less and less involved in the Great White Way. Even his close friendship with legendary film producer David O. Selznick, went by the boards as Jock gave every appearance of settling comfortably into his new role of paterfamilias.

Irene Mayer Selznick, Selznick's wife and the daughter of movie mogul Louis B. Mayer, had a front-row seat in the private drama of Jock's changing friendships, especially as they affected her husband. Reminiscing about the friendship that had led to the making of *Gone With the Wind*, she commented:

Apart from his family, David's single strongest emotional tie was to Jock. David called him Strongheart; it suited him in more ways than one, and it pleased him. Then I pointed out that it was also the name of a current star: a dog. When he took offense, I relented. Even in David's last years he referred to Jock by that name, and it never ceased to move me.

After the war, the mutual affection between David and Jock remained, but not the intimacy. It was not only the three-thousand-mile distance. Jock's life had changed radically and so had David's. When David complained to me, I had to tell him that if I were Betsey, I would not exactly have encouraged the relationship, certainly not at the outset of the marriage. . . .

Nothing was the same, nor should it have been. Liz [Jock's first wife] had always mockingly called Jock the Great Man. Well, that's what he was and then some to Betsey, who absolutely adored him, first, last and always, and gave him the kind of home he wanted.

I was more fortunate than David in this regard, because I was simply more adaptable. Also, I came to live in New York. Jock stuck with me through the years. I didn't have a better friend.

Another of Jock's show-biz cronies who did remain was borscht belt comic Joe E. Lewis. He continued to turn up every year for Jock's August 17 birthday bash, usually held at the Whitney home in Saratoga, New York. The gravelly-voiced master of Jewish humor never failed to send Jock into paroxysms of glee with his gags. This extracurricular gig among the highbrows was actually a sort of dress rehearsal for Lewis before he headed for the resorts in the Catskill Mountains.

Finance, sports, and theater were not Jock's only interests. In fact he had an abiding fascination with politics and a true concern for the welfare of the nation. He first got involved in politics as part of a group of young liberal Republicans, led by friend and fellow New Yorker Nelson Rockefeller. Jock served as head of the movie division in the Office of Coordinator of Inter-American Affairs in the Roosevelt administration. However, as America entered the fifties, Whitney began to move closer and closer to a moderate, middle-of-the-road Republican philosophy. It was at this time that business matters began to take precedence over sporting and social events.

Both Sara and Kate had proper coming-out parties but without the big splash that would have catapulted them into the headlines. The sisters first went to Manhattan's exclusive Brearley School, which a number of children of Betsey's friends attended. From there Sara went on to the Milton Academy, in Milton, Massachusetts, while Kate prepped at Miss Hall's School, in Pittsfield, Massachusetts. It was when Sara went on to study at Bryn Mawr College, near Philadelphia, that she met the six-foot-one, dark, handsome, and talented Anthony di Bonaventura, a Curtis Institute musical prodigy who was the son of an Italian immigrant barber in New York's Little Italy—not exactly the right side of the tracks by Whitney standards.

Sara Delano Roosevelt was a striking young woman with blonde hair and blue eyes, a wonderfully warm personality, and a great understanding of human nature. In this last respect, she greatly resembled her paternal grandparents, Eleanor and Franklin Roosevelt. Rather than going the standard post-debutante route—with its endless rounds of parties, teas, and dinners, all orchestrated on a lavish scale to let the world know that the year's crop of young debs were officially available for marriage—Sara opted instead to concentrate on education and travel, with and without her family. She had spent one summer as an exchange student in France, and in 1952 she had gone back to Europe with her family, when Jock decided to visit the family that had helped him after his escape during World War II. This gave her a remarkable amount of independence and sophistication, coupled with very high expectations from life, ingrained in her from earliest childhood by her shrewd mother and her exalted lifestyle.

Sara had grown up in the lap of luxury, but she never demonstrated the snobbery so typical of her peers. She had a great love and appreciation of all kinds of people from every socioeconomic walk of life, and never let herself be hedged in by the elite connections that inevitably surrounded a girl who stood to inherit millions. Given this bent for independence and her broad base of friends and acquaintances, Sara surprised few of her friends when she announced that she planned to marry the twenty-three-year-old di Bonaventura though she did catch her mother off guard. Betsey had apparently ignored all the warning signals, failing to believe that any daughter of hers would marry so far "beneath" her. In Betsey's eyes, such a match would represent the beginning of the end of the mystique that for nearly a quarter of a century had surrounded the lives and loves of the Cushing sisters. All three had snared men of great wealth and influence, and they—and the general public—expected no less of the next generation. Further, the far-ranging dynastic ramifications for this branch of the Whitney family, with its vast fortune, overwhelmed both Betsey and Jock.

Unfortunately for Betsey, however, Sara had her mother's and grandmother's steely determination. She was absolutely set on marrying her promising young pianist. Also unfortunate for Betsey was the fairy-tale quality of the love match between the heiress and the immigrant barber's son. No sooner had the press gotten hold of the story than it was headline news from coast to coast, capturing the collective imagination of the entire country. Americans, having emerged triumphant and prosperous from World War II and the Korean conflict, were justifiably proud of their nation and its values. Sara's romance with di Bonaventura was the very embodiment of American egalitarianism.

In any event, the marriage was essentially a fait accompli. Under the gentle guiding hand of Jock Whitney, the family—including Mrs. Vincent Astor and Mrs. William Paley—decided to accept the inevitable and make the best of the situation. Betsey and Jock hosted a dinner party at Greentree in the young couple's honor, inviting Anthony's parents, Fred and Rose di Bonaventura. When asked afterward by a reporter how they liked their son's in-laws-to-be, the di Bonaventuras commented, "They are nice people." To the same question, Jock Whitney provided the same answer: "They are nice people." Betsey, however, refused to say anything publicly, reserving her comments and opinions on the love match for her family's ears only.

Before long Fred and Rose di Bonaventura reciprocated with an invitation to dinner at their brownstone apartment in Little Italy. Rose served a typical Italian meal of pasta and rich homemade sauce, a zesty old family recipe from her native Abruzzi region of Italy. It was unquestionably a memorable meal for both families, albeit one that neither would ever in their wildest dreams have previously imagined themselves sitting through. The handsome and talented young man whom Sara had chosen to wed was definitely from a different world.

Fred di Bonaventura had brought his new bride, Rose, to the small West Virginia town of Follansbee, where he had established his own successful barbershop. Anthony was the youngest of four children, all born in the rooms above the shop and all musical. Sam, a Yale and Juilliard graduate, today teaches music and composition; Anna is a piano and violin teacher; and Mario studied music in Paris and has conducted and played at the famed Salzburg music festival.

The di Bonaventura family moved to New York in order to provide their talented children—especially little Anthony, who was playing the piano by ear at the age of four—with all the educational and ultimately professional advantages that a major city could offer. It was here that Anthony attended the Little Red School House, the New York model progressive school. He next went on to study at Public School 19, on East Fourteenth Street, and finished up at Elizabeth Irwin High School and All Hallows High, in the Bronx. He and his sister, Anna, played the organ at church every Sunday. Throughout his school years his musical ability continued to develop, and upon graduating from high school he seized the splendid opportunity to attend Philadelphia's prestigious Curtis Institute, where he and Sara Delano Roosevelt met at a party. The rest was history.

Sara's wedding was as small and unpretentious as her mother's and father's had been huge and grandiose. She arrived fifteen minutes late for the ceremony at the tiny Mary Helper of Christians Roman Catholic Church, located on East Twelfth Street. Yet there were also undeniable similarities to the lavish Cushing-Roosevelt wedding, for outside were thousands of well-wishers from the heavily populated tenement neighborhood. As the suspense mounted they jammed the street, crowding up against the specially erected barriers and several platoons of police. Sara's wedding was every bit as much a fairy tale as her mother's first one had been, and the crowd-drawing appeal was perhaps even greater, since this was truly a rags-to-riches story.

At last, with a dazzling smile for the crowd, Sara swept into the church on the arm of her adoptive father, Jock Whitney. Inside were only three wire-service cameramen; all reporters and other photographers had been banned, forced to remain outside, behind the barricades with the hordes, and the church was locked at noon to all but the invited guests. Noticeably absent were the bride's natural father and paternal grandmother, Eleanor Roosevelt; the globe-trotting former First Lady was in the Far East on a fact-finding tour.

Father Anthony Bregolato performed the ten-minute ceremony outside the altar area and without benefit of a mass, since the bride was not Catholic, and then the handsome couple stepped outside to an explosion of cheers and flashbulbs and a blizzard of shredded newspaper—the Lower East Side version of confetti—which the zealous onlookers tossed from the fire escapes and rooftops of the nearby tenements. The reception, given by Betsey and Jock at their 10 Gracie Square duplex town residence, set an obviously different tone, only serving to point out the great differences between the couple's backgrounds.

While the wedding had been a success, the honeymoon, at Mount

Katahdin Wilderness, in Maine, was an unmitigated disaster. Just four days after the wedding, while at the isolated resort camp, Anthony was stricken with acute appendicitis. He and his new bride roared out of the woods in an ambulance, traveling over thirty-odd miles of rough country roads to Millinocket and from there to Bangor's Eastern Maine General Hospital. Sara remained at Anthony's side throughout his hospital stay, and then the newlyweds headed back to Manhattan.

Anthony's career as a concert pianist never did live up to the promise of his youthful talent. The great violinist Efrem Zimbalist had praised the young pianist during his days at the Curtis Institute, and everyone expected great things of him. That these great things did not materialize may perhaps have been due at least in part to the enormous change in his lifestyle after his marriage to Sara. Certainly, similar sets of circumstances have throughout time impaired the achievement of equally promising artists. From a background of hard work and tenement living, Anthony suddenly found himself ensconced with his new bride in the lap of luxury, in a residence at 182 East Sixty-fourth Street. Within a year Sara gave birth to their first child, a boy named Anthony Christopher Peter, whom they called Christopher and who is today known as Betsey's favorite grandchild. Then, in 1956, Andrea Isabelle was born, followed the next year by Peter John. In 1959 Sarina Rosaria came along, and finally, in 1963, Betsey Maria arrived. Sara, in the Roosevelt tradition, had proved to be a good breeder. With so little need to work for a living and so many distractions, it is small wonder that Anthony did not achieve great success in his chosen field.

Unfortunately, the young di Bonaventuras' marriage was even less successful than Anthony's career. Recently a friend of the family summed the marriage up in four short words: "It was a disaster." Yet Betsey and Jock, so lukewarm about the marriage in the first place, were absolutely overjoyed by the births of their grandchildren. By the time Christopher arrived, Betsey was already planning the dynastic roles of this and all subsequent grandchildren, envisioning the part each would eventually play in the Whitney scheme of things. While of course the children were not genetically Whitney progeny, they were Jock's only grandchildren, and Betsey enlisted his aid in educating them about all the duties and responsibilities that would come with great wealth and power, and in providing all the necessary credentials to ensure that the youngsters would be able to attain the rarefied social and financial heights of the Whitney world. This was the principal task that Betsey and Jock faced in the latter half of the 1950s.

Jock's involvement in politics had escalated by this time. A staunch Eisenhower supporter, he played an impressive political and financial role in the campaign that led to Ike's election as the thirty-fourth president of the United States. At one point Eisenhower and some of his advisers seriously considered Jock as a vice-presidential running mate. For any range of reasons, Jock did not choose to pursue the vice presidency with Eisenhower. It is quite possible that Betsey did not want to rekindle her previous high-profile public lifestyle as she had during the FDR days. Also quite possible, Jock himself may have desired to keep his energies directed toward the diplomatic field, in which he would later emerge as a major figure. Of course, it is impossible not to wonder how differently the course of national politics might have turned out if Jock Whitney had become Eisenhower's vice president. In the meantime, Betsey had to deal with a more immediate and personal crisis: Minnie's announcement to her sisters that she planned to divorce Vincent Astor.

Betsey and, to a slightly lesser degree, Babe counseled caution. Although both the younger sisters had themselves divorced their first husbands, neither had kissed away a fortune comparable to Astor's, and the very idea of losing out on a $200- to-$300-million inheritance was unthinkable. Surely, they reasoned, all the health problems that had plagued Vincent for years, since his early childhood, would sooner or later take their toll. If Minnie could just hang in there for a few more years, she just might find herself to be an incredibly wealthy widow, still young enough to enjoy life. By this same logic, Minnie, as a widow without children, might well leave this vast fortune to her nieces and nephews, thereby absolutely assuring future generations of all the money they could possibly desire. This was a game plan worthy of European dynasties. But Betsey and Babe had not counted on Minnie's tenacity and stubbornness. The sisters met many, many times during the summer of 1953, but in the end, all their entreaties proved worthless. While Betsey, a great manipulator, made a strong case for Minnie keeping a cool head, she could not in the end persuade Minnie that the perks that went along with being *the* Mrs. Astor outweighed the emotional scarring and deep unhappiness that attended a marriage that had essentially ended the day it took place.

Betsey finally conceded defeat and retreated on this issue of Minnie's divorce, as did Babe, and returned to seeing to the comfort of the man who was, to her way of thinking, the most important in the world—Jock Whitney. Even after all these years Betsey thought that the sun rose and set around him. Recalling Betsey's hero worship of her husband, Dorothy Dillon Eweson (widow of Sydney Spivack, who was almost like a brother to the Cushing sisters) had this to say: "It was Jock, Jock, Jock! Jock likes this, Jock likes that." Betsey was deeply satisfied with the world she had created for herself.

15

A BOND IS SEVERED

*W*HEN Minnie at last divorced Vincent Astor, she had clearly won her heart's most ardent desire: freedom from a barren, stifling marriage. In addition, she collected an over $2-million settlement, which, according to rumor, included the St. Regis Hotel. All in all, not a bad deal, but the years ahead would show that the real winners were Vincent Astor and his third and last wife, Brooke Marshall Astor.

"The landlords' landlord" had finally found a woman he could relate to, one who would, under his expert tutelage, come to understand exactly the philanthropic direction he wished his vast fortune to take. The energetic, highly intelligent Brooke, while not totally identifying with Vincent's idiosyncratic personality, instinctively recognized his needy, vulnerable side and was able to provide the comfort and friendship he unknowingly craved. This in turn resulted in a mutual respect, which both Vincent and Brooke carefully nurtured from the very beginning of their marriage. Then, too, as Mrs. Vincent Astor, Brooke received all the wealth, power, and prestige of the Astor name, which in turn enabled her to gain the lofty status of the undisputed doyenne of New York's philanthropic and social world.

Betsey and, to an extent, Babe were all too aware of what Minnie had forfeited with her divorce and her remarriage to James Whitney Fosburgh, a painter of modest reputation and means—and an openly practicing homosexual, at that. In effect, Minnie's defection from the ranks of the fabulously rich, famous, and socially prominent was a blow to her sisters' pride and also, of course, to their hopes of eventually seeing the $200-to-$300-million Astor fortune filter down into the hands of their assorted Roosevelt, Mortimer, and Paley children and grandchildren. In addition, such a disastrous misalliance could not but detract from the mystique surrounding the Cushing sisters—a mystique that had become established nearly a quarter of a century earlier, when Betsey first stepped into the national limelight as the bride of Jimmy Roosevelt, and had subsequently grown with Babe's marriage to Stanley Mortimer and then to Bill Paley, Minnie's seemingly enviable match with Vincent Astor, and Betsey's phenomenal coup in marrying Jock Whitney. The sisters were hot copy, and every American knew that these glamorous women married big names and bigger bucks. And now, suddenly, Minnie was not playing by the Cushing rules. Betsey and Babe felt shamed by Minnie's behavior, as though Minnie's loss of prestige in some way lessened their own. They saw her divorce and subsequent paltry marriage as a sort of betrayal, and this greatly weakened the lifelong bond among the sisters, the bond established in early childhood and nurtured continually by the ever-vigilant Kate Cushing until the day she died.

Betsey, especially, resented the entire situation, and her resentment extended with a vengeance to Brooke Astor. Even to this day, a friend of Betsey's recently confided, Betsey bears a considerable grudge against the third Mrs. Astor. According to this same source,

At a luncheon where a group of friends were praising Brooke Astor's civic accomplishments, Betsey assumed the role of invalid, slumped back, looked confused, and asked, "Brooke Shields?" Everybody laughed, and no more was said regarding Mrs. Astor. Betsey loathes Brooke Astor.

This loathing seems to stem less from envy over Brooke's stellar civic and social image than from the fact that the Cushing sisters had lost out on Vincent Astor's vast fortune—and Brooke had scooped it up.

Despite their displeasure over Minnie's scheme, Betsey and Babe closed ranks around their older sister and saw her through her marriage to James Fosburgh. Kate had not only taught her daughters to marry well but instilled in them the major precept that top-drawer American families must always band together to save face, no matter how disgraceful the situation. Minnie's second marriage was just the sort of situation to bring this time-honored practice into play. And so, on October 23, 1953, just two weeks after Vincent Astor had wed Brooke Marshall in Bar Harbor, Maine, Minnie and James joined hands in holy matrimony.

The brief ceremony took place at the Congregational Church of Manhasset, performed by the pastor, the Reverend George C. Parker, in the presence of members of the immediate families. Pieter Fosburgh, one of James's brothers, served as best man, and Henry Cushing was once again pressed into service to give one of his sisters away. Bill and Babe Paley hosted a very small reception at their nearby home, Kiluna Farm. And Kate Cushing no doubt rolled over in her grave.

It might be noted that the groom's father, James B. A. Fosburgh, had been a partner of the late well-known financier and art patron Henry Clay Frick. The Fosburgh family name was certainly respectable enough, and Jim had attended St. Paul's School and Yale. By the time of his marriage to Minnie, most if not all of the Fosburgh money was gone. According to close friends, Jim was very defensive about not having the great wealth of his friends and especially his new in-laws, and he could in fact be quite petty and bitchy—in stark contrast to Minnie, whose disposition was constantly sunny, under any and all circumstances.

Minnie might, of course, have remained single after her divorce. She could easily have led a perfectly pleasant life, surrounding herself with most of the comforts that she had grown accustomed to in her years as Vincent Astor's wife. That she chose to remarry was undoubtedly due to the continuing influence of her late mother, Kate Cushing, who had always firmly believed that marriage was the only happy state for individuals. Minnie had made her bid for freedom but was undoubtedly hedging her bets by marrying Fosburgh. As a homosexual, he would provide companionship and the facade of marital security without making the demands that a more conventional husband would have made. In addition, Fosburgh had at least some artistic talent, a quality Minnie greatly admired, and he shared a number of Minnie's interests. Most important, his many connections in the world of art would give Minnie the opportunity to realize her dream of hosting the most brilliant salons in New York. In short, Jim Fosburgh was a perfect match for this particular Cushing sister.

Fosburgh's many highly talented gay friends would soon create a whole new guest list for Minnie's famed entertaining. With her husband's connections, she was at last able to gather together a select group of artistic, intellectual, theatrical, and social luminaries. The Fosburghs' Manhattan townhouse, on Third Avenue between Sixty-second and Sixty-third streets, was the place to be seen, the place to meet the most eclectic and amusing group of people. An invitation to one of Minnie's soirees was the hot social ticket of the era.

Jim Fosburgh, for his part, was equally happy with the marital arrangement, for now that he had his Lady Bountiful, he no longer had to worry about being able to compete with his ultra-rich friends—or even about whether he ever sold another painting. He did continue to paint, but he devoted equal energy to his newfound avocation—that of guiding Minnie into the role of Number One society salon hostess in Manhattan. In addition, he found himself constantly called upon to reassure his wife, a task that he accomplished admirably.

Soon the couple were entertaining such renowned individuals as Leonard Bernstein, Kitty Carlisle Hart, Tennessee Williams, Irene Mayer Selznick, Josh and Nedda Logan, John Richardson, Richard Feigen, Rex Harrison, Jimmy Donahue, Princess Margaret of England, and of course old friends like Jerome Zerbe and Duc Fulco di Verdura. From time to time Cole Porter would make an appearance, for he and Minnie adored each other. Occasionally family members would pop in at these gatherings. Among them were Pieter and Liza Fosburgh, sister-in-law Molly Fosburgh, Babe and Bill Paley—or more often Babe alone or with a friend—and even at times Betsey and Jock Whitney. Betsey, however, shied away from gatherings where the guests were too arty or too bizarre and restricted her visits to holiday celebrations and dinner parties in honor of important guests, especially British royalty or nobles, such as Princess Margaret or Viscount Anthony Lambton or Judy Montague, the princess's best friend.

Minnie's marriage to Jim took place at the beginning of a new era in the world of the arts in Manhattan, the barometer for the rest of the world. The Fosburghs would give much encouragement and comfort to many of the artistic and literary newcomers who were just gaining fame and fortune. By the latter half of the 1950s and the early 1960s these people were established, and thus, by having "discovered" them early on, Minnie was equally established as a hostess. Jim, of course, could take a great deal of the credit for having helped Minnie to achieve her lifelong goal, one that she had never quite reached during her years of marriage to Vincent Astor. For all his money and connections, Astor had neither the desire nor the ability to attract the intelligentsia that Minnie so desperately wanted to cultivate. But then, of course, there were trade-offs. Jim, in the role of host to so many talented and often beautiful individuals, especially the famous and successful men and their coterie of young male lovers, always had a ready supply of impressionable youthful admirers. Despite the unconventional nature of the Fosburghs' relationship, this could not have been an entirely comfortable situation for Minnie.

Nevertheless, Minnie was thrilled with her social success. At this time talented homosexuals were just beginning to establish their own culture in New York, and their myriad talents assured them of a prominent place in society. In fact, the results were dazzling, like a huge burst of fresh air, and Manhattan's socialites, with their vast wealth and power, took full advantage of this new trend.

Minnie, with that touch of fantasy so essential to creative minds, began to see herself as a twentieth-century reincarnation of the Marquise de Sévigné. The assembly-line parties for which Minnie was famous continued unabated both at the charming Third Avenue brownstone and also at the Fosburghs' country place, Cantitoe, in Katonah, New York, forty miles north of the city and in the heart of the

area that housed the various great Rockefeller family estates. A friend
in the arts and a frequent Fosburgh guest recently had this to say:

> Minnie and Jim were the last people in New York to have a grand
> salon. New Year's Eve and Christmas parties—if you were alone,
> you were always welcome. Many theatrical friends, the Oliviers,
> ballet people, painters, collectors—it was a kind of "high Bohe-
> mia." Entertained with great ease and charm. Often fifty to sixty
> people. Never place cards. Very informal. The third floor of this
> house had a famous red drawing room. The most festive room in
> New York.

The Fosburghs generally weekended at Cantitoe, a gracious house,
built in 1935 in a strictly English country style, and set on thirteen to
fourteen acres with extensive apple orchards, a pool, a poolhouse, and
an artist's studio. According to a friend who knew the house well, it was
decorated in excellent taste. The Fosburghs never had great pieces of
furniture, but the way the couple arranged their attractive things created
a charming, stylish ambience. The couple, while comfortably established, never had vast amounts of money to spend; yet they lived very
graciously and privately. And unlike her sisters, Minnie relied more on
her own decorating abilities than on those of famous professional interior designers.

The Fosburghs entertained nonstop at their weekend home, although
the parties were of necessity scaled down a bit. Here too, however,
"guests were people of interest and substance, not just golfers," as one
friend and frequent visitor once said. The couple was also notable for
generosity with friends who had nearby country places. For example,
the famed jewelry designer Fulco di Verdura, whose weekend place at
nearby Bedford had no swimming pool, was almost always welcome
to use the Cantitoe pool, although not between the hours of 4:00 and
5:00 P.M. Once, he arrived with a houseguest during that time slot—only
to find a number of German servants frolicking nude in the water.

In a recent conversation, Liza Fosburgh, the widow of Jim's brother
Pieter, provided an intimate look into Minnie's post-Astor years:

I did not know Minnie before she married my brother-in-law Jim Fosburgh. As to Betsey and Babe, I would only see them at prearranged luncheons when I was in Manhattan. I would go down to visit them at least once a month either in town or at their country place in Katonah. And on these visits either Minnie or Jim would frequently say, 'Let's call so-and-so for dinner. They had some of the most amusing and intelligent people as friends. Conversation was never dull. When they were in town for the winter Minnie and Jim were very social. They really picked up and collected people. Very selectively I might add. It was absolutely true that they had a salon. . . .

I recall our sitting up in the Adirondacks one summer day and Minnie, who was a great reader, was reading the latest big seller, *To Kill a Mockingbird* by Harper Lee. And Minnie turned to Jim and said, "As soon as we get back to the city we must invite her." They were not back in town two days and Harper Lee was at their home for dinner.

Yes, most summers were spent at the Fosburgh family's isolated camp on the grounds of the North Woods Club (the Fosburghs' grandfather was one of the founders of the club near the town of Minerva) [but] Minnie didn't much care for the Adirondacks outpost. She was really a city person. But she put up with it realizing it had been part of Jim's life for so long and it was one place he could paint with a passion. In addition to his well-known portraits, he did wonderful Adirondacks scenes—lakes and mountains. Some great still life.

In addition to reading Minnie was renowned for her needlepoint. And from time to time friends would come up to the camp for a weekend. I now live in a house that had belonged to Minnie and Jim. Most of the furnishings they had are still here. Some of the pieces are wonderful wicker. Minnie was fortunate enough to be in Saratoga when the furniture from the historical Grand Hotel [was] sold and she bought most of the original wicker porch chairs.

Yes, I would say with a degree of certainty that Minnie, Betsey, and Babe were very close knit. But all very different. Minnie enjoyed intimate gatherings. She always looked great. A stylish, conservative dresser. . . . Minnie and Jim thoroughly enjoyed each other. She was most supportive of his work. However Jim didn't paint as much in the city, they were too busy with people. Minnie was always most thoughtful of family and friends. If she thought you might be traveling to Europe, she might say, "Let me call the prime minister so he can receive you while you're in London." That kind of thoughtfulness was so typical of her.

As the years rolled by, Minnie continued to serve as a director of the Metropolitan Museum of Art, but she moved further and further away from the old-guard society. She continued to devote her time to the intelligentsia and always sought out the latest luminary on the scene— whether it was a David Hockney or Robert Motherwell in the field of art, an Alan Jay Lerner or Marlon Brando in the theater, or a Renata Tebaldi in the music world.

The years were not kind to Minnie's health or her looks. Always less attractive than her sisters, she lost her robust appearance and became increasingly frail and stooped; her blonde hair lost its healthy shine and became lank and stringy. As one friend of the Cushing sisters recently put it, Minnie looked "a little like ZaSu Pitts," a Hollywood comedienne of the thirties, forties, and fifties, whose screen image was that of a prim and proper dippy spinster. The same friend added that Minnie had "a personality a little like Babe's, but without the looks or the style. She needed constant reassurance." Also, according to this friend, "Minnie and Jim Fosburgh had a drinking problem. They both drank a lot. A friend once recalled seeing the Fosburghs in Arizona, and when the boot of the car was opened, it was filled with whisky bottles." This account, however, conflicts with remarks recently made by another friend and frequent guest at the Fosburgh home in Katonah. Although this person did not dispute the fact that Jim was a heavy drinker, he did not remember Minnie's ever having a problem with alcohol. She did, he asserts, become quite frail with age however. Ultimately, Jim's drinking did affect his career as an artist and take a serious toll on his health.

Despite their problems, Minnie and Jim continued to entertain nonstop, both in town and in the country. By this time they had sold the charming little Third Avenue townhouse and had purchased a huge apartment at 32 East Sixty-fourth Street, where Jim had a studio on the same tier as Kitty Carlisle Hart's bedroom. While this studio was not so spacious as the one he had had in the brownstone, that did not seem to matter, for he was painting less and less, devoting more and more time to his role of host.

The Fosburghs also gained fame as highly knowledgeable collectors. Minnie collected French paintings, including Cézannes and Toulouse-Lautrecs, as well as works by Winslow Homer and eighteenth-century drawings, sculptures, and furnishings, including some fine Louis XVI pieces. Jim had a creditable collection of nineteenth-century American art, which was destined to go to his alma mater, Yale. Both Fosburghs were regulars at the numerous auction galleries that dotted Manhattan.

The Fosburghs and their set dominated Manhattan's magical society scene from the mid-fifties through the early sixties. Then it would be the Paleys' turn to capture the limelight. Babe and her multimillionaire husband would rock the media back on its heels from the sixties through the mid-seventies. And while the artistic and literary world had beaten a path to the welcoming arms of both Fosburghs, the Paleys were sought out as guests. Their presence at a Manhattan social function guaranteed its success and won reams of publicity, regardless of whether the event was a public one or an intimate dinner party at the home of a close friend.

Yet Minnie and her second husband had created a splendid aura that was difficult if not impossible to duplicate. Mrs. Frank Whitney, one of Jim's aunts by marriage, summed it up best when she stated: "If the queen of England decided to make a private visit to America, she would first have lunch with Minnie and Jim and then go on to visit Betsey and Jock."

Despite their lingering resentment and wounded pride over their older sister's misalliance with her openly homosexual second husband, both Betsey and Babe continued to communicate with Minnie on an almost daily basis. Minnie, with or without Jim, seldom got together with the Whitneys or the Paleys. She quite simply operated in a completely different world, maintaining her own clearly defined agenda with her select group of arty friends. She seldom visited Kiluna Farm, and even more rarely got to Greentree. While still friendly with her younger sisters, she could not identify with them or their lifestyles—any more than they could identify with her or hers. The special closeness that had marked the sisters' earlier years had disappeared along with Minnie's first marriage. That special Cushing bond had been irreparably severed.

———

16

THE BEAUTY REGNANT
AND THE COURT JESTER

*I*N January of 1958 Babe Paley reached a monumental milestone in
her ongoing search for perfection. After more than a decade on the Ten
Best Dressed list, she was inducted into the Fashion Hall of Fame. With
this honor she was now truly at the very top of the fashion heap, along
with such all-time greats as the Duchess of Windsor, longtime friend
Gloria Guinness, and fellow socialite, gardener, and clotheshorse C. Z.
Guest. The award itself, a sort of standing ovation from the fashion
professionals and press, was given in recognition of Babe's elegant
perfectionism in dress, accessorizing, grooming, and bearing, which she
had made both an art form and very nearly a career. As her old friend
Tex McCrary once exulted, "In a ball gown, bikini, or ice pack Babe
Paley is the one woman all wives permit their husbands to admire. It's
a waste of time to envy the utmost." And this was in fact exactly what
Babe Paley had become: the utmost.

At first Babe continued to cultivate her glamorous fashion image in
order to please her demanding husband. But now that their marriage

had undergone subtle changes, she went back to pleasing herself. She derived tremendous personal satisfaction from her classically stunning looks, meticulous coiffure, flawless makeup, and unprecedented fashion flare. Her legendary attention to detail was a constant source of challenge and pleasure. The attention from the media, which she had always adored, was icing on the cake. Ultimately Babe reached the status of an international fashion deity—the standard against which all style-conscious women would be measured.

For more than three decades Babe was without equal in the world of fashion. Her approval lent an immediate cachet to almost any accessory, item of clothing, hairstyle, beauty product, or decorating scheme. Her appearance at a public event caused an outpouring of admiration and affection accorded only to a very few of her female contemporaries, such as the Duchess of Windsor and Jacqueline Kennedy Onassis.

At this point in her life, Babe was forty-three years old—and more stunning than ever. She stood five feet eight inches, with perfect posture and an unstudied natural grace. Her voice was low, with the finishing-school crispness that was a hallmark of her class. And with only the slightest change of expression she could manage to look primly sweet or icily imperious. Despite her horribly disfiguring 1934 automobile accident and subsequent reconstructive plastic surgery and dental bridgework, her face was absolutely beautiful. Purists—or envious rivals—might argue that her lips were a trifle too thin or that her jaw was a little too large or her nose too aquiline, but these features, augmented by her flashing dark eyes, sculpted bone structure, luminous skin, and long, swanlike neck, added up to an astonishingly aristocratic work of art. And this, plus of course Babe's impeccable social credentials, was what William Paley had bought and paid for. As Jack Dunphy, Truman Capote's lover at that time, once said:

> It wasn't the Cushing family in Boston that made her. It was Bill. She would have been nothing if she hadn't married him, and Truman wouldn't have had much to do with her, either. Whether he admitted it or not, he was attracted to money and power.

This may have been a slight exaggeration, for Babe had already made a name for herself, even making the Best Dressed list, before her marriage to Bill Paley. In any event, if she hadn't married Bill, she would undoubtedly have wound up with some other prominent, wealthy second husband. Nevertheless, it goes without saying that Bill's money and power enabled Babe to make the very most of her natural beauty and taste.

Despite all the glamour and chic that had become an integral part of the Paleys' aura, their marriage had taken a difficult turn, not only because of Bill's demanding nature. It was on one of their rare family vacations, in Cap d'Antibes, that Babe and Bill began to notice that their youngest child, Kate, not yet five years old, was losing her hair. The family was shocked, and became even more alarmed when, by the end of that summer trip, every hair on Kate's head and even her eyebrows had fallen out. Doctors diagnosed her condition as alopecia universalis, a rare disorder often associated with severe stress. To this day medical science has not found a cure for this condition, but the prevailing belief is that it stems from quite severe emotional disturbance.

"Babe went crazy," said a family friend. The Paleys consulted specialist after specialist—without results. Neither Babe nor Bill could accept the fact that any child of theirs could possibly contract such a malady—and that, once she had, all their considerable resources were not enough to find a cure. Some of the attempted cures bordered on the bizarre and only had the effect of creating further psychological problems for the growing child.

Predictably enough, Babe took Kate with her when she went to her hairdresser, the renowned Kenneth, and had the child fitted with a rather outlandish wig—a Buster Brown style with long bangs to cover her nonexistent eyebrows. To her credit, Babe did teach her daughter to wear wigs and to hide her baldness while getting into and out of the water, whether at a pool or the ocean, by cleverly manipulating a towel into a turban. But essentially, Kate's condition was a terrible affront to her parents' egos, and they could not even try to minimize the situation, let alone accept it. Like the parents of all disturbed children, they felt considerable guilt. The perfectionist in Babe led her to one conclusion: that she was somehow to blame for her daughter's malady. This simultaneous denial and guilt caused Babe to become more and more neurotic, and this of course began to affect both her marriage and her relationship with Kate and Billy.

Meanwhile, Babe's celebrity continued to grow, reaching its zenith in the 1960s. Despite the strain in their marriage, the Paleys were seen everywhere together during that time. Both Babe and Bill loved dining out, unlike Minnie and Jim Fosburgh. The Paleys held court at the best restaurants in Manhattan, rather than at their small pied-à-terre. Oddly enough, neither Babe nor Bill was remotely interested in the big charity-benefit circuit, which was so much a part of New York social life. And it is an established fact that Bill, unlike other Jewish tycoons, rarely if ever lent his name or his checkbook to the standard Jewish charities. In fact, he made every effort to avoid them, minimizing his contact with any activity that might remind society of his immigrant ethnic background.

Bill Paley's world revolved around self-promotion, whether through his phenomenal business success or his beautiful wife and her great family connections. Whatever extra time he had he devoted to his favorite extracurricular activity—ardent womanizing. Needless to say, all this left him little or no time for his children. In his memoir, Bill Paley barely even mentions his children. He pays lip service to his role as a parent by writing briefly and tritely on "the wonderful joy of childhood and youth" that they had brought to his life and his home. In fact, they were, like Babe, mere props on his stage. But Babe, of course, was more useful, for she greatly enhanced his public image and social acceptance. The children served no such purpose and so remained forever in the background.

Hilary and Jeffrey, Bill's two adopted children from his first marriage, were spared some of the feeling of rejection that accompanied his uncaring behavior toward his children, for they lived most of the time with their mother. Dorothy Paley Hirshon was a strong and loving mother, who tried in every way possible to make up for the total lack of love and attention her ex-husband accorded the children. Jeffrey, at his father's insistence, attended the Taft School and Harvard and established a creditable career as a newsman for the *International Herald Tribune* in Paris, a paper partly owned by Jock Whitney. When Jeffrey returned to the United States and attempted to join CBS's news department, he was thwarted at every turn by his own father. Realizing the futility of attempting to work for his adopted father, Jeffrey went on to earn a master's degree in economics at the New School for Social Research in New York, and proceeded to carve out a career for himself as an investment adviser. Creating his own success did not endear him to Bill Paley. In fact, if anything, it only served to increase the distance between father and son.

Hilary Paley, a beautiful blonde with an upturned nose, which pleased her father, had none of her mother's intellect or creative drive. After attending the Riverdale Country School in New York, Hilary willingly went on to the Shipley School, a fashionable finishing school on Philadelphia's Main Line, and later attended her mother's alma mater, Bennett College, for a year. She was presented to society not once but twice—by her father and stepmother at Kiluna and, several months afterward, by her mother at a dinner dance at New York's exclusive River Club.

If it can be said that William Paley paid enough attention to the six children to have selected a favorite, it was Hilary. Her beauty and great femininity were a nonthreatening source of pleasure. On occasion she displayed her father's toughness and could be very nasty in her remarks and comments about people. This, too, pleased Bill, since he was never on the receiving end. Hilary adored Babe and did her level best to emulate her glamorous stepmother at every turn. To an extent Hilary succeeded; she dressed like Babe, spoke like Babe, and after finishing her year at Bennett, even got a job at *Vogue*. She also managed to marry a wonderfully handsome man, whose social credentials were every bit as solid as Stanley Grafton Mortimer's. Young J. Frederic Byers III came from the family that had founded W. R. Grace and Company and Byers Steel. This additional social connection pleased Bill Paley immensely, and it actually brought Hilary a step closer to him.

The greatest victims of their father's neglect and lack of affection were his children with Babe, William and Kate. William, known as Billie, was a handsome youngster, combining as he did the best features of both parents and his mother's dark hair and big, dark eyes. He had a very kind nature, like his mother, and he was known to give away his toys and other childhood possessions to his playmates. Early on he developed an intense nervousness, rightly or wrongly attributed by some to his parents' determination to change his left-handedness. He went to a succession of boarding schools, some as far away as Switzerland, and even enrolled in Florida's Rollins College without first having earned a high school diploma. Certainly his father's influence must have had something to do with his being accepted by the college. He did not stay there for long. According to Sally Bedell Smith in her recent biography of Bill Paley, Billie has said of himself:

> I was a strange child. My parents thought I was crazy. I was sent to a psychiatrist when I was ten, got kicked out of schools, started smoking dope when I was sixteen and didn't have many friends. . . . I was different, that's all. I didn't want to alienate my parents. I loved my parents, but I hated them, you know?

Not a very auspicious beginning for the son of a self-proclaimed "self-made tycoon." Billie took off for Europe, then later became a combat photographer in Vietnam. It was there that he became a heroin addict.

Returning to the United States, he spent a time as a beach bum in Florida, then went into the restaurant business in Washington. One thing he had learned from his father was to appreciate good food and fine wines. When his business failed, Billie again drifted back into his old drug habits. Finally, in January of 1979, he received a suspended three-month sentence for possession of heroin and marijuana. Ultimately, to his great credit, Billie Paley kicked the drug habit, and he now runs a drug rehabilitation clinic in Washington. He and his wife, the former Alison Van Metre, have two young sons, Sam and Max.

Kate Paley's rebellion took the form of distancing herself from her family. She never got along with her siblings. When invited to tea or luncheon with her mother, she often failed to show up. Kate went to the right schools, first to the Green Vale Day School, on Long Island, and then to Madeira, an exclusive boarding school in Virginia. Early on she showed some talent for art, but she never really pursued painting or drawing. Kate had a proper coming-out, when her aunt and uncle Betsey and Jock Whitney presented her at a dinner dance at Greentree, and then attended the Rhode Island School of Design, but she dropped out before graduating. At last Kate found peace by becoming a born-again Christian, attending a fundamentalist Baptist church. As she became more and more involved with her newfound religion, she seemed to come to terms with her father, even moving out of her SoHo loft and into an Upper East Side apartment so as to be closer to him in his old age. She currently devotes much of her time to her church and to charity work.

Tony and Amanda Mortimer, Babe's children from her first marriage, fared a bit better. Of all the children, Tony, a pleasant young man with his mother's sweet nature, was her favorite and the one with whom she was on the most intimate terms—often to the chagrin of his stepfather, who expected Babe to devote herself entirely to him. Tony attended the Green Vale School, went on to St. Mark's and, from there, to Harvard. After graduating, he earned his law degree at the University of Virginia, returning to New York to complete his M.B.A. at Columbia. For all his intelligence, achievements, and excellent connections, Tony never was a favorite of Bill Paley's. In fact, their relationship was at best just cordial.

Amanda, or "Ba," as her brother Tony nicknamed her, rose far higher in her stepfather's esteem. Dark-eyed and raven-haired, she was a beautiful child and an even more beautiful young woman, with looks that rivaled her mother's a little too closely for Babe's comfort. Amanda's stepfather, never immune to beauty and style, was very nearly as fond of Amanda as he was of Hilary. Of course, this fondness never translated into a true parental role, but it was preferable to the total indifference that typified Paley's attitude toward his other children.

Despite her beauty and developing intelligence, Amanda was not a sparkling youngster. In fact, according to close family observers, she was a shy, withdrawn child who developed a great love of reading. She attended her mother's alma mater, Westover, and then came home to make her obligatory debut. Babe and Bill presented her in great style at Kiluna. Amanda then attended Wellesley College. Within a month of her arrival as a freshman, she met Harvard senior Shirley Carter Burden on a blind date. Burden was tall, blonde, handsome, rich, and glamorous, and he swept Amanda off her feet. The great-great-great grandson of Commodore Cornelius Vanderbilt, Carter was endowed with blue blood, as well as a background of great wealth and privilege, and this of course placed him among the ranks of New York's social elite.

His mother, Flobelle Fairbanks, had been an actress, albeit a cousin of Douglas Fairbanks, Jr. Carter's blue-blooded father, William Burden, a sometime investment banker and sportsman, had lost his Social Register listing when he married the actress. The Burdens lived on a large Beverly Hills estate, enjoying all the glamour and glitz of the Hollywood social scene. It was here that Carter grew up, before going east to school.

In the midst of the whirlwind courtship, Amanda apparently lost her academic aspirations, and soon she dropped out of Wellesley to prepare for her wedding. She converted to Catholicism, in deference to Carter's faith, and the couple said their vows in St. Mary's Roman Catholic Church in Roslyn, Long Island, on June 14, 1964.

Mainbocher, one of Babe's favorite designers, created Amanda's magnificent wedding gown. Departing from Cushing tradition, she had not Jerome Zerbe but Cecil Beaton behind the camera. The reception took place at Kiluna, where Babe with typical flair had erected a gigantic pistachio-green tent, which she filled with masses of white flowers from her garden and hundreds of chic guests from her social set.

Naturally, the wedding of twenty-year-old Amanda Jay Mortimer and Shirley Carter Burden was the event of the season, occasioning all the press and fashion media fanfare that seemed an inevitable part of her Cushing heritage—and, not surprisingly, a foreshadowing of things to come. The bride and groom would almost immediately become the hot young couple among Manhattan's glittering new generation of social blue bloods. Their names would be an absolute must on every fashionable guest list—and in every gossip column. Photographers as well as reporters would have a field day with the glamorous young Burdens, who somehow invited epithets like the Young Locomotives and New York's Number-One Fun Couple. They lived in the elegant old Dakota, a newly trendy co-op apartment building on Central Park West (later the site for the filming of *Rosemary's Baby* and home of John Lennon and Yoko Ono, among numerous other celebrities). Of course, on weekends, they had their own cottage at Kiluna. *Vogue* ran a ten-page feature article on the Burdens and their life at the Dakota. The title—"The Young-Joyous Life"—said it all.

Bill Paley adored Carter and no doubt wished that he could have had a son like young Burden. And Carter returned his father-in-law's affection. At Paley's urging, the young man finally made the decision to enter the political arena, running for and winning a seat on the New York City Council. With all the Burdens' wealth and glamour, the White House did not seem so terribly far off.

James Bloodworth, a fellow tenant in the United Nations Plaza building occupied by Truman Capote, was familiar with Babe Paley, having seen her any number of times coming in and out of the building on her visits to Capote. He recently recalled election night at Carter Burden's dingy storefront campaign headquarters on East Seventy-ninth Street:

Burden's district took in not only Manhattan's Upper East Side but a goodly part of Spanish Harlem. It was a mob scene that night, with campaign workers—the "muffets" from Long Island's North Shore, the Puerto Rican political activists, and the many highly placed political operatives, such as the Kennedys' Jerry Bruno and Burden family member Douglas Fairbanks, Jr.—all crammed into this small space. I can remember Babe and Bill Paley arriving about ten P.M. They were immediately greeted by Carter Burden. He was so obsequious toward Mrs. Paley, just panting. She didn't return the panting but was very polite. Amanda arrived with a prominent member of the Catholic clergy. She looked like she had just stepped out of a bandbox. There was no great show of affection between Amanda and her mother. When Amanda had trouble ascending to the platform, the Paleys exchanged decidedly knowing glances. . . .

The Paleys remained by themselves; the group of campaign workers, family members, and friends, if so inclined, came to them. Mrs. Paley, who appeared quite knowledgeable about the election process, began to explain to Mr. Paley the numbers as they came in from the various precincts. She was very made-up, which surprised me. It was amazing to see that evening young eighteen- and nineteen-year-old girls going gaga over this woman. And if you asked them what qualities she had, they couldn't give you an answer. Dignity, she had that about her, and she gave a genuine impression of being well bred. Other women of similar position were often silly, artificial, pushy, and rather like superannuated high school cheerleaders. Mrs. Paley had none of that.

This tremendous social and political success delighted everyone except Babe. Long accustomed to the limelight, she found that she did not particularly enjoy sharing it with her beautiful daughter. Oddly enough, she viewed Amanda not as her own creation but as her rival. The celebrated mother had a decided, though subtle, jealous streak, and Amanda had just a bit too much of her mother's beauty, ambition, and savvy. Babe, whose self-esteem depended so heavily on her public image, greatly feared that her daughter might usurp her title of reigning number-one society beauty, and this fear was not entirely unfounded.

The Paleys remained the most talked-about, socially revered couple in New York's social and fashion circles. Amanda might be the chief pretender to the throne, but the queen was not yet ready to abdicate.

Bill Paley, too, had his insecurities. He had too long borne the stigma of being an outsider, and he could never come to terms with his Russian Jewish immigrant upbringing. Nothing bolstered his ego so much as being surrounded by beautiful women, for he needed constant reassurance that he was the most fascinating, most attractive man around. Babe helped him to transcend all but the hardest-core anti-Semitism and snobbery. Of all Babe's connections, Jock Whitney was the single most important, for to Bill Paley Jock represented everything that had long been denied him. For all the years that Bill and Dorothy lived next door to the WASP prince, they had never managed to attach themselves to him socially. And even though both men served on the board of the Museum of Modern Art, Bill had never achieved more than a nodding acquaintance with the person he most admired. Actually, Jock Whitney had quite actively avoided Bill Paley for many years. His marriage to Babe changed all that. Bill suddenly had his long-awaited opportunity for friendship with the ultimate upper-crust WASP. Paley, in so many ways an arrogant and demanding person, was appropriately and almost naively delighted by this friendship and he never lost sight of the fact that he owed it all to Babe.

Bill greatly admired Jock, but he also envied his new brother-in-law. It was not Jock's wealth, for Bill had more than enough money and business success. Rather, it was the Whitney breeding, background, exalted social position, and universal acceptability that the more-or-less self-made multimillionaire coveted. From time to time this envy would surface, often in a most ungentlemanly fashion, as it did after a billiard game in which Jock defeated Bill. Bill, never a good loser, complained that Jock had probably had a pro teach him to play bottle pool.

Jock may well have had his share of insecurities, but he never displayed them publicly, never struck out at others to cover up feelings of inadequacy. Bill Paley, on the other hand, had a decidedly unpleasant habit of punishing those closest to him—family, friends, and especially business associates. In 1969, for instance, Paley, as president and trustee of the Museum of Modern Art, summarily dismissed Bates Lowry as the museum's director. Another trustee, Ralph Colin, protested, and so without a single qualm Paley fired Colin as his private and corporate counsel—thus ending a forty-year association. Colin reported that when he told Paley he hoped they would remain friends, the broadcast tycoon replied, "I've never regarded you as a friend—only as an employee."

Bill Paley, undoubtedly realizing that such a reply would do nothing to help his public image, denied having made that statement, but he did add that he and Mr. Colin had never had any "personal relationship." Paley further justified his decision to dismiss Colin as his lawyer on the grounds that the CBS staff counsel had advised him to switch to a larger firm. This incident and hundreds of others like it told a great deal about Bill Paley's sense of decency and honor—and pointed to the sharp contrast between him and Jock Whitney. It may well have been such differences that led Bill to admire his new brother-in-law so greatly.

Jock was an athlete and a gentleman—not necessarily in that order— as well as a man of letters. He was truly a Renaissance man, but one with an entirely modern outlook on life. He had had the best of educations, attending Groton and Oxford, an unassailable position in society, and a tremendous popularity among outstanding people in the arts, politics, business, and show business. His friendships extended beyond the confines of society to include a great many individuals whom the more snobbish members of his class would not have tolerated. Jock's was a lusty, strenuous, swashbuckling way of life, with extraordinary variety in interests, activities, and relationships. Once Bill Paley was "family," Jock unreservedly accepted and befriended him.

But even Jock's friendship, family relationship, and sponsorship could not get Paley voted into Washington's highly prestigious Metropolitan Club; nor could Jock get his brother-in-law past the gates of the exclusive Brook Club for a game of golf. Babe's entreaties to a longtime friend to sponsor them for membership in the Bar Harbor Club came to naught. No matter how rich or powerful or well connected Bill Paley might be, he still could not gain admittance to certain extremely selective, extremely snobbish inner circles—the very circles that were so important to him.

E. J. Kahn, Jock's biographer, had this to say:

A lot of people took Jock to be a kind of lightweight—polo, horse racing, money, all that—but he wasn't. I suspect that Paley, quite apart from being his brother-in-law, recognized this and appreciated it. They were probably very lucky to have found and profitted—obviously not in a monetary sense—from each other.

While this was undoubtedly true, and while the two men shared a warm friendship, Paley often carped about his status in this heady society of old money and older bloodlines. Despite their immense popularity and chic, Babe and Bill were both labeled early on as social climbers—at least by the loftiest of the old guard. This was quite a dilemma for the ambitious Bill and for the somewhat naive Babe. It had probably never occurred to her that her credentials and Bill's would be averaged by the people who viewed their marriage from certain vantage points. Obviously, Babe's beauty and social connections had given Bill Paley quite a boost up the society ladder, but Bill's Jewish immigrant background had brought Babe down a rung or two in some people's opinion.

Through a fortuitous meeting, the Paleys found their muse in the small, effeminate person of Truman Capote, who had become the literary rage of the country, especially New York. The brilliant, ubiquitous Capote would soon become their court jester, Babe's particularly, garnering reams of publicity for the couple as they traversed the globe with him in a rather curious trio.

Reared in a scrub-poor Alabama town, Truman Capote had, in the early 1950s, soared to the top through the sheer genius of his writing and his notoriously bitchy repartee. In no time he became the pet of New York's social and literary sets. By the time his play *House of Flowers* opened, he had established a friendship with Jacqueline Kennedy, then the wife of the glamorous but still relatively unknown senator from Massachusetts. From the sheer magnetism of his conversational prowess he was able to insinuate himself into the life of Babe Cushing Mortimer Paley. In fact, Capote became so close to Babe that he enjoyed a position in her life even her children could never attain.

Capote entered the Paleys' life in January of 1955 when David Selznick and Jennifer Jones, his wife at that time, were about to spend time with the Paleys at their home in Round Hill, Jamaica. The guests asked if they might bring Truman along. Of course, Bill and Babe readily agreed to the scheme, adding that it would be an honor. Bill, so the story goes, assumed that David and Jennifer were talking about Harry Truman, and was both astounded and disappointed when he saw the elfin writer boarding the Paley private plane. Even before the plane left the ground, Babe and Truman were deep in conversation. And so began the intimacy that would ultimately set *le tout* New York on its ears for the next decade. Theirs was an intimacy established by their instant platonic love for each other, a love born out of the very depths of their troubled souls.

Bill, too, warmed immediately to Capote, but in a completely different way. The broadcast mogul viewed the writer as he viewed all other celebrities—as a person whose fame and celebrated connections would enhance his own importance. Bill could see in a glance that Capote would be socially useful. Babe, on the other hand, had recognized a kindred spirit, a human being whose pain was as deep-seated and well disguised as her own. In Truman Capote, she believed, she had found her personal confessor, perhaps the one human being she could confide in and who would understand her innermost thoughts and feelings. Here at last was a platonic mate, someone she could relate to completely and who would accept her when she removed the mask of glamour which she had donned as her signature from the first moment she had stepped into the world of society and fashion. What she did not consider during the first of many magical moments that she and Truman would share over the next two decades was the danger of confiding the most intimate secrets of her troubled life to a writer, especially to a writer like Capote, who was fast emerging as Manhattan's premier gossip.

From that January day on, wherever the Paleys went, Truman Capote, like designer luggage, was likely to be along. They were almost inseparable from the mid-fifties to the early seventies. The café society crowd had either died off or gone into hibernation after the inebriating decade of the forties, and the jet set had taken over center stage. New York's very social literati dubbed this era the Capote Years. It was a time when money still mattered and when society was still top drawer. Power remained in the hands of a select few and was not dispersed, as it would be in the yuppie-infested eighties.

New York society of the fifties and sixties was like a particularly decadent court masque, filled with intrigue, lavish display, and gossip. And Babe, Bill, and Truman were among its leading players. Capote was in many ways like one of the dwarfs in the court of Philip IV of Spain, depicted in the brilliant and slightly satirical royal portraits by the great painter Velázquez. These elegantly dressed little people were the constant companions of the princes and princesses of Spain, and thus were privy to all the secrets and intrigues of the Spanish court. So too would Truman Capote see and hear every single juicy tidbit of gossip that made the rounds of socialites' dinner and cocktail parties, weekend house parties, and longer jaunts on private jets and oceangoing yachts. He was quite literally a genius, and he lavished as much of his incredible intelligence on ferreting out the "dirt" as he did on writing his few but critically acclaimed and memorable books. Sadly, many Capote admirers felt that he never lived up to his literary potential. But when it came to gossip, he surpassed himself. New York was the ideal place for scandal-hunting, and Capote dug up an incredible number of family skeletons, dirty laundry, and "dangerous liaisons." Soon the strange little man knew who was sleeping with whom, how often, and whether the involved parties had any kinky preferences. He learned whose title was phony and whose was legitimate, who had real money and who was merely a pretender or a hanger-on. He was like a human sponge— soaking up all the sordid news of which tycoons were keeping which girlfriends in which chic East Side flats, and which society matrons employed gigolos for sexual and escort services. He also knew the most intimate details about the actual sexual encounters of the rich and famous—even which society women had sex while menstruating and who had what sorts of sexual proclivities. And if—heaven forbid—anything happened to escape his notice, his gossipy bevy of socialites was ever anxious to let him in on it. In fact, most craved the chance to outscoop the notorious brewer of scandal broth.

Capote never missed an opportunity to learn or impart gossip, and he managed to capture every nuance and to catalog and save it for the day when it might prove useful. He was not a blackmailer, but he was a clever writer, which turned out to be just as bad—or even worse—for many of those he had taken up with. In fact, it was fatal for quite a few supposed pillars of society, and doubly fatal for him.

It was all great fun while it lasted, and it did last for many years. Capote enshrined his special madonna—Babe Paley—as well as the pantheon of other society beauties who surrounded him. Given their looks and his imagination, Capote took to calling them his swans. Babe led the pack; Gloria Guinness, C. Z. Guest, Slim Keith, Marella Agnelli, and Pamela Churchill also numbered among these goddesses.

Babe, to Capote's mind, "had everything." Gloria Guinness, born in abject poverty in Mexico, survived several disastrous marriages before ending up with British banking magnate Loel Guinness. C. Z. Guest, the only Boston Brahmin in the crowd, had rebelled against her snobbish and proper background by becoming a showgirl and also by posing nude for the Mexican artist Diego Rivera. C.Z. finally settled down with polo great Winston Guest, making the round of society parties and establishing a great reputation for her gardening expertise. Slim Keith started out in Salinas, California, but soon took her willowy figure and all-American beauty back east and, through her friendship with *Harper's Bazaar* editor Carmel Snow, appeared in almost every issue of *Vogue*'s chief rival. Slim first married director Howard Hawks, then wed producer Leland Hayward, and finally ended up with Lord Keith, a British tycoon. Marella Agnelli was the wife of the Fiat giant and, through her husband's American grandmother, a relative of the Mortimer family. Her great patrician beauty dazzled Truman Capote. And last but hardly least was Pamela Churchill, ex-daughter-in-law of Winston Churchill. Pamela finally won the very social Leland Hayward away from Slim Keith, and upon the great producer's death, went on to even greater glory and material rewards by marrying Averell Harriman, who was renowned for his fabulous wealth and fascinating life. The couple remained together until Harriman's recent death. Pamela Harriman, long involved in political philanthropy, is now viewed as the godmother of the Democratic Party.

All Capote's swans returned in at least equal measure the ardor he showered on them. In this way he was living out the fantasies of his lonely childhood—fantasies of living in a world of wealth and beauty. Money and power per se did not interest him. But style did. As Capote once said, "Style is what you are," and his swans had it—either innately or acquired early on. This is no doubt what drew him to Babe Paley. The fact that he was not obsessed with money didn't mean that he was not attracted to the people who had it and knew what to do with it. He fully expected them to flaunt it, but always of course with taste and style. If there was anything that he detested, it was the nouveaux riches, like the Florida land developers and Hollywood movie-magnates-turned-art collectors. Neither was he attracted to the blue-blooded old guard, as exemplified by Mrs. William Woodward, Sr., and Jock and Betsey Whitney; nor, in truth, were they attracted to him. Capote's crowd was the wonderfully stylish rich, who knew just how much of their wealth to display. They also knew how to have fun. And now that they had their own town crier, every gossip columnist and talk-show host reported on their every move—when they stepped onto and off their private jets and at what private island hideaway they would be rendezvousing during any given season.

Inviting Truman Capote was the in thing to do. His name was an absolute must on the top-notch guest lists, for his presence at a party virtually ensured its success. He had carte blanche at Kiluna, and he turned up frequently both on weekends and for special occasions at other times. He kept dinner conversation rolling with his pithy comments and bitchy gossip, made all the more amusing by his effeminate, high-pitched drawl. Babe for her part constantly consulted with Truman, as if he were her best girlfriend—and rightly so, for like many homosexuals, he understood the female psyche better than many of his heterosexual counterparts. Truman gave as much as he received. He was not an idealist. He understood precisely why he was in the midst of this beauteous society, why he was so ardently courted. And each time he departed, these "right people" felt better for having been in his company.

Capote was invariably on the scene when Babe and Bill would go to spend a month each summer at Piencourt, Loel and Gloria Guinness's home near Deauville, and then to sail the Mediterranean aboard the Guinnesses' yacht. After that Babe and Bill—without their children, needless to say, but often with Capote—would spend some time at Mautry, the Normandy estate of Baron and Baroness Guy de Rothschild. Next perhaps they would go on to the Greek Isles, usually aboard either the Guinnesses' or Marella and Gianni Agnelli's yacht.

On all these vacations, the central theme for Bill Paley was not scenery or culture but food. Whether in France, Greece, or Italy, Bill's chief cultural excursions were to the best local restaurants. On these gastronomical tours he would think nothing of having two different lunches and then following them up with a seven-course gourmet dinner in the evening. Food, like sex, was Paley's idea of nirvana. Nevertheless, after a period of overindulgence, his vanity and health concerns would win out, and he would go off to Baden-Baden for the therapeutic waters and cure his father had first introduced him to.

Babe preferred to remain in Paris while Bill went to Baden-Baden. The Paleys always had the same elegant suite at the Ritz Hotel, overlooking the Place Vendome. During these Parisian interludes she spent a great deal of time with Brose and Virginia Chambers, whose charming house in Paris had once been the home of Cole and Linda Porter. It was Virginia who had introduced the Cushing sisters to art authority John Richardson, Virginia who served as an expert guide when any of the sisters wished to search for fine antiques.

In all Babe's shopping ventures—whether hunting treasured antiques in London or Paris, fine leather goods in Venice, or designer clothes and accessories in Paris or Rome—she chose carefully and wisely, using money from the trust fund Bill had established for her in the early 1950s. Most years, the trust provided her with an income of close to $160,000— ample spending money, to be sure, but considering her way of life and the cost of maintaining her fashion and decorating image, not enough for thoughtless extravagance. In any event, Babe did not dare to indulge her every whim, for she knew all too well Bill's niggardly ways, and she did her very best to please him and to avoid his wrath. Once, without notice, he had ordered his CBS accounting minions to cancel Babe's magazine subscriptions, which he considered frivolous, as he could easily bring the magazines home from the office. On the other hand, when it came to showing his WASP princess to her best advantage, he spared no expense. He wanted to see her maintain her glamorous image, and no price tag on a designer gown was too expensive. In fact, the more expensive the better. He reveled in Babe's best-dressed status and would have been appalled if she had settled for anything but the best. The same held true for jewels, which Bill gladly paid for. Babe's collection was worth well in excess of $1 million—at preinflation prices. Among her most treasured pieces were a ring set with one perfect 30.92-carat cabochon emerald, surrounded by thirty-four round diamonds totaling 7 carats, a magnificent necklace with thirty-one emeralds weighing in excess of 700 carats, and a solitaire 21-plus-carat, cushion-shaped canary diamond. Babe and her friend Gloria Guinness were quite competitive when it came to fashion and jewels, and Babe was a bit envious of the Mexican import's great chic and title of the Ultimate. The two women were at least as serious about their rivalry as they were about their friendship.

Babe was in no real danger of losing out to Gloria Guinness. In fact, every time Babe stepped out her door, she received admiration, adoration, and idolization. On the surface she did indeed have it all. But beneath the surface was a tortured world of pain and insecurity, of self-pity and feelings of falling short of the perfection that, she believed, might have earned her husband's true appreciation. Naturally, this dramatic aspect of her life was not common knowledge. The press, the public, and all but a tiny handful of her closest friends had no inkling of the pain she endured in silence behind her perpetual appearance of good cheer. Indeed, Babe Paley seemed to be the luckiest and most perfect woman in America, if not the entire world.

However, early on in her marriage, Babe had reached the sad conclusion that her supposed love match was nothing more than a platonic pact between two people who needed each other for the most superficial of reasons. Despite the fact that Babe loved Bill, she realized all too soon that she was nothing more to him than a highly prized public relations prop. Through his actions, he constantly reminded her that he had married her for her legendary beauty and her superior social and family connections. The anti-Semitism that she and the Paley children endured because of Bill's heritage hurt Babe deeply. And among the worst perpetrators of such hateful barbs was Jock Whitney's sister and brother-in-law, Joan and Charlie Payson. Joan once told a friend, "Watch out for Bill Paley. He'll take the gold right out of your teeth."

According to close friends, Babe did a superb job of concealing all the hurt that stemmed from her marriage, the hours upon hours she spent trying to please Bill, the pavement-pounding she did to search out exotic delicacies to please his demanding palate. Sometimes Babe even had these gourmet items crated and shipped aboard the CBS jet when she and Bill took up residence either at their retreat in the Caribbean or for the few weeks they spent at their Squam Lake home. Babe was on a timetable, just as though she were in a job that required her to punch a time clock. Her taskmaster was the man she had married and whom she continued to love even after she had lost most of the starry-eyed illusions and tremendous respect she had had for him from the earliest days of their relationship.

Yet Babe had learned Gogsie's lessons well, and she was incapable of wearing her troubled heart on her sleeve. The Cushings never aired the family's dirty linen in public, and in fact often conspired to keep their problems away from the press and curious hangers-on. Saving face Cushing style always took precedence over personal satisfaction or even happiness, and Babe followed that cardinal rule to the letter, as had her sisters. When in the past their unhappiness had led to divorce, all three had endeavored to keep a stiff upper lip and end their marriages as discreetly and quietly as possible. When one or more sisters disagreed with a family member's decision, they would nevertheless rally round to give at least the appearance of family solidarity.

The sisters had always told one another—and after Gogsie's death, *only* one another—everything. But now Babe, out of her quiet but heartrending desperation, had broken one of the principal tenets of Cushing law; she had brought into her confidence and into their midst one who was not only an outsider but an author—and one who was becoming increasingly known as the single most outrageous gossip in jet set society. Truman Capote had entered Babe's private world, which, up to that time, she had shared only with her mother, Minnie, and Betsey. It was as though Babe had created a fourth sister, but a sister who in essence had no family of "her" own and so could focus almost unlimited attention on Babe. And this Truman Capote did without reservation. In so doing, he became privy to all the most intimate details of the Paley marriage—all the good and all the bad.

Truman, in Babe's own words, "opened up avenues" for her. Until she met him, perhaps because of her limited education, she had not been an intellectual; in fact, she was not particularly well read. But Truman soon had her devouring Willa Cather, Edith Wharton, Flaubert, and all the works of Proust, and Babe became an avid student in other areas as well. Babe, in turn, passed along to Truman her considerable knowledge of antiques and decorating. Theirs was a mutually beneficial relationship, and the Paleys, especially Babe, came to depend on Truman Capote in many different ways, just as he came to depend on them. They spent many a sunny afternoon together, sometimes at the Paleys' blue and white villa in Jamaica and sometimes at their sumptuous Long Island estate. This close three-way relationship seemed destined to last a lifetime.

While Babe, Bill, and Truman went on providing hot copy for every major gossip columnist in the country, even for those in their various haunts throughout the world, Betsey and Jock Whitney avoided the press like the plague, basking in the very private satisfaction they received from heading and indeed embodying the old guard blue-blooded set, which deemed itself above such carrying-on as the jet setters, like the Paleys and Capote, seemed to dedicate their lives to.

17

HAIL BRITTANIA

*T*HE Whitney family had traditionally been affiliated with the Democratic Party, and Jock was no exception. In fact, for most of his adult life he had avidly supported and greatly admired Franklin Delano Roosevelt, feeling a social and political kinship with the presidential giant. After Roosevelt's death, Jock's politics underwent a rather dramatic change. To the surprise of many of his family and friends, he abandoned the Democratic Party to become actively involved with the group of eastern Republicans who were backing General Dwight David Eisenhower in his soon-to-be-announced run for the presidency. Editor Russell Davenport and Senator Howard Duff of Pennsylvania were Jock's closest associates in the independent fund-raising endeavor to capture the White House for the conquering hero of World War II.

And capture it they did. Apparently, Jock's political instincts were right on target, for Ike marched into the White House with a landslide victory. When it came time for the popular president to make his bid for a second term, he again sent out feelers, hoping this time to convince

Jock that he would make an ideal vice-presidential candidate. Instead of running on Ike's ticket during his campaign for a second term, however, Jock preferred to turn his substantial talents to fund-raising. This time, he began to work within the party, rather than continuing with the loose-knit group of independents who had been so instrumental in winning the 1952 election. Thus Jock Whitney assumed the chairmanship of the prestigious United Republican Fund, a title which had formerly been held by banker Winthrop Aldrich.

Eisenhower, having won again in 1956 and looking forward to another four years in the highest office in the land, privately informed Jock that he intended to name him ambassador to England. Thus Whitney would follow in his grandfather's footsteps, for John Hay had represented the United States in Britain in 1897. This was a post far more to Betsey's liking. Long an Anglophile, she had nothing but fond memories of the time she had spent at Hyde Park with the late King George VI and Queen Elizabeth, now the Queen Mother, and was delighted to have the opportunity to associate more often and perhaps more closely with the royal family, which she had for so many years admired and emulated. In addition, the lofty yet relatively private role of ambassador's wife was infinitely better suited to Betsey's notions of propriety than was the uncomfortable fishbowl existence of a politician's spouse.

Shortly after Eisenhower's private consultation with Jock, the president sent the Whitneys a highly personal Christmas gift, obviously a token of his esteem. It was a painting he had just finished, an amateurish work entitled *Mountain Lake*. At first the president had hesitated to send the gift, for he knew full well Jock's reputation as a connoisseur and collector of fine art, but whether from vanity or simple good will, Eisenhower overcame his doubts. Thus the painting depicting snow-covered mountains and a lake bordered by trees—which, the Whitneys reasoned, had been inspired by some fanciful postcard—eventually wound up in the upstairs hall of the ambassadorial residence in London.

On January 29, 1957, Eisenhower announced Whitney's nomination for ambassador to the Court of St. James. A short time later Congress confirmed the nomination without a whisper of opposition, and immediately thereafter Jock and Betsey began making plans for the move to London.

Whitney family and friends greeted Jock's appointment with joy and immediately began feting the ambassadorial couple. The grandest party of all was the top-drawer shindig that Jock's sister, Joan Whitney Payson, gave in their honor at her Long Island estate. Among the guests paying tribute to the ambassador-designate were Babe and Bill Paley (apparently Joan was able to put aside her prejudices for so important an occasion), *Newsday* publisher Alicia Patterson, Broadway producer Richard Halliday and his famous wife, Mary Martin, *New York Herald Tribune* publisher Ogden Reid, comic Sid Caesar, and Senator Jacob K. Javits. Not among this stellar cast, however, was one of the guests of honor—Betsey Whitney. She was in the hospital for gastric ulcer surgery and so she had to content herself with a special tape recorded for her. Betsey, since her earliest days in the Roosevelt White House, had suffered with a chronic ulcer condition, which would be alleviated in part by the pre-ambassadorial posting to London.

Tex McCrary gave an equally festive farewell party—a stag dinner at 21. The exclusive guest list included such names as those of Robert Woodruff, Shipwreck Kelly, Alfred Gwynne Vanderbilt, Lucius D. Clay, Henry Cabot Lodge, and Bill Paley. While toasting the new American ambassador to Britain, Bill must have had mixed feelings, for he had himself so coveted that plum assignment, assiduously lobbying any number of well-placed friends in the administration and in Congress— only to learn that his brother-in-law had unwittingly and effortlessly beaten him to the appointment.

By the time the Whitneys were set to take off for London, Betsey was well enough to travel, although not totally recovered from her chronic ulcers. Unfortunately, the following years would not be a time for stress-free rest and recuperation, since the Suez crisis was creating a great deal of tension in Anglo-American relations. The situation was enough to give a healthy person ulcers, and it certainly did nothing to help Betsey's condition, but she was not about to let diplomatic considerations spoil her enjoyment of the regal lifestyle she had always envisioned for herself. It was a politically trying time for Jock—"the gifted amateur," as *Time* magazine called him—but he positively thrived on the challenge and on the upper-crust British ambience, which appealed to him as it did to Betsey.

In Jock Whitney the British got an ambassador worthy of his title. He soon proved himself to be a highly competent and forceful chief diplomat, one of universal appeal to the citizens of the United Kingdom. His history of wartime service in Britain and his prowess as an all-around athlete—adept at boxing, rowing, tennis, polo, and golf—as well as an owner and breeder of top-notch racehorses, immediately endeared him to the sports-minded proletariat, most of whom had an especially keen interest in racing and regularly found at least a couple of bob to place on a favored horse. And Jock Whitney was not the least bit snobbish or standoffish. As an editorial in one Scottish paper commented, "Mr. Whitney is of the type of rich American who disguises with easy breeding the possession of 100 million dollars. It is hard to think of a more ideal envoy from a Republican administration."

Jock's involvement with horse racing made him as popular with the upper echelons of British society as with the working classes. He had always maintained a large stud operation in England, which Jeremy Tree managed. At first Jock was reticent about racing his horses during his tenure as American ambassador; he feared that it might decrease his status by making him seem more a sporting type than a statesman. But he needn't have worried, for the English in general were great race fans, and even the royal family had long been involved in racing, as well as other horse sports. Owning a fine stable of racehorses and attending the celebrated racing events could only add to Jock's already considerable consequence. At the insistence of many highly placed British friends, including Prime Minister Harold Macmillan, who considered Whitney "the best American ambassador in many years," Jock acquiesced.

In fact, Whitney thoroughbreds had long enjoyed a fine reputation; among the most famous were the steeplechaser Easter Hero and the flat-racing stars Tom Fool and Capot. Even though Jock's thoroughbreds were the top money winners for several years in a row, he never did get to wear his bowler into the winner's circle at either the Derby, which was the most important flat race, or the Grand National, the ultimate steeplechase. The vicissitudes of the life of a racehorse owner gave him a ready-made topic of conversation and immediate grounds for mutual congratulations and commiserations with the horsy royal family—most particularly the queen and the queen mum, both of whom were inveterate racing fans, as well as horse owners.

Jock's horses were by no means his only link with the cream of British society. His early days at Oxford, his tremendous wealth, and his exalted family and personal connections would have provided him with far more than adequate credentials to establish him in the very most elevated of circles. In 1957 *Fortune* magazine reported that Ambassador Whitney had an estimated fortune of between $100 million and $200 million, as did his sister, Joan Whitney Payson. This clearly made Jock the wealthiest American ambassador to England in memory. The U.S. ambassador serving in France at the time was Corning Glass heir Amory Houghton, whose fortune was very nearly equal to Whitney's.

Jock was related by marriage to the Paget family—Pauline Whitney had married Almeric Paget—among whom was the very lively Olive, Lady Baillie, the owner of the fabled Leeds Castle in Kent, once home to Anne Boleyn. And Jock's liberal-minded aunt Dorothy Whitney Straight Elmhirst was another pillar of British society. Her son, Whitney Straight, was an executive of Rolls-Royce. Jock also had the good fortune to have a family member on his staff—his aide-de-camp, James W. Symington, son of Senator Stuart Symington and the senator's first wife, Eve Wadsworth Symington, onetime café society singer and a granddaughter of John Hay.

Then too, Jock had many upper-crust friends from his wartime service in England. Although Betsey may not have wished to examine the facts too closely, one of her husband's great friends from those earlier wartime days in London was none other than Pamela Digby Churchill, ex-daughter-in-law of Winston Churchill. In fact, while a relationship has never quite been documented, rumors had once circulated linking Jock and Pamela romantically. True or not, these whispers from the past kept Betsey on her toes. Over the years she maintained a careful eye on the ravishing upper-class Englishwoman, who had long ago learned her way around the rich and mighty on both sides of the Atlantic.

However leery Betsey might have been of Pamela Churchill's intentions, she could not deny the glamorous divorcée's great social importance and so did not hesitate to send her to Babe for a weekend visit during the early years of Jock's ambassadorship. Since the Whitneys were in London and could not be at Greentree to welcome Pamela, Betsey called Babe and asked her to do the honors. Babe, as socially aware as anyone, knew all too well what would be expected of her.

Entertaining any guest from abroad even for a weekend entailed any number of arrangements, and these were greatly complicated by the fact that this particular guest was an extremely high-profile divorcée, whose charms were avidly touted by a legion of admirers, including Elie de Rothschild, Prince Aly Khan, Jakie Astor of the English branch of the Anglo-American clan, Averell Harriman, Aristotle Onassis, Edward R. Murrow, Stavros Niarchos, Gianni Agnelli, and even Jock Whitney.

Babe reluctantly set about arranging for the arrival of this celebrated mantrap, planning an elegant dinner party at Kiluna and a Broadway outing. Of course, it was imperative to find an escort for Pamela, one who was prominent enough to satisfy even this connoisseur of famous and wealthy men, yet who was also presumably safe from her clutches. Knowing that her friend Slim Hayward (the future Lady Slim Keith) would be out of town during Pamela's visit, Babe asked Slim if she would mind letting her husband, multimillionaire producer Leland Hayward, serve as Pamela's escort to a Broadway show. Slim, lovely and confident after thirteen years of marriage, readily gave her consent, and the rest is history. The evening at the theater expanded into a week-long interlude, and by the end of Pamela's brief stay in New York, the wildly attractive Hayward had fallen in love with her. Unlike Pamela's other famous paramours, after a discreet few months he announced his intention of divorcing Slim and marrying Pamela Churchill. And so it was that Pamela became the third Mrs. Hayward (he had previously been married to the actress Margaret Sullavan) and ultimately Leland's widow.

Both Babe and Betsey were stunned and saddened by this perfidious chain of events, mortified that they had unwittingly played a role in it. But they would not have been quite human if they had not breathed a sigh of relief that Pamela had finally bagged her own millionaire and so would not, at least in the near future, be casting her well-lacquered tentacles in the direction of either Jock or Bill. And breathe a sigh of relief the sisters did. However, they never once relaxed their guard whenever Pamela was around. A family member recalls a weekend at the Whitneys' place on Fisher's Island in the period between Hayward's death and Pamela's remarriage to an even bigger catch—her wartime London paramour, Averell Harriman.

The sisters always dreaded the arrival of Pamela, for she caused so much consternation in the normal household routine, arriving with her own maid, her silk Pratesi sheets. And her dressing table during this stay resembled a well-stocked cosmetic counter with all the perfume bottles, jar after jar of creams, bottles and bottles of nail lacquer, her hair needs—everything to maintain her well-endowed beauty.

Pamela Churchill did not set her cap for Jock Whitney, and it was just as well, for Betsey could more than hold her own in any struggle for marital or social primacy. She not only held on to her extremely desirable husband but almost instantly became a social figure to be reckoned with in the royal circles of her dreams. The fact that Britannia, the symbol of Britain, was a woman was not lost on Betsey Whitney. She played her role of ambassador's wife to the utmost, reveling in the social power it afforded her. After nearly two decades she quickly and easily renewed her friendship with her particular role model, the "queen mum." And the U.S. ambassador's residence, Winfield House, was as elegant a backdrop as she could have wished for.

Once a royal hunting lodge, the enormous cream-colored Regency mansion had been built in 1825 for the third Marquis of Hertford, who, it was said, used it for his harem. Situated on twelve and a half acres of expansive lawns and gardens, it had been known at that time as St. Dunstan's Lodge. Just before World War I the American banker Otto Kahn acquired the lodge, but he never used it, and once the war was over, he sold the property to the press magnate Lord Rothermere. In 1936, after a disastrous fire, the property wound up on the auction block, where the highest bidder was none other than the madcap Woolworth heiress, Barbara Hutton, who was at the time newly married to the second of her seven husbands, Count Court Reventlow.

Rather than building her "honeymoon home" on the ruins of St. Dunstan's, Barbara elected to construct a massive, three-story pink brick Georgian-style mansion of fifty-odd rooms, naming it Winfield House after her grandfather Frank Winfield Woolworth. On the recommendation of her friend Lord Louis Mountbatten, she hired the prestigious architectural firm of Wimperis, Simpson and Guthrie to carry out her dramatic plans for the property. As the dime-store heiress was well known for her largesse, everyone was most eager to be of service. The Duke of St. Albans, who had originally sparked Barbara's interest in the property, received a handsome commission, as did Lady Sheila Milbanke, who acted as Barbara's decorating assistant. Soon enormous, elegant rooms began to appear; there were vast kitchens, a music room, a library, a pillared parlor, a gymnasium, indoor and outdoor swimming pools, and numerous wardrobe and storage closets. The grounds themselves were equally spectacular, with huge manicured lawns and great chestnut trees, three greenhouses, a generous stable for fine horses, and a clay tennis court. This pastoral setting made visitors feel as though they were out in the country instead of in the heart of London. As a private residence, Winfield House was second only to Buckingham Palace. The dime-store heiress ended up spending, in 1936 dollars, $4.5 million on the mansion and another $2.5 on the furnishings and decor.

When Barbara returned to London after World War II, she was appalled by the run-down condition of her dream home, and so she immediately deeded it over to the American government as an ambassadorial residence. At first the newly minted president, Harry Truman, hesitated, no doubt worried about the astronomical cost of restoring and maintaining this colossal home. But he then wrote Barbara Hutton a gracious letter accepting her extremely generous offer.

Winfield House opened officially on January 8, 1955, with Queen Elizabeth and her consort, Prince Philip, in attendance. The first American ambassador to occupy the residence was Winthrop Aldrich. Jock Whitney was the second. Fortunately, the departing Aldriches had warned Betsey and Jock to bring along or have shipped such personal items as vases, rugs, pillows, reference books, breakfast trays, clocks, mantel ornaments, and coffee tables—in short, all the amenities. Naturally, Betsey had not skimped in this department; in fact, she even threw in a king's ransom worth of Impressionist and postimpressionist paintings, including the works of such artists as Cézanne, Degas, Picasso, Monet, and Braque, as well as of a variety of American painters— among them brother-in-law James Fosburgh and Ike. This enviable collection of eighty-one works—a mere fraction of Jock's total stockpile—was a rare treasure to behold in an American ambassadorial residence, but of course Jock Whitney was no ordinary American ambassador.

In a typically modest moment Jock once said of his art-collecting prowess:

> I've always been a bit finicky about calling myself a "collector."
> Collector to me means someone who specializes in painted plates
> with strawberries or one school of art. I'm interested in anything
> from modern American to Corot. I started buying prints when I
> was at Yale. Now I suppose I have twenty paintings that might be
> considered masterpieces and another twenty near-masterpieces.

In later years Jock had the advice of experts such as art historian John Rewald, who was the Whitneys' paid consultant and who helped them build one of the best and most complete collections of Fauvist paintings in America.

Meanwhile, Jock's eclectic art provided Betsey with an instant and truly magnificent "portable decorating scheme." While another foreign service wife might have tossed a few trinkets or even good pieces of jewelry into a travel pouch, Betsey called in Cartier to pack and ship her extraordinary collection of jewelry, including no doubt her diamond tiara. In addition, the Whitneys took over what remained of the Aldriches' wine cellar, for which Jock paid $1,078.99—quite a hefty sum in those days. And so it was that the Whitneys arrived well equipped to handle very nearly any social contingency.

According to E. J. Kahn, Jr., Aldrich offered the Whitneys his butler but warned them that the man had an ulcer. Jock decided to keep him on despite his infirmity, reasoning that since Betsey also suffered from ulcers, this mutual ailment would create an instant upstairs-downstairs bond. Of course, the Whitneys also brought along a number of their own staff from Greentree, to ensure a smooth transition and to maintain the level of comfort to which they had always been accustomed. An impecunious ambassadorial couple would no doubt have found life in Winfield House intolerable, but it suited the wealthy, aristocratic Whitneys to a T. Unintimidated by the number and size of the rooms, Betsey rolled up her proverbial sleeves and went to work, adapting the enormous house to her tastes and requirements.

Dorothy Rodgers, wife of Broadway composer Richard Rodgers and a great friend of all three Cushing sisters, had this to say regarding Betsey's astonishing success in this endeavor:

> When John Hay Whitney was our ambassador to Great Britain, I saw the power of personal treasures demonstrated on an enormous scale. The residence of the United States ambassador in London is a formidable house, where it would be no trick at all to lose five hundred people. One huge room opens into the next, ad infinitum, and no amount of furniture could make the place look cluttered, let alone cozy. But with the aid of a number of Jock Whitney's beautiful Impressionist paintings, his wife, Betsey, proceeded to work miracles. The touches she added were personal; in addition to the paintings, she used pieces of her exquisite porcelain, intimate photgraphs of the family and their friends, small needlepoint rugs here and there, and flowers absolutely everywhere. (I remember one great Sevres vase holding a marvelous arrangement.) True, the paintings were fabulous, and the weekly flower bill was probably one that only Jock Whitney could have afforded to pay. But the chill was killed not just by spending vast amounts of money. What really mattered was that Betsey picked the things she added with such care and love that you could feel the warmth even in those mammoth rooms.

Jock installed a portrait of his grandfather and ambassadorial predecessor, John Hay, in a place of honor in his own ambassadorial office on Grosvenor Square. Then, at exactly high noon on February 28, 1957, John Hay Whitney, our eighteenth ambassador to the Court of St. James, presented his official credentials to Queen Elizabeth II at Buckingham Palace. Following long-established tradition, Jock rode to the palace in the black-and-gold-trimmed landau from the royal stables. Also according to tradition, Jock was attired in white tie and tails, sporting his decorations: the Legion of Merit and the Bronze Star from his wartime service, along with that of the Commander of the Order of the British Empire. Betsey followed right behind in their chauffeur-driven Bentley.

At the palace Jock removed his top hat at the exact moment dictated by traditional etiquette, then approached the throne, bowing at the precise second decreed by court decorum. Her Majesty asked him, just as she and her royal forbears had asked hundreds of envoys, "Did you have a good journey?"

"Yes, ma'am," Jock replied, "but very uneventful."

The official Court Circular appearing in *The London Times* reported,

His Excellency the Hon. John Hay Whitney was received in audience by the Queen and presented the letters of recall of his predecessor and his own Letters of Credence as United States Ambassador Extraordinary and Plenipotentiary to the Court of St. James. . . . The Right Hon. Selwyn Lloyd, M.P. [secretary of state for foreign affairs], who had an audience of the Queen, was present and the Gentlemen of the Household in Waiting were in attendance. Mrs. Whitney had the honor of being received by Her Majesty.

On the down side of Jock's enviable appointment to the Court of St. James was the less-than-princely yearly salary of $27,000—approximately the sum that the Whitneys spent per *week* at home to maintain their lifestyle. The annual entertainment allowance was set at $10,000, an amount that could barely have kept Betsey in flowers. And even an especially frugal ambassador could not entertain the queen on that kind of money. The Whitneys ended up supplementing this allowance to the tune of a good $50,000 per year in order to properly wine and dine Queen Elizabeth and Prince Philip, who were frequent guests at Winfield House. Other members of the royal family also supped splendidly at the Whitney table. Of this exalted company, the Queen Mother was by far the closest to Betsey and Jock, for she too had fond memories of the time she and President Roosevelt's former daughter-in-law had spent together, happily munching hot dogs at Hyde Park in those last days before the war.

Other Whitney guests included Prime Minister Harold Macmillan,

Sir Harold Nicolson, Baba Metcalfe, Jeremy and Michael Tree, the not-yet-disgraced John Profumo, and Lord and Lady Louis Mountbatten. Babe and Bill Paley and Minnie and Jim Fosburgh were also frequent and welcome guests whenever they got to England. Even though Betsey lived an ocean away from Babe and Minnie, the three Cushing sisters were, as always, in constant touch by phone and by mail. And they usually managed to spend holidays together, either in England or in the United States when the Whitneys were able to get away from their ambassadorial duties.

Betsey, with her strong sense of family, had insisted on bringing over her daughter Sara, Sara's husband, Anthony, and their two young children, Christopher and Andrea Isabelle. The di Bonaventuras soon found themselves ensconced in a luxury flat in the posh Grosvenor Square area of London and immersed in all the pomp and circumstance surrounding embassy life. While this experience might have been a fabulous opportunity for many young families, the ambience was hardly geared to furthering the budding career of a would-be concert pianist from New York's Little Italy. The distractions of this luxurious, easy life were too many and the incentives for hard work and pavement-pounding too few. But Sara and Anthony had had little to say in the matter. As many family friends have observed, Betsey could be very controlling, and she had made up her mind to have her elder daughter, son-in-law, and grandchildren by her side. Her wish was apparently their command.

Once Betsey had recuperated sufficiently from her ulcer surgery, she began in earnest to undertake all the official duties connected with her position as American ambassadorial hostess. Regardless of the ups and downs of diplomatic relations between Britain and the United States, social relations never really suffered; in this area America remained firmly entrenched in its "most favored nation" status.

There has long been an unwritten alliance between the elect of *Debrett's Peerage* and the *American Social Register,* a fact that is reasserted each year at the queen's Buckingham Palace presentation parties for selected debutantes. These very exclusive afternoon tea parties, two per year, officially open the London "season," the time when all sufficiently established persons give and attend an incessant whirl of parties launching the current year's debs into polite society. American girls are the only foreigners presented to the queen; not even young women from other Commonwealth countries are so favored. No one seems to know how this situation came to pass, but it has been part of British social tradition for more than half a century.

The custom of the court presentation began in Tudor times for a very specific purpose. Mothers of the cream of the annual crop of debutantes brought their daughters to court, ostensibly to be presented to the queen but in fact to be looked over by eligible courtiers, in the hope of receiving advantageous offers of marriage. Some of the young ladies gained fame and influence after merely being seen at court, and others married Henry VIII, who was also looking them over. Of course, any enjoyment these particular ladies might have gained from being on the receiving end of subsequent presentations would be short-lived. In any event, the custom continues to this day, for more or less the same purpose, but changing slowly and subtly over the years to reflect to some extent the changes in mores and fashion.

In 1957 Mrs. John Hay Whitney presented the twelve American girls (selected from a list of twenty) at "Thursday's court," on the first Thursday in April. The parents were not in attendance at either the presentation or at the lavish buffet tea preceding it. The actual presentation to the queen took place in the great ballroom in the state apartments at Buckingham Palace. Queen Elizabeth and Prince Philip were seated on red plush chairs at the far end of the room, with the wife of the American ambassador close by. According to strict court etiquette, the young women's sponsors entered the ballroom; each in turn handed a card to a functionary, who handed it to the Lord Chamberlain, who then read the particular debutante's name in a loud voice. The young woman walked forward until she was opposite the queen, made a deep curtsey, continued on to the prince consort, repeated the curtsey, then moved away from the royal presence.

Among the debs presented at Betsey's first big Anglo-American social event were Daphne Fairbanks, daughter of Douglas Fairbanks, Jr.; Beatrice Lodge, daughter of John Davis Lodge, the United States ambassador to Spain; and Nicola Lubitsch, daughter of the late Ernst Lubitsch. Then, as now, the American girls who made it to court were from families that were politically, as well as socially, well connected. In fact, those with the most congressional sponsors were almost certain to beat out the competition. In this case Cushing connections seemed to pay off at least as well. Both Daphne Fairbanks and Beatrice Lodge had a direct "in" with Betsey, for Douglas Fairbanks, Jr., had known all three Cushing sisters since their earliest days on the New York social scene and Beatrice's maternal relatives were the Braggiotti clan, all of whom were close to Betsey, Babe, and Minnie.

At a later date both Betsey and Jock would participate in another very elite state function. This time their invitation was due not to tradition but to the queen's great personal regard for the ambassadorial couple. She granted them the singular honor of making them part of her official party when, in October of 1957, she made a five-day state visit to the United States to celebrate the 350th anniversary of the Jamestown settlement.

Betsey and Jock were as close to Queen Elizabeth and Prince Philip as any American representatives could ever have hoped to be—so close in fact that the royal couple called them by their first names. They, of course, could not respond in kind but had instead to answer according to strict protocol, with "ma'am" or "sir." Even though they were often weekend guests at Windsor Castle and at other royal residences throughout the kingdom, the Whitneys never deviated from the rigid rules governing all speech and actions in and around the royal presence.

It was an absolute that the queen's guests must never keep her waiting. This fact was brought home to Betsey one weekend when she was visiting Windsor Castle for the races at Ascot. Since she was a little behind schedule in dressing for the evening, she informed the royal page stationed outside her bedroom door that she would be a bit late for dinner. "Quite all right, madam," the page replied. "You have thirty seconds." Betsey paced herself accordingly.

On another occasion, when the Whitneys were guests of the queen in the private quarters of the royal family at Buckingham Palace, they began to discuss the lost art of enameling with her and Prince Philip. During the course of the conversation, merely to illustrate a point, Jock took off his enamel tie clip, which was the work of Fulco, Duc di Verdura. The prince so greatly admired it that Jock immediately gave it to him. Not long afterward Jock received a note from the prince, which said in part, "Dear Jock, Thank you so much for the pin! I enclose mine in exchange." To Jock's amusement the enclosure turned out to be a common safety pin—obviously a friendly touch of royal humor.

Anglophiles that they were, Betsey and Jock bought a country home at Wentworth, near the Ascot racetrack, where they could retreat after a busy round of social and official functions in London. This weekend place delighted Betsey, and it proved very convenient for Jock, who liked to see his horses in action. Of course, like Winfield House, it was the scene of almost nonstop entertaining—both private and official. On very nearly any given weekday Betsey would plan and smoothly carry off a business lunch, dinner, or reception at Winfield House. And not surprisingly, she was a superb hostess, having learned from her childhood, her regrettably unhappy years in the White House, and from managing the far larger Greentree house, grounds, and staff. Once they had finished their own entertaining, Betsey and Jock invariably went out, singly or together, to similar functions. While often exciting, the jobs of both the ambassador and his wife were very demanding, costly, and just plain hard work. Hardly a week passed without some American politician's showing up and expecting to be wined and dined or introduced to British VIPs.

Once a congressman, a real hayseed from a rural district of a Midwestern state, met at Winfield House with Sir Patrick Dean, the British deputy under secretary of state. During the course of the conference, the knowledgeable Sir Patrick commented on the magnificent Impressionist paintings that adorned the room they were meeting in. "It's always such a pleasure to come to this house and be able to see these pictures," he said.

"Yes," the congressman replied, "and I didn't even know the ambassador painted."

One year, toward the end of November, Vice President and Mrs. Richard Nixon arrived in London for a visit. While Jock had little admiration for Nixon or his political past, the ambassador was duty bound to entertain the highest-ranking administration official to set foot in England since Whitney had taken command of the embassy. He and Betsey decided to give a traditional Thanksgiving Day dinner, to which they invited the queen, the Harold Macmillans, the Duchess of Devonshire, Lord Louis and Lady Edwina Mountbatten, the lord chief justice of England, and Sara and Anthony di Bonaventura, with Nixon serving as nominal host. The traditional meal was to consist of roast turkey, sweet potatoes, cranberries, and pumpkin and mince pies. For the first course Betsey had selected oyster stew. As was customary, the menu was announced in advance, and it was left to the master of the queen's household to send Jock a handwritten note informing him that Her Majesty was not particularly fond of oysters and suggesting that perhaps the Whitneys might consider substituting a fruit dish, such as melon or grapefruit. The master of the household ended his note with the following escape clause: "I might add that the Queen has no idea that I have written to you and will probably undermine my good intentions by eating the oysters after all." Betsey immediately instructed the chef to serve the queen a bowl of chicken soup, thus saving the day and saving face. Even for so accomplished a hostess, entertaining royalty was never really simple.

In October of 1959, the Whitneys were in the States for the impending wedding of Betsey's younger daughter, twenty-three-year-old Kate Roosevelt, to William Haddad, a reporter for *The New York Post*. They had not announced their engagement and the reason may have been that Kate's much publicized engagement to photographer Dennis Stock in September of 1958 had not officially been broken. Stock, an ex-navy man and native New Yorker, met Miss Roosevelt in a professional way. She too was a photographer. However, this scenario came as no surprise to Cushing-Whitney-Roosevelt watchers. Both Sara and Kate married very strong men—a fact that did not guarantee happiness for either sister—at least, not the first time around.

The simple wedding ceremony took place in the presence of only the immediate families at the Protestant Episcopal Church of St. Matthew and St. Timothy, at 26 West Eighty-fourth Street. The rector, the Reverend James Gusweller, officiated. The bride wore a simple street-length dress of white faille, fashioned with a boat-shaped neckline and a full skirt. Atop her head was a wreath of pastel flowers, and in her hands was a bouquet of matching blossoms.

Jock gave his adopted daughter in marriage, and Sara Roosevelt di Bonaventura was her sister's only attendant. Peter Braestrop was Haddad's best man. This wedding was a far cry from Betsey's lavish trip down the aisle.

The groom had been an officer in the merchant marine, and at one time had served as an aide to Senator Estes Kefauver during the senator's national campaign for the Democratic nomination for president. Now, it seemed, Bill was looking forward to a brilliant career in journalism. Kate, after a brief honeymoon, returned to her job as a nursery-school teacher. By this time Betsey seemed to have resigned herself to the fact that neither of her daughters was destined to marry the kind of money and social position that she and her sisters had. Or perhaps she was counting on the fact that first marriages weren't necessarily forever. Or maybe once again Betsey, like her mother before her, was simply putting on the best face possible under the circumstances. Since she had ensured her daughters' future by having Jock adopt them, she could at least content herself with the knowledge that neither Sara nor Kate would ever want for anything. Nevertheless, Kate's marriage must certainly have been a disappointment for Betsey's dynastic ambitions.

Whatever Betsey might have thought of her second son-in-law or he of her, Bill Haddad had nothing but praise for Jock Whitney. "An incredible man," he enthused. "A first-rate human being who has kept all of the attributes that usually erode in others of his position." Indeed, almost everyone felt this way about Jock Whitney.

Shortly after the wedding the Whitneys returned to London for the final months of their official duties, entertaining and being entertained at breakneck speed both officially and among English and American friends. One who enjoyed a number of visits to Winfield House during the final days of Jock's ambassadorship was Irene Selznick, ex-wife of David. While Betsey had either directly or indirectly contributed to the cooling of Jock's friendship with David, Irene remained friendly with the Whitneys. Irene of course was only one of many who found themselves on the receiving end of the Whitneys' legendary magnificent hospitality, always dispensed with a deceptive appearance of ease.

In any event much of Jock's time during his last months in his London post was devoted to preparing for the day when he would be returning to the private sector and his vast business empire. Of course, there were the honors and the accolades that would demonstrate the deep respect and affection that the British felt for this very special human being who represented his country with great distinction.

Jock himself offered one last gesture of friendship to the British people by lending his fabulous art collection to the internationally acclaimed Tate Gallery for a six-week exhibition. Sir John Rotherstein, director of the Tate, who had often seen and admired Jock's paintings while a guest at Winfield House, had approached the ambassador about the possibility of mounting an exhibit. The Whitneys only considered fifty-six of the eighty-one paintings they had with them to be "major" ones—not quite enough for a real art show. Thus Jock and Betsey arranged for John Rewald in New York to select and ship a dozen more works from their collection. Jock's only stipulation before allowing the show to open was that there be no discussion of the monetary value of any of the works. Even so, a critic at one British newspaper asked Rewald to place a price tag on the collection. Following Whitney's instructions, the art historian replied, "If you were invited to dinner at Buckingham Palace, would you ask Her Majesty how much her china was worth?"

The six-week show opened at the Tate Gallery on December 16, 1960. Among the paintings on display were the works of Degas, Courbet, Monet, Pissarro, Seurat, Toulouse-Lautrec, Utrillo, and James Fosburgh. The exhibit was a tremendous popular success, and Jock and Betsey were pleased for the most part by what the critics had to say about it. Especially to their liking was a remark by critic John Russell in *The Sunday Times*: "It remains, in the true sense, a family collection."

Then the farewell celebration began, with the queen feting the Whitneys with a luncheon at Buckingham Palace after she had viewed the show at the Tate. Prime Minister and Mrs. Harold Macmillan also gave a farewell dinner at Admiralty House (10 Downing Street was undergoing extensive repairs), with most of the ambassadorial couple's British friends in attendance. On the exalted guest list were Lady Alexandra Metcalfe, Solly Zuckerman, Lord and Lady Mountbatten, the Whitney Straights, the Earl of Home, the dowager Duchess of Devonshire, and a score of others.

The Queen Mother wrote Betsey,

My dear Betsey,

Thanks for all you and Jock have done during the last four years to bring our two dear countries even closer together. Goodness how we shall miss you!

The Whitneys left many close friends behind, but they would return over the years following their official departure, to renew friendships and also to keep tabs on Jock's racing establishment. And each time the Whitneys would return to Britain, Jock would inevitably make a stop at Davies & Son, in Hanover Street, for they had been his London tailors since his student days at Oxford.

For Betsey the London years would always evoke fond memories. As she and her husband alighted in New York from their London flight, she turned to him and said with deep feeling, "Thanks for giving me the best four years of my life."

18

"A GREAT LITTLE TRIO"

*W*E were a great little trio," said Truman Capote of his close relationship with Babe and Bill Paley. He truly loved Babe and eventually found more to like than dislike about Bill. And so it was that for more than twenty years he traveled the world with them—mostly at their expense. The friendship deepened from the mid-fifties through the jet set sixties, heading on into the seventies on a collision course with destiny.

Wherever the Paleys were, their impish court jester was sure to be close at hand, whether at their getaway retreat at Round Hill, in Jamaica, close to Noël Coward's home; on celebrity-packed weekends at Kiluna Farm; on a cruise down the Dalmatian Coast aboard the Agnellis' yacht; or from time to time throughout the Mediterranean aboard the Guinnesses' equally glamorous yacht, known far and wide for its "cargo" of swans and multimillionaires.

Of course all these chic entertainments had a price, and Truman quite willingly sang and joked and gossiped for his supper, playing his amusing role to the hilt. He had long since realized that his swans required not only constant admiration but his particular brand of outrageous tidbits of gossip, which he dished out to them at frequent intervals. That many of these bordered on slander mattered little. It is difficult to understand why these sophisticated women would confide in him when they knew his penchant for carrying tales, but perhaps each swan flattered herself with the belief that her own relationship with Truman was so special that her juicy carryings-on were sacrosanct. This seems especially to have been the case with Babe, who did indeed enjoy a special place in Capote's heart. Or perhaps Babe so badly needed a nonjudgmental shoulder to cry on that she ignored the warning signs of Capote's loose tongue when it came to others. Babe's trusting nature, coupled with her love for Truman, led her to believe that he would never betray her secrets. In any event, she told him everything—absolutely everything—repeatedly lamenting the fact that, although she was barely past forty and was still recognized as the ultimate in beauty, style, and glamour throughout America, her robust and virile husband had abandoned her sexually.

Capote peddled without compunction this and many other privileged communications to their mutual jet set friends, just as he would fill her in on the most scurrilous gossip about the Guinnesses; the Bouvier sisters, Jackie Kennedy and Lee Radziwill; and any number of other glittering luminaries. Oddly enough, no one ever clued Babe in; not one of her closest friends ever informed her that Truman was bartering her most closely guarded secrets for favored status among others of her social set. During all the years of their friendship, Babe saw him as an equally troubled soul, which was true enough. It was that fact above all else that had cemented their relationship from the moment they first met. In addition, Babe and her jet set friends saw themselves as responsible for the international fame and critical success of this pet-sized prose poet from New Orleans. This of course was far from the truth, but the notion persisted, further endearing Truman to the rich, stylish crowd he had always cultivated.

Babe did many things to help her dearest friend, seeing that his material needs were met, entertaining him on a grand scale, and giving an enormous party in his honor during the writing of *In Cold Blood,* his literary masterpiece based on the Clutter family murder. Yet it never once occurred to her that Capote was a writer who up to that point in his literary career had made his reputation on works based essentially on his own personal memories; nor did it occur to her that, as his celebrity grew, so did his renown as a world-class gossip.

Babe and Bill continued to spend tremendous amounts of time with their highly amusing little friend. Capote's witty repartee provided them with untold hours of delight. Babe felt a deep and abiding affection for this young genius, an affection that far surpassed that which she had ever displayed toward her own children.

In January 1966, when *In Cold Blood* hit the bookstores, Capote's name became a household word throughout the world. At last the hanger-on became one of the movers and shakers. While his newfound fortune was not in a league with the Paleys', the book was estimated to have earned him a healthy pre-inflation $2 million plus. Even after paying fees to agents, lawyers, and the Internal Revenue Service, Truman found himself financially independent, with a very comfortable income, which Bill Paley helped him to invest wisely.

As the book climbed on the bestseller lists, so did Truman's ambition to get out of his dank basement flat in Oliver Smith's house, in Brooklyn Heights, where he had lived with his lover, Jack Dunphy, for eight years. Babe and Minnie had helped Truman to decorate the apartment, minimizing the flat's basic lack of appeal. While Truman had opened up new intellectual and literary vistas for Babe, she and Minnie had a trick or two up their sleeves when it came to furniture and decor. They taught him about various periods in decorating, paintings, all the things that stem from longtime exposure to great wealth. And Truman never lost an opportunity to express his gratitude. As quoted in Gerald Clarke's biography of Capote, the writer had this to say:

> Babe taught me a lot of things. How to look at a room, for instance. She showed me how to decorate by throwing things together, expensive things with cheap things from the dime store. She showed me that a room could be fun and personal and that's the way I've decorated ever since. I taught her a lot of things too. Such as how to read and how to think.

Babe, Minnie, and Betsey, like others of their generation and class, had ended their formal education with secondary school. The world of great literature was unfamiliar to Babe until Truman introduced her to it; when he did, she became an avid student. Always bright, her mind hungered for this sort of enrichment—and undoubtedly the escape it offered from her high-stress day-to-day existence.

And so Truman and Babe continued in this symbiotic relationship for many, many years. He loved being with the "Beautiful People." In fact, he once told an interviewer just how much it meant to him to be part of their world:

> Beautiful People have something more than that. It's a level of taste and—freedom. I think that's what always attracted me. The freedom to pursue an esthetic quality in life is an extra dimension like being able to fly where others walk. It's marvelous to appreciate paintings, but why not have them? Why not create a whole esthetic ambience? Be your own living work of art? It has a good deal to do with money, but that's not all of it by any means.

And that more or less summed up the basis of the great bond between the Paleys and their eccentric little southern sidekick. Of course, had he really thought things through, he might have realized that the Beautiful People were no more free than the nobodys—maybe less. Babe Paley was not free to sit in bed and pop bonbons into her mouth; to walk about in a housecoat, scuffs, and curlers; to let herself get lazy, fat, and old. She had always to strive for perfection, to live up to the glamorous, high-profile image of a "living work of art" that she had created for herself. This at times made her life undeniably stressful, especially since all her efforts never seemed to be quite enough to please her demanding husband. In effect, taste, wealth, and freedom had provided the means for her to dig herself into a trap, one from which she could rarely if ever escape.

In any event, Truman was undeterred in his zeal to become one of the Beautiful People. And that meant trading up in housing and location. Now that he had the wherewithal to create his own little living space, he picked a two-bedroom apartment in what one fashion writer termed "the most important new address" in Manhattan: the United Nations Plaza, located at First Avenue and Forty-ninth Street, adjacent to the East River and the United Nations. Truman had never lived at so dignified or trendy an address, and for $62,000—a big price tag for an apartment of the era—it was all his. Decorator Evie Backer set about making a comfortable living space—but one with very elegant restraints. Capote's home gradually filled out, like a sumptuous Vuillard painting with great colors and textures—seafoam green carpeting with a yellow and orange Bessarabian rug tossed over it, beige silk wall coverings in the living room, straw-blue silk for the bedroom walls, red lacquer paint in the dining room, green velvet upholstery for the Directoire sofa, the rich brown of the antique tables, and china cats, antique French paperweights, even a Faberge box, scattered everywhere. Truman's portrait, painted earlier by Jim Fosburgh, hung over the sofa, and all the little antique mementoes that he had searched out with Minnie and Babe (primarily on Third Avenue) were placed with great care throughout the twenty-second-floor apartment. And to top things off, there was a magnificent panoramic southern view of lower Manhattan and beyond.

A friend seeing the finished apartment for the first time commented, "Somehow reminds you of the contents of a very astute little boy's pocket."

Of course, the move to Manhattan's newly chic East Side neighborhood was only part of the author's larger scheme to place himself center stage in society—a position he hungered for from his earliest childhood. He might not have had the looks to be a Cinderella, but with his talent, inventiveness, and newfound financial and literary success, he could provide a proper setting for all the Cinderellas who had become a part of his world.

The years following *In Cold Blood* were highly accelerated ones. In February of 1966 he was with Jack Dunphy at the home they had just purchased together in Verbier, Switzerland, and by April he was back in America. That spring he gave a reading of some of his short stories at Town Hall, keeping the glittering audience spellbound, despite his high-paced nasal drawl. Afterward, Babe commented, "It was a very moving moment for me."

That summer found Capote briefly in Portugal with Lee Bouvier Radziwill, and then he joined the Agnellis for a cruise down the Adriatic. Returning to New York refreshed, he began immediately to put into motion plans for what he saw as the "best goddamn party" that anybody had ever heard of. He saw it as not just a party but a social and creative event, an esthetic coup of a magnitude not far beneath that of his wildly successful book.

By October 8, 1966, 540 invitations to Truman Capote's Black and White Ball were in the mail. The *bal masqué* was to take place on Monday, November 28, at the Plaza Hotel, and Katherine Graham, head of the family that owned *The Washington Post* and *Newsweek*, was to be the guest of honor. Truman's selection of the publishing magnate, whom he had met through Babe several years earlier, was just one more example of his genius for publicity.

With this masked ball Capote hoped to rekindle the romantic fire of great fetes of the past. The minute the invitations arrived, hundreds of New York socialites and their show business sidekicks began casting about for the most inventive masks. Bergdorf Goodman's youthful milliner, Halston, had this to say about the preparations: "I've never seen women putting so much serious effort into what they're going to wear."

Halston had to stop making hats for a while and concentrate on masks. Within days of receiving their invitations, Babe Paley, Anne Ford, Robin Butler, Molly Phipps, Anita Loos, and Brooke Astor had all placed orders with this inspired young hatter. Jayne Wrightsman had ordered two masks, white for herself and black satin for her oil-magnate husband, Charles. "Each mask is going to be totally different," said Halston. "Some will be worn but most will be carried on sticks." He did design Mrs. Graham's so that she could keep it on while she stood in the receiving line and needed to have her hands free for pats, shakes, and hugs. Gloria Guinness was one of the high-profile guests who did not get her mask from Halston. She flew in from Europe just to attend Truman's party and brought with her masks from Paris.

Of course, no woman would have been caught dead in the "same old thing" people had seen her in before, and besides, clothing had to conform to the prescribed color scheme. So Halston, who specialized in hats, found himself commissioned to create some of the gowns to be worn to the party. Jean Harvey, then Mrs. Alfred Gwynne Vanderbilt, dressed herself in a black and white fantasy gown by the young designer. Truman's party may in fact have been Halston's proverbial foot in the door to clothing design. In any event, virtually everything worn at the ball, except for the blazing jewels, was brand new and highly individual. The party itself was like a mobile checkerboard, since all the ladies had been instructed to wear black and/or white, and the gentlemen of course had no choice in the matter.

With the flurry of planning in full swing, Truman managed to keep a tight rein on every aspect of the party. From his dictum that no one would be permitted to bring an uninvited guest to his determination that a number of the guests should give small dinner parties beforehand and that the diners would arrive in groups, to ensure that not one woman would have to bear the "humiliation" of arriving unescorted. Babe and Bill Paley invited, among others, Mr. and Mrs. Alvin Dewey of Garden City, Kansas; Dewey was the FBI agent who conducted the inquiry into the murders described in *In Cold Blood*. And Truman and his guest of honor dropped in for drinks before repairing to Capote's suite at the Plaza for what he described as a quiet little "bird and bottle" picnic supper.

Throughout it all, Truman maintained a casual demeanor. Just days before the event, he was quoted as saying, "They just don't understand. This is purely and simply a party for my friends." The trouble was, no one quite believed that Truman's 540 most intimate friends included the likes of Sammy Davis, Jr., Rose Kennedy, Walter Lippmann, James Baldwin, the Marquis and Marchioness of Dufferin and Ava, the Baron and Baroness Guy de Rothschild, and the Maharaja and Maharanee of Jaipur. But the truth of the matter was that Truman Capote possessed an almost endless entrée into the world of great wealth and glamour.

At last the magic moment arrived; the doors of the Plaza Hotel's gold and red ballroom burst open, and the near-mythical evening began. Leo Lerman from *Mademoiselle* observed, "The guest book reads like an international list for the guillotine."

The newly minted millionaire host and the powerful Washington publisher took their places in the receiving line near the scarlet tables in the gilt candle-lit ballroom. Kay Graham was gowned in a white wool crepe ballgown, and perched on her nose was a matching wool crepe mask sprinkled with jewels. Capote, true to form, wore a thirty-nine-cent domino mask from F.A.O. Schwartz.

The host and guest of honor received guests until nearly midnight, and Truman had a word for everyone. "Oh, Billy, that's fantastic," he said to decorator Billy Baldwin as he walked by in a unicorn headdress of black and gold.

Most of the guests unmasked before the appointed hour of midnight. Alfred Gwynne Vanderbilt, who had worn his black velvet cat mask under protest, was heard to complain, "It itches and I can't see," as he pulled it off and stuck it into his pocket. "That's a lot better," he announced.

Mrs. William Woodward, at that time the grande dame of old-moneyed New York society (and the mother of Bill Woodward, whose showgirl wife, Ann, shot him), had been giving and going to elegant parties since before World War I. She was in a black-feathered mask that talk-show hostess Arlene Francis had gotten for her. "We used to do this sort of thing in Newport in the old days," Elsie Woodward commented. "Why I remember when we all dressed up in lavish costumes and the Ziegfeld Follies came up from New York to perform."

Capote's fabulous ball achieved for him a nodding acquaintance with the goal that had kept him going all his life—to be a real part of the world of glamour and old money. With this fantasy party he personally felt that he had reached a status on a footing with that of Caroline Astor (*the* Mrs. Astor at the turn of the century), who had established New York society's upper echelon when she had limited her invitations to just four hundred guests.

Humorous columnist Russell Baker, in an astute postparty observation in *The New York Times,* offered the following comment:

Capote's social success will help the writer take a healthier attitude toward his career. Most writers surely will experience an instant inflation of self-esteem from the knowledge that one of their colleagues has seized Mrs. Astor's former role as social arbiter. . . .
If one writer can make Henry Ford, Andy Warhol, Walter Lipp-

mann, Tallulah Bankhead, Stanislas Radziwill, Marianne Moore, Frank Sinatra and several hundred other equally eminent personages dance to Peter Duchin, then surely another writer can have the Carlsons, Blairs, and Adamses (everyday folk) in for cheese dip and whiskey. . . . With a single fling, Mr. Capote has given the writer the right to social dignity.

By 3:30 in the morning, it was over. More than two hundred stalwarts had stayed to the end. To his departing guests the impish Capote, a half-smile playing across his youthful face, continued to insist, "I just wanted to give a party for my friends."

So it almost might have seemed, but in a moment of nearly understandable weakness, he gave *The New York Times* his guest list, not bothering to cross off the names of those who had regretted or who just did not come. Those included a handful of ambassadors, Governor Nelson Rockefeller, New York's Mayor Lindsay, and Jackie, Bobby, and Teddy Kennedy. The published list changed the private fete into an overly publicized public event, thus giving gossip columnists and sociologists a chance to move in. "Almost a joke," said Cleveland Amory, author of *Who Killed Society?*

But Kay Graham said fondly, "I can't bear to think that there may ever be another party like this." She might as well not have worried, because to date there has never been a society event to duplicate Truman Capote's Black and White Ball.

Socialite Gloria Guinness had to remain in bed for two days, for she suffered from severe neck pain caused by two monstrous necklaces, one of diamonds and one of rubies, that had completely covered her elegant swanlike neck.

With this extravagant ball, Capote seemed to have taken on an omnipotent air. His party remained the talk of the town for months; he had become the darling of talk-show hosts, and magazine and newspaper profiles of him proliferated worldwide. So great had his reputation become that every important host in New York vied for his attendance at a get-together; Truman's very presence virtually guaranteed social success. Yet even as the memories of that grand night wafted in the rarefied air of New York top-drawer society, storm clouds were beginning to darken the horizon, and the glittering sun of Capote's fame, popularity, and glamour was slowly starting its descent. For the time being, he remained surrounded by his swans, each of whom had a consuming passion for gossip as long as it focused on the others and not on their own intriguing lives. However, as his celebrity grew and his name became a household word throughout the nation, Capote's personality became more and more unpredictable. For years he had been dependent on amphetamines and alcohol, and this habit began to take its toll. Worse yet, Truman Capote fell into the trap that had snared so many celebrated people, whether politicians, actors, authors, or dictators—he began to believe in his own celebrity and act accordingly.

The Black and White Ball became the capstone of his fame. Within a year of that spectacular event, Capote would begin his ever-so-gradual fall from grace. The tragedy was that the feeling of social invincibility along with pills and booze caused him to trigger his own destruction. The descent would not stop with his celebrity and popularity but would translate to his writing genius. Capote would ultimately find himself almost completely ostracized from the world he had worked so hard to make his own—the world populated by beautiful swans and multimillionaires, private jets and yachts, glamour and savoir faire.

19

THE CIRCLE NARROWS

*A*LL three Cushing sisters, with their husbands in tow, attended Truman Capote's Black and White *bal masqué* in 1966. By this time Minnie, Betsey, and Babe had come a long, long way from the days when their mother had begun to curry them for their spectacular marriages. Each sister had in her own fashion attained the social and economic heights Gogsie had envisioned for her daughters. And each in her own fashion had paid an enormous price for this success.

From the moment the Cushing sisters had set foot in top-drawer American society, they had made headlines around the world. Their every move had been immediately chronicled in Cholly Knickerbocker's "Smart Set" column, as well as in myriad other gossip columns. Their names—like it, as Babe did, or not, as Betsey did not—were household words. Changing with the times, the sisters had entered the smart set, made a brief stopover in café society, spent a far longer time as members of the jet set, and had finally settled in comfortable dignity into old-guard New York society. True, Minnie had pursued a more arty path, and Betsey had found her old-guard niche early on, but each sister in her own way had reached the pinnacle of social success. American women adored, envied, and emulated these stunning, dashing Cushings, for in the eyes of the press and the public theirs was a fairy-tale existence even if their "princes" didn't provide coronets and (with the exception of Jock Whitney) weren't particularly charming.

Babe Cushing Mortimer Paley took great pride in being the wife of her super-rich media magnate despite the fact that he lacked the WASP credentials so important to her generation and her class. And even as the decade of the seventies dawned, she still enjoyed her perennial status as an icon of fashion and beauty.

By 1970, when Babe was a gorgeous, well-preserved fifty-five years old and Bill was an active and aggressive seventy, the Paley's had arrived at another turning point in their dramatic relationship. Bill had become more and more involved in the day-to-day operations at CBS, and when he did have some leisure time, he tended to spend it in the company of other women (a lifelong activity that he had never outgrown), rather than at home with his wife.

Babe continued to live up to the public image that had now become central to her existence. Like so many celebrity and society couples, the Paleys began to lead distinctly separate lives. Babe had long since come to terms with the fact that the sexual side of her marriage was over. While the hurt remained, she no longer grieved, and in fact came to view her celibacy as somewhat of a relief. Then, too, she had learned from her parents' relationship that when a man pursued his own business—and extracurricular—interests, his wife could do little but patiently await his convenience and see to it that he was comfortable when he happened to honor her with his presence.

Thus Babe's role became one of hostess and escort. She knew in no uncertain terms that she had to maintain her beauty, provide a grand yet comfortable home and spectacular meals, and appear on Bill's arm at important social and business events, like a very expensive ornament. The very things she most valued were also a constant source of stress. Being perennially "best dressed," most beautiful, and wife—albeit in name only—of the fabled founder of CBS and equally fabled womanizer was not as easy as she made it look. And of course the older Babe became, the harder it was to keep up her image. *Vogue* had once written of her, "She makes excellence look easy." But the truth was that it had never been easy and it was becoming more and more difficult. Much of Gogsie's early teaching had centered upon the appearance of ease in the midst of attention to the most minute, perfectionistic details, and Babe had mastered her mother's lessons. As Gogsie had once demanded perfection of her, Babe now demanded it of herself—and Bill expected nothing less.

Babe could never simply be a devoted, hard-working wife and mother; she had always to be the manager of great establishments. And this was a twenty-four-hour-a-day occupation. Outwardly Babe never showed signs of the stress associated with constant pressure to perform and with the increasing certainty that her second marriage was as loveless as her first had been. Inwardly she lived with the stress every minute of every day.

At a time in her life when she might have wished for the companion-ship of her grown children, she and Bill had become totally estranged from their children. Billie was bumming around, living a hippie life and indulging in his serious drug habit. Kate was living a bohemian life in Greenwich Village and rarely made contact with either her parents or her siblings.

Amanda, too, was lost to Babe, at least partly because of Babe's envy of her own daughter. It was hard for the still beautiful but aging mother to accept the fact that Amanda had become the darling of New York's younger social set and a media princess. In fact, Amanda and Carter Burden were the most talked-about young couple on the Manhattan party circuit.

At the time when they had hit the headlines as New York's "fun couple," Halston had declared the young woman ". . . the most beauti-ful girl going." Chestnut-haired and hazel-eyed, with exquisite features and flawless skin, the lovely young socialite and her politically ambi-tious Vanderbilt scion husband had taken the town by storm. "Ba," was not merely a pretty face and form. She had dropped out of Wellesley to marry Carter, but she had always been a great reader. After her mar-riage, she studied at the New School, Columbia, and the Art Students League. In 1966 she was elected to the top spot on the Best Dressed list, a position previously occupied by her mother.

Given Babe's rather unhappy situation, it is perhaps not so surprising that she should have felt a bit envious of her daughter, who was blossoming into a strikingly beautiful young society matron just as Babe's star was descending. Amanda was doing all the things that her mother longed to continue to do—and so much more.

Yet Amanda had more in common with her mother than beauty and a flair for fashion, for even as she appeared to have it all, this highly social media darling was having trouble in paradise. In one way, Amanda was not like her mother, for according to a *New York Times* story, she had a reputation among her friends for throwing frequent temper tantrums whenever anything displeased her or did not go her way. Nevertheless, she did manage to get her degree in public planning, an accomplishment that neither her mother nor her aunts had achieved. Although since meeting Truman Capote, Babe had become increasingly aware of her own ignorance and had made great strides with her reading, she nevertheless felt intellectually insecure and so was very envious of her daughter's degree and the potential for independence that went with it.

Babe continued to establish a close relationship with her oldest child, Tony Mortimer. As she and Bill became more and more estranged, she took great comfort in this relationship. With Tony and Tony alone, of all her six children and stepchildren, she managed a real parental role. Babe and Tony would have lengthy telephone conversations each day, and he would often stop by after work to have cocktails with his mother. Babe in turn shared confidences with Tony that she shared with no one else in her family. Bill, in true dog-in-the-manger fashion, deeply resented these mother-son intimacies.

Truman Capote continued to be Babe's closest confidant. As her frustration with her marriage grew, he was there to lend an ear and gain a first-hand insight into her troubled soul. As Babe's depression deepened she unwittingly conveyed more and more juicy confidences to her dearest friend's eager ear.

In an interview with journalist Sally Bedell Smith, the photographer Horst (a longtime friend of Babe's) summed the situation up in very simple terms: "He [Paley] wore her down. He was a bit too much in command. She was not happy. He kept her too busy. 'Look at the list of what I have to do,' she would say."

Biographer Gerald Clarke quotes Truman Capote as saying,

[Babe] loved, loved, loved [Bill], hated, hated, hated him. I never
met anybody who was so desperately unhappy as she was. Twice
I saved her when she tried to kill herself. One time she took pills
and the other time she cut her wrists. Once she tried to leave him
and I sat down and said, "Look you don't have any money and
you've got four children. Think of them. Bill bought you. It's as
if he went down to Central Casting. Look upon being Mrs. William S. Paley as a job, the best job in the world. Accept it and be
happy with it."

This advice was precisely the sort that Gogsie would have imparted, had
she been alive. She had understood with perfect clarity that love and sex
had little if anything to do with the type of marriage she had engineered
for her daughters. For Gogsie Cushing marriage was a business—a very
serious one, with its ups and downs, its joys and frustrations. "Job-
hopping" was something that she had always frowned upon, and she
would have rolled over in her grave if she had known that Babe was even
contemplating such a move at this relatively advanced stage in her
life—especially since there was no other, better offer on the horizon.
Truman Capote, no less practical than Gogsie had been, immediately
grasped the true basis of Babe's marriage to Bill Paley and was appalled
by the idea of her chucking it all in for mere personal happiness.

Perhaps Babe shed more than a few tears, but true to her class and
her upbringing, she went on gallantly playing her role. Before her marriage to Bill, she had had a brief fling with diplomat Elim O'Shaugh-
nessy. However, despite his elegance and handsome looks, his financial
prospects were so slim that Gogsie had eliminated him from her list of
eligible bachelors. In the 1960s rumors circulated linking Babe and
Belgian banking heir Jean Lambert, but nothing ever came of the relationship. And Babe's common sense and probable consultations with
Truman brought her back to the realization that the best possible job for
her was that of being Mrs. William S. Paley.

Still, hers was no easy job, and her chores and burdens didn't grow
any lighter as the years passed. In the mid-1960s, when most of the
children had left Kiluna, Bill surprised Babe by purchasing a twenty-
room duplex at 820 Fifth Avenue, overlooking Central Park. Neighbors

in the building included Jeanne and Alfred Vanderbilt and Charles Wrightsman. The enormous apartment was a far cry from their intimate pied-à-terre at the St. Regis, which they had maintained throughout their entire married life. So monumental was the task of decorating the duplex that Babe enlisted the services of no fewer than four of New York's top decorators, among them Billy Baldwin, Stephane Boudin of Jansen, the great French decorating establishment, and Sister Parish and Albert Hadley of the firm Parish-Hadley.

Billy Baldwin, always a great favorite of Babe's, re-created their old St. Regis living room, which he had installed originally as a jewel-like library, complete with its antique needlepoint rug and rococo painted and guilded Venetian clock, gayly suspended from the ceiling. The same shirred brown and beige chintz hangings covered the walls, creating a perfect backdrop for Picasso's *Pink Lady* and Matisse's *Odalisque,* with its Oriental flavor.

Stephane Boudin worked with the Paleys on their new apartment. The long entrance gallery was a very distinguished space with bookcases floor to ceiling on all but the central wall opposite the entrance door. Picasso's *Boy Leading a Horse* was the dominant feature.

A magnificent antique parquet floor was installed, and a soft shade of sage green was used on the walls in contrast to the white trim and rich, highly polished mahogany doors.

Paneling was installed in the drawing room, which was a scaled-down reproduction of a room from one of the great houses in Paris. Parish-Hadley obtained from a dealer in Paris an exceptional carved and painted, late-eighteenth-century chimney piece with simulated marble finish. A rich golden yellow was eventually used for the paneled walls. No less than five different shades were used to create a subtle though dramatic background for the Paleys' collection of paintings, sculpture, and extraordinary furniture and decorative objects.

In each of the two end bays of the long entrance gallery, large rectangular red lacquer Oriental tables were placed, each with its own bronze dore library lamp. In true personalized Cushing fashion, the table was piled high with books and every current magazine imaginable.

The small elevator vestibule was a rectangular space with a magnificent pair of ivory-handled paneled doors centered on the long wall

opposite the elevator. Parish-Hadley painted and glazed the walls a deep
bourbon color and applied small squares of the thinnest wavy German
glass with tiny gilded metal rosettes.

The classically laid-out dining room was large with architectural
detail designed by Boudin. Parish-Hadley chose a heavy printed cotton
for the walls, curtains, and the white painted Louis XVI chairs. The
warm earth tones of the floral design were intensified by bright tangerine
corded wall-to-wall carpeting.

Mr. Paley's bedroom was redesigned with a rich printed fabric of
Oriental inspiration for walls and curtains. The subtle shading of earth
tones became a background for the furnishings and his collection of
superb paintings and drawings.

Throughout the apartment, covering every table top, were the fruits
of Babe's travels throughout the world and up and down Third Avenue—precious antique objects of every size and kind. Babe loved to go
antiquing with her sisters or, more often, with her longtime friend
Natalie Davenport, and she chose each object with love, taste, and an
unlimited budget. Her apartment was a veritable treasure trove, and yet
the overall effect was one of almost cluttered but tasteful homeyness.

The duplex housed the sizable Paley art collection, most of which Bill
had acquired during the time when he had been married to Dorothy.
Never one to waste money, he had purchased the majority of the pieces
directly from the artists, thus saving the dealer's fees. Rousseau's *Vase
of Flowers,* Gauguin's *Queen of Tareois,* Van Gogh's *Washerwoman at
Arles,* and Toulouse-Lautrec's *Montmartre Madam* were among the
great works that graced the living room.

While all this may sound incredibly luxurious, the new apartment,
increased household staff, and more frequent at-home entertaining only
added to Babe's work load. While in the old days she had been able to
leave almost everything up to the staff of the St. Regis Hotel for her
large-scale parties, she now had to manage every detail personally.
True, she had plenty of household help, but directing so many servants
was no mean feat.

In addition, Babe's days in the city were scheduled to the hilt with
luncheons and occasional committee meetings. She was a highly active
fund-raiser for both the Association to Help Retarded Children and the

North Shore Hospital, a pet charity of Betsey's. Babe was usually up and about by eight-thirty in the morning, though she was occasionally known to sleep until just before lunch at one o'clock. From time to time she attended drawing and painting classes at the Art Students League on West Fifty-seventh Street. If she was driven to the school or on one or more of her many other errands, she frequently chose to walk home. She felt compelled to keep fit, but calisthenics were not for her and she was never an avid athlete. She did enjoy walking, especially in the early part of the day. Fortunately, Babe was blessed with a healthy metabolism, for she had a hearty appetite and a fondness for cakes and pies. If she did find herself gaining an extra pound or two, she immediately put herself on a strict diet.

Babe was one of the original "ladies who lunch," and she found luncheons with friends and family members to be festive and relaxing. She was a fixture at the most glamorous New York restaurants—Henri Soule's Pavillon, the Colony, La Grenouille, and La Côte Basque among them. After lunch she would often shop or have a fitting, activities which she scheduled to the minute: a dress fitting from 3:30 to 3:50, shoe shopping from 3:55 to 4:10. Anyone who has ever waited in line, searched in vain for a salesperson, or failed to find a desired item can appreciate just how impressive a feat this was. But Babe had shopping down to a science. She had every stop charted out before she ever left her apartment, and she never failed to make sure that everything would be ready when she arrived at a favorite designer's showroom. Babe Paley was not just any shopper, and the designers and salespeople jumped through hoops to do her bidding, although she was in no way supercilious or demanding. She—and they—simply considered punctuality to be her due.

When Babe was in New York, she always reserved Mondays and Fridays around lunch hour for her hairdresser—first Kenneth and later Monsieur Marc. At this latter salon she would invariably partake of a hearty lunch, which she washed down with a beer. Never one to waste a minute, Babe generally brought a book along to read during every free second.

In the evening, if she and Bill were going out for an early dinner, she took the chauffeur-driven Bentley to Black Rock, the CBS building, to collect her husband as he left work. This sometimes meant sitting in the car for up to an hour. Babe would often turn to her needlepoint to pass the time while Bill finished taking care of the day's business. Babe may have led a cushy life, but she was never idle.

When not shopping, dining, or partying in New York, the Paleys could generally be found indulging in those same pastimes in Europe, usually in the summer and again in January. Billy Baldwin describes one such trip:

The Gaynors [Rosie and Bill] and the Paleys were all in Paris having a real holiday. It was the height of the Fine French Furniture Fever in New York, and everybody who had any money at all had to have a splendid piece of it, no matter what it looked like, and no matter whether they even cared about it. French furniture was a signature of taste, of fashion, and absolutely a must.

My job with them [the Paleys] was finished except that I was to help them find a French commode for the drawing room. I cannot say that it was a must. There really were plenty of pieces of furniture that we had seen in New York that would have been lovely, but Bill had a strong idea of collecting only for a name, and he was determined to find what he wanted in Paris.

So the Paleys had come with the Gaynors to look. Rosie, it is quite true, had grown up with lovely French furniture, which belonged to her mother when she was married to William Vanderbilt, and she had always known a great deal about it and had a great deal of taste. Bill Gaynor knew nothing about anything except being the best-looking man in Southampton and being a brilliant doctor.

I had the most marvelous agreement with the Paleys. They had asked me to be their guest in Paris for a week in order to look for the French commode, and they wanted me to go with them every day. I agreed to be their guest and to help them, on the condition that I would not take a commission if we found the right thing. That way I could have the pleasure and the fun of freely and totally expressing myself, which I think is very hard for anybody to do honestly if money is involved.

Bill Paley had the strength of ten and it was great fun to go to all the terribly expensive and most fashionable antique shops with them and find everyone staring at Babe. She looked extraordinary that summer, with her beautiful manners and that divine smile. The city of Paris was at her feet.

One day Bill said to me, "I think you, Babe, and I should go alone tomorrow afternoon. I've heard about a piece of furniture that I want to see."

So off we went in the late afternoon to a very well-known antiquarian, and ther we saw a black lacquer commode which was positively guaranteed to have belonged to Madame DuBarry. The price was absolutely staggering. The dealer who owned it knew the Paleys and had even been to their house on Long Island, and he said to Bill, "Mr. Paley, if you take the commode and put it in your salon, it will immediately make it the most important room in New York."

Bill said, "I don't doubt that. It is magnificent."

Magnificent it was, but I knew if we got the commode into their drawing room that it would look like a whore. It was much too elaborate, much too fancy, and it would not be right at all. Because of my agreement with the Paleys I was in a lovely position to say exactly what I thought the minute we left that gentleman's shop.

"Well," Bill said, "No, I can't see that, but the important thing is that I'm starving and I've got to have some herring right away."

"Well, darling," said Babe, "of course you must, indeed."

"Billy," he said, "do you like herring?"

"I love it," I said.

"There's only one place on earth that has really good herring, and it's right here on the Champs Elysees," said Bill.

We stopped at quite a strange restaurant, and it was true. It had the best herring I've ever eaten.

Whether pursuing postimpressionist paintings or a marvelous boiserie, thoughts of food were never far from Bill Paley's mind. When seized by a craving for some particular food, he wanted only the best— immediately, at that—and Babe was expected to drop everything, fall into line, and either produce the desired food or endure such impromptu pilgrimages as the one Billy described.

Whenever the Paleys were in Paris, they made a point of seeing Pamela Churchill (in the days between her divorce and her subsequent marriage to Leland Hayward). This pilgrimage, too, was more Bill's idea than Babe's. Nevertheless, Pamela was the hostess to be entertained by, and a visit with her was almost mandatory for anyone with claims to social and fashion status. Bill, like his brother-in-law Jock Whitney, found Pamela most beguiling, and Babe, like many another wary wife, found the dashing divorcée threatening in the extreme. In fact, Bill's somewhat fawning attention to Pamela was a source of great irritation to Babe.

Ultimately, the years of intense perfectionism, lunching, shopping, entertaining, and globe-trotting, coupled with the constant pain of Bill's rejection and the effort to appear calm and cheerful, created more strain than Babe could handle, affecting her physical well-being. Slowly but surely she became aware that her health was failing her. A smoker since the days when she and her sisters had to sneak their cigarettes to avoid their father's wrath, Babe had become more and more dependent on nicotine as the years—and pressures—wore on. For many years she smoked more than two packs of L & Ms a day. Although she had tried to stop on various occasions, she always picked up the habit again whenever a crisis erupted. For her, cigarettes were a crutch without which she felt she could not get along. This habit was certainly damaging to her health. In addition, depression had taken its toll. Always somewhat fragile and having suffered some major health problems in the past, Babe found herself with less and less energy and less and less time to slow down, so great were the demands of the role of Mrs. William Paley.

As matters went from bad to worse, Babe's greatest strength was her friendships. She took great comfort not only from her sisters, Tony, and Truman but from various others who were generally very sympathetic and supportive: Jeanne Murray Vanderbilt, C. Z. Guest, Katherine Auchincloss, Sibilla Clark, Irene Selznick, Louise Melhado, Slim Keith, Jamie Choate, and Marietta Tree. Babe often lunched and shopped with these fashionable women—and sometimes shed a few tears on their shoulders. In addition, she had a large group of single, highly creative male friends. These men, including Patrick O'Higgins, English director Peter Glenville, writer Frederick Eberstadt, Boaz Mazor, and art historian John Richardson, offered her wonderful platonic relationships, bolstering her sagging ego with their adulation of her great beauty, taste, wealth, and sweetness.

One of these men, Boaz Mazor, one of the wittiest raconteurs on the Manhattan social scene, met Babe through John Richardson in the very early 1970s. Although not one of Babe's most intimate friends, Mazor was often a guest of the Paleys before her death. He recently reminisced about his first impression of Babe—her glamour, beauty, and great style. Babe's perfectionism did not escape Mazor. Commenting on their house in Nassau, he said, "It was just perfection. Nothing could touch the Paleys." But Babe's sense of style was such that she did not always feel compelled to spend a fortune to achieve her fabulous chic. Mazor remembered having taken Babe a strand of Kenneth Jay Lane's faux baroque pearls as a housewarming gift: "Babe had the real pearls just like them. She was very gracious and said, "I will never wear just one again. I will mix them up, and I love the idea that people will try to guess what is real and what is fake." She would later come into the back at KJL and buy jewelry. Babe took pride in making costume jewelry into a chic thing. On her legendary beauty, Mazor remarked,

> She had everything that we consider classic beauty—a long, long neck. She was not today's beauty. Today's beauty—Jane Fonda, the blonde girls today, all the girls we know (Judy Taubman, Carolyn Roehm, Ivana Trump)—are very attractive. Babe and Marella Agnelli were in another league. Their beauty was like an old Roman coin.

Like almost all Babe's other friends, Boaz had memories of her kindness and consideration. In 1976, when he had to spend five weeks in the hospital with hepatitis, she sent him copies of *Apollo*, a favorite publication of antiquarians. She also sent little parcels and phoned frequently. "She was always so concerned about her friends," Mazor noted.

There were times, however, when Babe would indulge her competitive instincts. Among her closest friends were a number of great beauties. She and Gloria Guinness were friendly rivals, and Gloria was capable of rather catty practical jokes. In at least one case, according to Mazor, Babe gave as good as she got:

> Often when [Gloria] invited the Paleys [aboard the fabulous Guinness yacht], she would deliberately tell Babe to dress simply. (Babe would arrive in a simple dress and sandals to find herself at a gala.) Gloria would wear all her jewels and upstage her. Babe, who was very competitive, was very upset. I'm sure it meant a great deal who was the more elegant, the more stylish.

Babe waited her turn to get back at Gloria. For years Babe, Gloria, and Francoise de la Renta had tried to outdo one another in serving the tiniest possible baby vegetables. The moment arrived when Gloria and husband, Loel, arrived in New York to attend a dinner party the Paleys were giving in honor of Oscar and Francoise de la Renta. And Babe had her moment of triumph over both these elegant ladies who prided themselves on being superb hostesses. After that evening neither of them was ever able to outmatch Babe again in this area of culinary art.

Babe's social and economic status was perhaps the hook that helped her form her numerous friendships, but it was her caring and generous nature that kept them. She was as ready to give as to take comfort, and she was invariably thoughtful. Despite her busy schedule, she always remembered birthdays and anniversaries, and always took the time to find just the right gifts for special occasions. Like her mother before her, Babe shopped all year long for Christmas gifts, taking advantage of off-season sales and instantly buying "the perfect present" for someone wherever and whenever she came across it.

Sibilla Clark, once wed to A&P heir Columbus O'Donnell, gave great insight into the Paley marriage and Babe's special qualities:

> Babe was very attentive to Bill. He liked to have attractive people around. There was always lots of superb food around (he loved lots of food). The flowers were always incredible. Babe's life was spent with houses, travel, parties, and gardening.

I saw the Paleys both in New York and Nassau. And remember Truman Capote well. Found Capote to be silly. I mean, that voice! The others liked him. He was always making some sort of little wisecracks at somebody's expense.

. . . Babe was a role model for me. She always found time for everything. Had great depth of feelings. Babe and Betsey were both a bit shy. Babe gave me clothes. At times she would invite me to her home to pick things out that she had set aside for me. Designers included Norell, Mainbocher, Valentina, and Mila Schoen.

Sibilla Clark would continue to be a guest at the Paley homes after Babe's death and would frequently see Bill in Nassau at their respective homes. Both she and Slim Keith would also spend time at Kiluna.

Another great friend of Babe's and her sisters was Jeanne Murray Vanderbilt, the second wife of Alfred Gwynne Vanderbilt. Jeanne remembers with great fondness Babe's kindness to her during difficult times:

When I was getting my separation from Alfred and news of it was in the press every day [and] newsmen [were] parked outside our building, Babe rang me up from Kiluna and said, "Vander, you come out here this minute." And she sent the car to collect me. I went out to Kiluna on one of those long holiday weekends and with the help of Babe and Bill I began to sort things out in a much more rational manner. David Selznick was also there and he gave me a lift back into town and with his marvelous intelligence and knowledge of life he gave me . . . a stern lecture about getting myself together and going on with my own life. He was such a wonderfully strong person and what he said on that drive made so much sense and went a long way to helping me through a difficult period in my life. And that weekend with Babe was only one of many kindnesses that she directed toward me.

While Babe found comfort and strength from her many friendships, her sister Betsey gained her greatest happiness from her immediate family. Her marriage to Jock Whitney was, of all the sisters' marriages, the one great love match. In measuring how well Minnie, Betsey, and Babe did in their various multimillion-dollar marriages, Betsey unquestionably got the best deal. As Jeanne Murray Vanderbilt said rather generously of the Cushing sisters, "They were known and remembered for having fallen in love with men who happened to be very rich." Even if love had been the primary motivator for Minnie and Babe (and especially in Minnie's case this seems doubtful indeed), the eldest and youngest Cushing sisters wound up in what could at best be considered marriages of convenience—more likely, inconvenience. Betsey, on the other hand, adored her second husband, and he adored her. Most important, the passing of years brought them closer rather than further apart. Tex McCrary had this to say recently about the sisters: "The Cushing sisters made every man they married far better men than they really were."

Besides landing a kind and loving man, Betsey stepped into the rarefied atmosphere of old money, insuperable social standing, and the most extravagant, elegant lifestyle imaginable. Greentree was the most magnificent private residence in America, and Betsey knew how to make the most of her fabulous surroundings. Perhaps even more important, she managed to secure the Whitney fortune for herself and her children. In Betsey's case, Gogsie's strategy worked out perfectly.

Archibald L. Gillies, of the John Hay Whitney Foundation, recently made this observation:

> Betsey was terribly loyal to Jock but not in a cloying way. She seemed to worship him—nice quality . . . Never negative. I never saw any sharp words or digs or anything of that sort. That's very nice, unlike so many married couples who get in their digs. Not Betsey and Jock. Betsey was definitely a helpmate. Not just my impression only. I'm sure he talked to her about one project or another. Jock, I'm sure, consulted with her on foundation matters.

The postambassadorial years were filled with family activities for Betsey, with a growing breed of grandchildren surrounding her at Greentree, and with increased business ventures for Jock, who nevertheless proved to be a very attentive husband. By the end of the 1960s, eight grandchildren were constantly in and out of the estate. Sara and Anthony had five children, and Kate and Bill had three daughters. Sara's son Christopher (christened Anthony, Jr.) was clearly Betsey's favorite, although she doted on them all. Betsey's dynastic sense of family led her to incorporate her grandchildren into her very elite Whitney world at Greentree and all their other lavish homes throughout the country. Soon Sara's and Kate's children were more Whitneys—with all the perks, of course—than di Bonaventuras or Haddads. It was Betsey's show, and sons-in-law either fell into line or by the wayside.

During the post-London years Betsey also took an active role in the John Hay Whitney Foundation and was involved in all the decisions the board made. It was she who was responsible for Jock's hiring Sydney "Spiv" Spivack to help formulate social policy for the foundation and to review the structure and effectiveness of a number of similar philanthropic organizations. Spiv had long been like a brother to all three Cushing sisters.

Jock had a rule of thumb for allocating his considerable income; quite simply, one third of his fortune went for personal expenses, one third for J. H. Whitney & Company, and the remaining third for philanthropy. Spiv urged him to become more deeply involved in publishing ventures and also to set aside a larger portion of the foundation's funds for scholarships to black students. This latter policy became one of the chief interests of the foundation, a move Betsey wholeheartedly endorsed.

Spiv later married Dorothy Dillon Eweson, sister of C. Douglas Dillon, investment banker, onetime United States ambassador to France and secretary of the treasury. Minnie, Betsey, and Babe were delighted and quite frankly relieved when their old friend, a highly volatile man, at last found happiness and settled down with Dorothy, a woman whose ideals were equal to his. All three sisters attended the wedding, which took place at the Dillon family estate in Far Hills, New Jersey.

Dorothy recalls that Spiv was closer to the sisters than was their own brother, Henry. Spiv had also been a great friend of Gogsie's. Reminiscing about the three Cushing sisters, Dorothy Dillon Eweson had this to say: "Babe and Minnie were so generous with their time. Both were so . . . visible socially, Betsey less so. But their closeness was remarkable.

Each day of their lives they would spend hours on the telephone talking to one another." On the subject of Greentree, Mrs. Eweson spoke almost reverently: "Greentree is a remarkable private residence. The magnificence of the paintings is so overpowering that one doesn't notice the furnishings. The house and its furnishings have changed little since the early days of Jock and Betsey's marriage." Dorothy also remembered an incident that spoke volumes about Betsey's daughters' relationship with the Roosevelts: "I recall being at the Waldorf-Astoria for a very large function with Sara and Kate Roosevelt, and Jimmy and Elliott Roosevelt were also there. And one of the girls turned to me and asked, 'Is that Dad?' "

Clearly, Betsey's daughters looked to Jock Whitney as a father figure. And Betsey positively doted on him. She and her sisters had set quite different priorities and agendas, and Betsey's primary concern was Jock's well-being. And she had reason for concern, for Jock was working extremely hard, juggling the chores of the *New York Herald Tribune,* of which he was editor-in-chief and publisher, and his duties at Whitney Communications, the Whitcom Investment Company, and the John Hay Whitney Foundation. As it turned out, the *Herald Tribune* was one of Jock's few failures; he poured some $26 million into the newspaper before having to close it down in 1966.

It was during his stewardship of the *Herald Tribune* that Jock became very ill and had to enter New York Hospital, suffering from a severe case of influenza and a mild cardiac disorder. Upon being discharged Jock and Betsey went to their estate at Thomasville, Georgia, for him to recuperate and to begin a strict diet that his doctors had ordered him to maintain for life. Needless to say, Betsey saw to it that Jock adhered to the rather stringent health regime. She genuinely loved her husband and made a great effort to take care of him.

Greenwood, the Georgia plantation, had been one of the favorite retreats of Jock's Uncle Oliver Payne. The land held vast pine woods and an abundance of wild game. Jock had always delighted in having friends down during the winter months for bird shooting. Dwight Eisenhower was a frequent guest, as were Jock's wartime colleagues generals Carl Spaatz and Ira Eaker. The Whitneys and their guests always traveled to Georgia by Jock's C-47 transport plane, which he had converted into a luxurious private aircraft.

The main house at Greenwood was small by Whitney standards—a mere seven bedrooms—but there was ample room for company in the various cottages on the estate. Betsey made great improvements on the grounds, engaging the services of the Italian landscape architect Umberto Innocenti. He had planted camellia bushes in the area near the house and had flanked the driveway with magnolia trees. Meanwhile, the Whitneys had also worked the plantation, turning it into a profitable producer of timber and corn feed.

Another favorite Whitney retreat was Fisher's Island, off New London, Connecticut, where Betsey and Jock would spend a few weeks each summer in the house they had built in 1949. Departing from Roosevelt Field, on Long Island, they could be on Fisher's Island in less than a half hour via their private plane. The island provided the privacy that both Betsey and Jock valued so greatly. Here they could be alone or with close friends in an extremely simple setting. Betsey had decorated the house with bright colors and white wicker furniture, filling it with the natural beauty of masses and masses of flowers in wicker baskets— courtesy of the spectacular Greentree gardens. The time they spent on Fisher's Island was always quiet and restful, a time of renewal.

When at home, Betsey kept very busy with a few select charities, all related to her role as Mrs. John Hay Whitney. Among these were the Museum of Modern Art, Yale University, and New York Hospital. However, probably the largest portion of Betsey's caring and time went to the North Shore Hospital. Once only a small village hospital, it grew under the auspices of the Whitneys and the Paleys into an impressive and respected medical center, known as the North Shore University Hospital. Jock and his sister, Joan, donated the fifteen acres on which the institution was built. The hospital came into being when, in the mid-forties, a group of Long Islanders saw the need for a regional hospital and pitched in seed money to show that they meant business. They then went to the Whitney family members for help. Plunging into the project with great energy, Joan and Jock rounded up the administrative and necessary medical expertise and donated $2 million to get the financial ball rolling. Jock's friends, Tex and Jinx McCrary, turned themselves into dervishes for the cause, roping in dozens of celebrities for benefits. As the hospital's president, Joan signed the construction contract for the first building, which opened in 1953. Together with

Betsey and Babe, she took an active hand in the interior design. Babe founded the Women's Auxiliary. Over the years the Whitneys continued to give support and leadership to what now stands as a major regional medical center.

In the years that followed their relatively public ambassadorial life in London, Betsey and Jock reverted to their very private, very low-key life. Betsey never had the flair or the figure to excel in fashion, as Babe did. Nor did she even try. She had always bought extremely expensive clothing, all beautifully tailored but decidedly on the conservative side. Givenchy was her favorite designer. In truth, at one point Betsey had made an effort to compete with Babe. Intimidated by her sister's high fashion profile, Betsey had soon given up on trying to make a fashion statement and had contented herself with being well and expensively dressed.

However, Betsey did excel on a par with her sisters in her role as chatelaine of Greentree. Boaz Mazor recently spoke of a visit he made to Greentree:

> Without question, it is the most magnificent private residence in America. It has the largest drawing room of any home I've seen in this country, with comfortable traditional furniture and lots of chintz and everything set off by those fabulous paintings collected over the years by Jock Whitney. And I might add that Betsey's teatime service is very special, with the most elegant and tasty tea sandwiches I've ever had anywhere. Incomparable!

While Betsey was happy and secure in her role of Mrs. Whitney and mistress of Greentree, Minnie did not fare quite so well. It seems almost certain that over the years she must have had an occasional doubt about her decision to abdicate her place as Mrs. Vincent Astor. Certainly she and Jim had their difficulties, and their marriage could not have been especially fulfilling, in a traditional sense. Nevertheless, Gogsie's deeply implanted legacy of stoicism enabled Minnie to persevere in her chosen path. Like her mother and sisters, Minnie did not look back once she had elected a given course of action.

The eldest Cushing sister continued to be active in the arts, both as a trustee of the Metropolitan Museum of Art and as a force behind struggling young artists. She offered them encouragement and also introductions to the right people. Her salon in New York had an international reputation. Their East Side apartment was constantly filled with famous and important people, whether for private parties or for fundraisers. Minnie was a great supporter of ANTA (American National Theatre). Another pet charity was the Henry Street Nursing Service.

After the move from their townhouse, Jim painted less and less. His health began to take a downward turn. Psychologically, he may well have been depressed. His depression may have resulted from his waning energy or may indeed have caused it. In any event, he seemed to feel that there was little left to live for. Certainly being married to Minnie made few demands on him. Their relationship had almost surely never been a sexual one, given his openly avowed homosexuality and the rumors surrounding Minnie regarding her sexual preference. From her earliest days in New York her close relationships with women friends had stirred gossip. As has been noted, Minnie shared her first apartment in New York with Cleveland department store heiress Kay Halle, a woman long thought to be a lesbian. And then, according to a close friend of all three Cushing sisters, it was revealed in a recent interview that Minnie may have had an affair with French actress Annabella; dress designer Valentina is another name that crops up in this regard.

With Jim doing so little painting, the Fosburgh marriage became strained. According to Jerry Zerbe, "As the years passed it was less and less fun going to Min's." Even so, Minnie did her very best to keep up appearances. Her closeness to her sisters, despite the subtle changes her marriage to Jim had wrought, became almost a refuge for Minnie. This closeness had always been a source of strength to all three Cushing sisters, and it may well have proved to be Minnie's salvation. She took great delight in her nieces and nephews. The Roosevelt girls, Sara and Kate, had always been particularly fond of their Aunt Min. As the years took their toll on her health, their visits were a great boon for Minnie.

Dorothy Dillon Eweson recalls, "Of all the sisters, Minnie was a real city girl, so I'm not surprised that the months spent at the Fosburgh camp in the Adirondack Mountains were trying for her."

As Minnie and Jim entered the decade of the seventies, they enter-

tained and traveled less frequently, primarily because of their frail
health. They did continue to entertain family and a relatively small
coterie of friends. Jerry Zerbe may have found these times less stimulating than they had been in the past, but most of the Fosburghs' close
friends still viewed Minnie's celebrated drawing room as the one place
in New York where they could meet highly amusing and intellectually
stimulating people. Even as her health declined, Minnie remained a
great salon hostess—perhaps the last New York hostess to maintain the
great eighteenth- and nineteenth-century European tradition of the artistic and literary salon.

20

***

BETRAYAL?

*A*PRIL of 1973 found Babe Paley in a Shanghai hospital, with a fever of 104 degrees. She and Bill had been on a whirlwind nonstop tour of China. Bill had been unrelenting in crowding twenty-four hours' worth of tourism into ten-hour days. Babe became physically incapable of going on. The Chinese physicians diagnosed her illness as pneumonia.

Amanda Burden remembers her mother's preparations for the trip to China. According to Amanda, Babe, who was not known for traveling light,

> was told that the luggage carriers there were older women. She decided to take only one suitcase with her because she said that she would be embarrassed to have her luggage carried by an older person and she wanted to be able to handle it by herself. . . .

Although Bill Paley showed proper concern over his wife's condition, even calling his own physician, Isadore Rosenfeld, in New York, he was

convinced that her illness was simply a routine and transitory problem
that could be cured with treatment and medication. Two weeks after
Babe's initial hospitalization, she and Bill returned home where she
immediately saw a battery of doctors, who confirmed that she did
indeed have a severe case of pneumonia and strongly advised that she
stop smoking. Although Babe followed their orders, her belated kicking
of this lifetime habit could not prevent the growth of a small tumor on
her right lung discovered in January of 1974. Babe checked into New
York Hospital for surgery. When the tumor turned out to be malignant,
the team of doctors, headed by Dr. Paul Ebert, removed a third of the
affected lung. They felt quite optimistic that they had checked the spread
of the cancer.

Sadly, their optimism proved to be not justified. A little over a year
later, in May of 1975, Babe entered Memorial Sloan-Kettering Cancer
Center, where doctors removed the remainder of her cancerous right
lung. Up to that point Babe had continued to entertain and travel her
usual social route on the town, if on a slightly reduced scale. After this
second surgery, she never really regained her old strength and verve.
Radically curtailing her social life, she did continue to see her sisters and
a few close friends—Irene Selznick, Slim Keith, Jeanne Murray Vanderbilt, Sibilla Clark, Truman Capote, Sister Parish, and Natalie Davenport. Everyone was well aware that she was only making a heroic effort
to keep up appearances.

Bill initially scoured the globe, looking for a magical cure that would
heal Babe. Invariably accustomed to having his own way, he simply
could not accept the idea that his efforts might be inadequate, that her
time might be limited, and that he might find himself without a "prized
possession." Most of the Paleys' friends perceived his solicitousness to
be as temporary as any of his moods or superficial interests.

Capote visited frequently. When Babe was strong enough, she continued to visit him at his United Nations Plaza apartment.

He was as attentive and supportive as ever during the health crisis in
Babe's life. Ironically, he chose that very moment to have one of the
chapters from his still-unfinished novel, *Answered Prayers*, published in
the November 1975 issue of *Esquire*. This novel, Truman believed,
would be the American equivalent of Proust's *Remembrance of Things*

Past. Unfortunately, Capote had become entangled in what he himself termed obsessive perfectionism, which led him to rewrite as many as thirty pages to change twenty words and to go months on end without writing anything at all. He had gotten a $750,000 advance in 1966 to write not only this book but two others, and was still struggling through *Answered Prayers* when the excerpt, entitled "La Côte Basque 1965," appeared. It was indeed the bombshell that Truman had hoped it would be, but he was in no way prepared for the violent reactions of his friends, who saw in it themselves and all their dirty linen aired in a most unflattering and revealing way.

Clearly, the little court jester considered his swans' confessions fair game. They knew he was not only a writer who drew on his experience but also a consummate gossip. As an old Spanish proverb so aptly states, "Whoever gossips to you will gossip of you." After hearing the tales Truman carried about their closest friends, how could they not have known that they were risking exposure of their most intimate secrets by entrusting them to him? Capote, like other writers then and now, found it convenient to cozy up to his subjects. Just as he had turned the confidences of the good people of Garden City, Kansas, into his tour de force, *In Cold Blood,* he stored up his swans' gossip and confessions against the day when he would produce an even greater work—or so he thought. That he was able to maintain their friendship for as long as he did was due quite simply to the fact that, while submerging himself in their glamorous fast-lane existence and overindulging in the idiosyncrasies that endeared him to them, he found himself incapable of producing the work that would forever bar him from their ranks.

The 13,000-word excerpt centered around a luncheon between "Lady Ina Coolbirth," a fortyish woman, many times divorced and on the rebound from an affair with a Rothschild, and the supposedly naive narrator, "Jonesy," at Henri Soule's haute monde Manhattan restaurant. While drinking champagne and eating a souffle Furstenberg, just across the room from Babe Paley and Betsey Whitney, Lady Ina gossips about the international set, telling all about everyone, including herself. Capote peopled his story with real persons, using their real names in some cases and thinly disguised pseudonyms in others.

The tales included that of "the governor's wife" and her sordid sexual encounter with a social-climbing Jewish tycoon, "Sidney Dillon," and another of the poor white-trash woman named "Ann Hopkins," who tricked a blue blood into marrying her and then murdered him after he discovered that she'd never divorced her first husband. Capote also carried tales of the Duchess of Windsor's never picking up the tab, Carol Marcos Matthau's foul mouth, Oona O'Neill Chaplin's fluffing off a youthful J. D. Salinger, and Joe Kennedy's taking sexual advantage of an eighteen-year-old school friend of one of his daughters. In fact, nearly everything that Truman Capote had learned on his constant rounds of society homes and haunts was there, in the pages of *Esquire,* for public consumption.

The story created instant scandal and consternation. The tale of the governor's wife and the social-climbing Jewish magnate could not possibly have been about anyone other than the late Marie Harriman and Bill Paley. In "La Côte Basque 1965," the governor's wife just happens to be lunching in the restaurant at the same time as Lady Ina and Jonesy, and Babe and Betsey. According to Lady Ina, Sidney Dillon had found himself sitting next to the governor's wife at a dinner party. He had always had an interest in her. The fact that she had once owned a Manhattan art gallery only made her more appealing. Since both his wife and the governor were out of town at the time, he invited the woman back to his Pierre Hotel pied-à-terre (certainly, a clear reference to the Paleys' apartment at the St. Regis), where he proceeded to lure her into bed. The encounter proved disappointing, for she had failed to warn him that she was menstruating. When she departed the pied-à-terre, according to Lady Ina's detailed account, she left the sheets covered with bloodstains. Naturally, the tycoon was frantic, since his wife was due back early in the morning and he had to do something about those stains. He began soaking the sheets in the bathtub and trying to get the blood out with the only thing he had on hand—a bar of Guerlain's Fleur des Alpes scented soap. At last he succeeded in removing the monstrous stains and then dried the sheets by baking them in the oven of his tiny kitchen. After all that he remade the bed, jumped in, and fell into a such a deep sleep that he never even heard his wife enter. When he awoke, he found a note on the bureau:

Darling,
You were sleeping so soundly and sweetly that I just tiptoed in and
changed and have gone on to Greenwich. Hurry home.

Of course Capote insisted that all Lady Ina's gossip was pure fiction,
but no one had any real doubts as to whom Capote was depicting in
such devastatingly intimate detail. And no one was immune. Lady Ina
managed to carry tales of Slim Keith, Fleur Cowles, Pamela Harriman,
and many of their friends. Perhaps most hurtful of all was the brutally
unflattering portrayal of the womanizing, social-climbing, deceitful
"Sidney Dillon" and his wife, "Cleo Dillon," who loved only herself.

Babe read the story the minute it hit the newsstands and was reported
to have called Slim Keith for her reaction. The only thing Babe got from
Slim was that the whole thing was a piece of fiction and should be
treated accordingly. Nevertheless, Babe reportedly got on the horn and
informed all her family members that, from that moment on, longtime
friend Truman Capote was persona non grata. Despite Babe's angry
retaliation, her close friends realized that the *Esquire* story had been
devastating for her. First and foremost Babe was loyal to her family,
always keeping the skeletons carefully locked away in the closet and the
dirty linen in the laundry. She could not interpret Truman's revelations
as anything other than complete and total betrayal. That the person she
viewed as her closest friend had so callously publicized her confidences
was almost more than she could bear.

Society's favorite rumor at that time was that Truman had phoned
Paley to ask him what he thought of "La Côte Basque 1965," and Paley
supposedly replied, "Well, I started it and dropped off to sleep, and
when I woke up, they'd thrown it out." When Truman protested that
it was important for Paley to read it, his old friend said wearily, "Truman, my wife is ill. I really haven't time for it."

It soon came to pass that almost all Capote's jet set friends, the
so-called Beautiful People, whom he had catered to all his working
career, turned their backs on their onetime bosom pal. Not only the
Paleys but the Whitneys (who had never really cottoned to Truman in
the first place), Gloria Vanderbilt, and Loel and Gloria Guinness,
among others, dropped him like a hot potato. The gilded doors on Park

and Fifth avenues that had for so long been welcomingly open to him slammed shut with a resounding thud—a sound that would ring in the author's ears and mind for what remained of his life.

The swans did not view gossiping among themselves in at all the same light as seeing that gossip in print. Undoubtedly Capote had taken some literary license to make the gossip even juicier for the general public. How could he not have known that his swans would be deeply angered and offended?

One friend of the Cushing sisters and a man-about-Manhattan saw Truman just a little differently: "He was such an enchanter, he could get anybody to talk. Before he became an alcoholic monster, they would tell him these crazy stories . . . Having Truman was like having your private court jester. He was magical."

Nevertheless, according to Joanne Carson, Johnny Carson's ex-wife, with whom Truman stayed in California at the time, he looked like a baby who had been slapped. Perhaps he felt that he had adequately disguised his subjects. Or he may even have thought that they would be amused by his ultimate bitchery, overlooking the segments where they themselves appeared in an unflattering light or interpreting their own scandalous characterizations as highly fictionalized. He didn't say anything to Joanne, but she would find him in his bedroom reading and rereading the section that appeared in *Esquire,* as if trying to figure out what had gone wrong.

For the record, he was feisty at first, saying things like "Wait till they see the rest; they'll have to go live in igloos in the North Pole." Then he was almost matter-of-fact, reasoning, "They always knew I was a writer; what did they expect?" And then he was sad, when he realized that he and Babe Paley would never again be friends. He had told a tale about a man everyone assumed to be her husband, even including an unkind word or two about Babe ("Cleo") herself. Still, Capote continued to tell any and all who would listen that Babe Paley had been his "best friend. I really loved her," he insisted. "One of the saddest things is that while she was sick I couldn't go to her."

Yet in many ways the nature of Truman's relationship with Babe and the others of her class made this end inevitable. With the 1948 publication of *Other Voices, Other Rooms,* his first literary success, he had become both the "in" writer and the most celebrated gossip in New York—twin talents that catapulted him into instant fame and stardom. He had become the darling of high society, the resident wit and intellectual of the Beautiful People. He had basked in the radiant light of their glamour and savored the sweet flavor of their social life, travels, and entertainments. And he had thrived in this rarefied atmosphere where bitchery, hauteur, and snobbery were the coin of the realm—a fact that made him very rich indeed. Capote had sipped the rare vintage wines and cruised on the enormous and luxurious yachts of the kings of society and industry. All the while he had tattled and told on everyone—and to everyone. As he spooned up the delicious souffles at La Côte Basque and other equally glamorous restaurants, he never failed to titillate them with the most outrageous current tidbits of gossip. He commanded their undivided attention, and they thought him the most entertaining little imp in Christendom.

At some level Truman Capote, like so many writers, had found sweet revenge in the written page. Capote viewed himself as a great talent who had gotten himself trapped into acting as court jester and father confessor to a group of society women. As Carter Burden stated, "You were always aware of that. Truman couldn't just come for the weekend and sit in his room. He had to amuse; he had to be happy."

For years and years, he had played the role that the socialites expected of him, realizing full well that his swans tolerated him only for his amusement value. He had been little more than an odd little mascot, a lightweight social climber who had always to struggle to please and entertain in order to remain in the good graces of his high and mighty society chums. He had also to market his homosexuality, which made him seem all the more manageable and "safe" among his bevy of beauties and their powerful husbands. Even as he reveled in his glamorous life, he must surely have felt resentment over the role he had to play. By publishing "La Côte Basque 1965," a small part of what he was convinced would be his masterpiece, he was letting them all know that he was just as powerful as they were. This obvious hostility and apparent ingratitude infuriated them.

For all his cuteness, Capote was essentially a first-class troublemaker. His screwball image, complete with open homosexuality, alcoholism, drug addiction, and a wildly eccentric way of dressing—as when he coupled a Savile Row jacket with a Black Panther T-shirt—was all part of a carefully crafted pose. This persona, along with his wit and true genius, was what enabled him to gain access to the gilded lives of his society darlings, his swans.

As the controversy swirled around him, Capote retaliated with a statement that clearly and bluntly revealed the resentment he had for so many years harbored over what he viewed as the Beautiful People's condescending attitude toward him. "Yes," he said, "they have always made that mistake about me! Why, if anybody was ever at the center of the world, it was me, so who is rejecting whom in this?" For all his bravado, Truman was heartbroken by the end of his carefully nurtured relationships.

Writer Patrick O'Higgins, an aristocratic, exuberant Irishman, a pal of Elsie Woodward's, had this to say of Truman Capote:

> [He's] gone downhill. People think, "What a shame that a great talent should be reduced to writing gossip." Some people are really hurt because they've been kind to him. The Paleys were always so fond of him. But Elsie hasn't been hurt. She didn't even read the piece. She couldn't care less. All she'll say is "Je ne le connais pas"—isn't that perfect?

Of course, as is almost always the case in social blow-ups, Capote had his defenders, as well as his detractors. Dotson Rader was among the former group, applauding the *Esquire* piece as

> Marvelous, beautiful writing. It's unimportant whether it's true or not, since it is presented as fiction. Truman was always treated by these people as a kind of curiosity, expected to do his act. That was humiliation coming from people who had no qualifications other than being rich and social. Everybody in the world has been telling Truman their deepest confidences for years and he never said he wouldn't use them.

Columnist Liz Smith, took a slightly different tack: "Staying alive and well in society," she wrote in *New York* magazine, "means never zigging when you should zag." And Truman of course had most definitely zigged.

An even more emphatic pro-Capote diatribe came from screenwriter Joel Schumacher—who was highly critical of society:

This same world (society) thinks it supports art and artists, but never understands that all a writer has is his experience. These people feel a good press is owed them. Why? In the fame-and-fortune game, whether it's society, show business, big business or politics, everybody lives on a plane of incomparable elitism, more money, more privilege than others. So why are they so shocked when anybody tells even a slightly unattractive truth about them?"

Truman also defended himself—loudly and repeatedly in private conversations, printed interviews, and even on national television.

I've been seriously writing this for three and a half years. I told everybody what I was doing. I discussed it on TV. Why has it come as such a great big surprise? This thing [the *Esquire* story] was only a chapter. My God, what will happen when "Unspoiled Monsters" comes out? . . . Lord, I have a lot to say, baby! I haven't even begun to say it, though the book is eighty percent written.

Capote considered his book-in-progress including the *Esquire* excerpt, to be a serious work of art, and honestly seemed unable to understand why his society friends would ostracize him. But ostracize him they did, with the exception of C. Z. Guest, whose late husband was a cousin of Winston Churchill. During all the uproar surrounding the appearance of the story, C.Z. said quite matter-of-factly, "Everyone knows the man's a professional, and they told him these things, anyway. He's a dear friend of mine, but I wouldn't discuss very private matters with him. I don't even know who these fictional people are."

Gloria Vanderbilt, who had not been quite so discreet as C.Z., said tersely, "I have never seen it [the *Esquire* piece] and have heard enough about it to know I don't want to." However, Gloria's husband at that time, Wyatt Cooper, expressed himself in far more depth:

I hate talking when my feelings are negative. It isn't constructive.
I'm very fond of Truman. We used to have lunch, gossip, and it
was fun. But lately it wasn't. His viciousness ceased to make it fun.
I even talked to him about it. . . . I think this destroys all the things
he has built up. He can't really pretend to sneer at these people in
the jet set. He worked too hard to be "in" himself. Of course
Gloria is offended! He made Carol Matthau come out tough and
bright, but Gloria vapid and dumb, in a very unfair way.

Of course, there was a great deal of truth to both C.Z.'s and Wyatt's
statements. Capote's Beautiful People knew all too well that he would
not hesitate to make the most outrageous statements about others, even
his closest friends—even about himself, for that matter. In an interview
with columnist Liz Smith, which appeared in *New York* magazine, he
blithely said,

As for my personal life, I don't care what anyone says or writes
about me personally. I have been a public exhibit all my life. So let
them go ahead and make me a monster. I was a beautiful little boy,
you know, and everybody had me—men, women, dogs, and fire
hydrants. I did it with everybody. I didn't slow down until I was
nineteen, and then became very circumspect. But everybody knows
where everybody else is sexually. There are no secrets, and that's
why I can't understand the shocked response to "La Côte Basque
1965!" What is all this business? Are all these people living in some
other medieval century? I'd never sue anyone for anything but I've
been lied about my whole life. I'm just surprised they don't hire a
hit man.

In fact, Slim Keith did consider suing and went so far as to consult
an attorney, but he and her friends advised her against this course of
action on the theory that it would serve little purpose other than to
create even more publicity for Capote.

Truman wrote two long letters to Babe, but both went unanswered.
He tried enlisting the aid of mutual friends to bring about a reconcilia-
tion with her—but to no avail. In fact, a valued employee of Babe's

recently recalled, "Friendship with Truman Capote ended abruptly with *Answered Prayers*. When Gerald Clarke, who was writing a biography of Capote, contacted Mr. Paley, he refused to cooperate."

Truman would never be able to make peace with Babe and Bill. According to a mutual friend of theirs and the other Cushing sisters', "Babe always spoke of Truman with total loathing as this 'snake' who had betrayed her."

So deep was the hurt that Babe was furious when her brother-in-law Jim Fosburgh maintained his friendship with Capote, frequently lunching with the author and also entertaining him at home. Babe constantly called to upbraid Jim. How could he show such disloyalty? she demanded. Yet behind these outbursts lay the sad truth that Babe, like Truman, had lost her best friend. Her sorrow was at least as great as her anger. For the most part, Babe suffered silently.

Not so Slim Keith, who had always had a hard-luck image. Although she gave up the idea of a lawsuit, she continued to campaign actively for revenge. She felt wronged and wanted to get even, apparently having forgotten that it had been Truman and Jack Dunphy who, while living in Spain, had taken her in and massaged her damaged ego at the time her husband dumped her for Pamela Churchill.

In order to escape some of the flack over his story, Truman fled to Southern California, where he played a very minor role in Neil Simon's movie *Murder by Death*. Capote's friend Joanne Carson had rented a Beverly Hills house for him and his lover at the time, John Knowles, an unemployed bartender. Joanne was one of Truman's most loyal friends during this difficult period of his turbulent life, and she remained loyal to the end.

In the late seventies, Babe's cancer seemed to have stabilized after treatments with interferon, then in an experimental stage. In the summer of 1977 she even felt well enough to cruise the Mediterranean with Bill aboard the Guinnesses' yacht. The sea air and the bonhomie seemed to be the perfect tonic for Babe, and she truly prospered. This turned out to be the last perfect moment in her life, for upon her return to New York, she went into a terminal decline.

To his credit, Bill Paley became genuinely concerned, perhaps for the first time, with the well-being of his gravely ill wife. Possibly this change of heart was due to the fact that he could no longer delude himself with the notion that his will would prevail, could no longer deny that he was going to lose her. He took great interest in all aspects of her care and treatment, hired private nurses to be with her around the clock, and was in constant touch with her doctors. Bill read medical journals almost obsessively, searching for any hint of a new or experimental cure for cancer.

The Paleys entertained less and less, and when they did have guests, Bill frequently played host alone, while Babe took what nourishment she could from a tray in her room. According to a close acquaintance of Babe's, who requested anonymity after a recent interview, "If she was up to it, guests came in after dinner to briefly pay their respects at her bedside."

The drugs and radiation caused Babe's hair to fall out—a horrifying reminder of what her daughter Kate had experienced since early childhood. Babe took to wearing wigs or winding a scarf around her head, turban fashion.

For a brief time, she and Amanda grew closer, probably because of Amanda's divorce in 1972 from Carter Burden, after eight years of marriage and the birth of two daughters. Perhaps both mother and daughter could empathize with each other's plight. Or perhaps Babe's envy had turned to admiration, especially of the courage it took for Amanda to leave her marriage and to go it alone. It is also entirely possible that Babe had begun to see Amanda not as a threat to her supremacy but as a means of gaining immortality. As Babe prepared to abdicate her throne, she could probably begin to see her beautiful daughter, once a potential usurper, as a suitable heir.

Hilary, Babe's stepdaughter, was frequently at her bedside, but Jeffrey continued to remain at a distance from the Paley household, a course he had chosen long before. Billie Paley began coming around to visit his mother once he realized the seriousness of her condition. Kate Paley, on the other hand, stayed away, unable to put aside the tremendous hurt she had suffered throughout her childhood from what she could only view as neglect or, even worse, rejection. Not even in Babe's final moments could Kate bring herself to let go of those old yet still painful feelings.

When Babe was up to seeing visitors, her secretary, Addie Wallace, would come into her room in the morning and post a list of the day's guests on a picture frame. Babe's son Tony came almost every morning on his way to work and returned almost every evening on his way home, bringing great joy to his mother and leaving little doubt in anyone's mind that her first-born child was indeed her favorite.

Patrick O'Higgins, himself a cancer victim, also became very close to Babe at this time. His wonderful, cheerful spirit and witty repartee were a source of pleasure to her, enabling her to forget her pain and troubles for a time. Boaz Mazor also joined the small circle of family and friends who gathered around Babe as she struggled for her life. A blithe spirit like O'Higgins, Mazor lent a degree of levity to Babe's final days. Meanwhile Babe, her parents' daughter to the end, took a stoic approach to her illness, maintaining an upbeat attitude about her prospects despite her realization by the mid-seventies that she was slowly but surely dying.

December of 1977 found the Paleys at their Lyford Cay home for their last Christmas together. Among their guests were Patrick O'Higgins and Hilary and Jeff Byers. Billie Paley also joined them, flying down later from his home in Washington, where he had recently begun a restaurant venture. His hippie appearance—long hair, a full beard, and a gold earring—did nothing to endear him to his father. Sibilla Clark also saw Babe on this last holiday in the sun.

The Paleys' return to New York was fraught with tragedy, for on New Year's Eve Hilary's husband, Jeff Byers, leaped to his death from the young couple's Manhattan duplex apartment. This handsome, blue-blooded Paley son-in-law was deeply in debt, and his suicide note spoke of mounting "business problems." This time, unlike other instances in the past, Bill Paley had refused to bail him out.

And Babe's illness was reaching its final stages. That winter and the early spring of 1978 her health continually deteriorated. A close Cushing-Paley observer who was in the household for many years recently commented:

Mrs. Paley was really amazing. She was never so thin! And as her health deteriorated, she got even thinner, but her face did not change at all. It was fantastic; it did not change at all. It was just as beautiful as before. She was not drawn at all. It was astonishing!

Bill Paley was shocked to find that as Babe's condition worsened, she became openly hostile toward him. Since the beginning of their marriage, she had silently borne his constant manipulation of her life. But once she was fully aware she was dying, she seemed to want to get back at him for all the indignities and slights he had caused her to suffer in the past. As her illness began to make greater inroads on her overall health, Babe no longer felt the need to play the role of the perpetually sunny-tempered Mrs. William Paley. She began to criticize him openly to colleagues and friends. According to Paley biographer Sally Bedell Smith, a senior CBS executive was stunned when Babe first called him to ask, "What's the old SOB doing today?" Smith cites another incident between then CBS network president Jack Schneider and Babe at a New York dinner party. "How do you put up with him?," Babe asked. "How do you stand him? We are going abroad tomorrow and I can't see how we will ever get off. He is so disorganized."

Perhaps it was therapeutic for Babe to let loose with an occasional diatribe against the man who had been her consort for thirty years. For his part, Paley remained extremely patient during the final years of Babe's illness. He continued to search out cures, consulting doctors both at home and abroad. Whenever he encountered doctors, he badgered them, inquiring about some new breakthrough in the battle against cancer. Friends of both Paleys were pleasantly surprised at Bill's genuine attentiveness, a quality he had rarely exhibited in the past.

He did not, however, go so far as to forsake his old habit of womanizing. In fact, to relieve the great pressure of Babe's illness and antagonism, he became involved with a thirty-year-old woman whom he had met casually at a New York social function. She was Jan Cushing, the soon-to-be-divorced wife of the old-guard New York and Newport socialite Frederick Cushing—no relation to the Cushing sisters. This old and illustrious family did not consider Dr. Harvey Cushing and his famous daughters to be social equals. Over the years they had made every effort to set themselves apart from the better-known Cushings. Jan had previously been married to slot-machine and casino magnate Del Coleman, and like Paley, she was Jewish.

Those who knew Jan and Bill never believed that theirs was a serious affair. Rather, Jan seemed to serve more as a sounding board for Paley's anguish over his wife's terrible illness and the barrage of invectives she was constantly leveling at him. Almost certainly this interlude was platonic rather than romantic. Within a few short months the pair, by mutual consent, stopped seeing each other. In any event, there was never any thought of marriage. In addition to being Jewish, Jan and Bill had one other thing in common: Both greatly valued their place in WASP society, and neither would ever have considered jeopardizing this status by remarrying anyone without WASP lineage and credentials.

During those last months, in the late winter and early spring of 1978, Babe rarely went out, and when she did, it was only to visit Minnie and Jim Fosburgh, both of whom were, by tragic coincidence, also suffering from cancer. Babe's family and friends were all too well aware that it was only a matter of time until Babe Cushing Mortimer Paley and her legendary beauty would slip into history.

And so, as if preparing for a royal death, these devoted individuals began their final vigil.

21

THE CURTAIN FALLS

*I*N 1930 the curtain had gone up on what would prove to be one of the longest-running shows in the history of American society. In that year Betsey Cushing had wed James Roosevelt, son of the most prominent and popular politician in the country, thus attaining instant stardom. With this wedding, really a dress rehearsal for the future brilliant marriages of all three Cushing sisters, Betsey found herself center stage in the world of top-drawer, blue-blooded society. While the constant glare of the limelight was most disconcerting, she did not despise the social recognition and elegant lifestyle that went with it. Soon her two sisters would join her on stage, and there they would remain, also in starring roles, for very nearly half a century.

In 1978 the curtain began to fall on what had most definitely been a hit. Part comedy, part tragedy, but always dramatic, the story of the lives and loves of the glamorous Cushing sisters had reached its final act. The early months of that year found both Babe and Minnie dying of cancer, more fragile than ever, and Jim Fosburgh in even worse shape, very nearly a recluse due to the severity of his own cancer. According to his sister-in-law Liza Fosburgh, "He almost never went out, and when he did, it was only to have lunch with longtime family friend Eddie Warburg. Those luncheons with Eddie were the sole exception!"

Fosburgh, a former glider pilot in the 101st Airborne Division, had crossed the Rhine with his unit and had also served with the first division that ultimately liberated Norway. He had inherited a comfortable estate and had enjoyed reasonable success as a still-life and portrait painter, selling his canvases to a limited but appreciative public. In fact, he was really quite a gifted portrait artist, and his painting of President John F. Kennedy now hangs in a place of honor in the Fifth Avenue apartment of Jacqueline Kennedy Onassis. In addition, through his wife's great ambition and flair, Jim Fosburgh had found himself at the very hub of the New York art scene, serving as host to some of the most brilliant and important people in the arts. An avowed homosexual, he had spent nearly a quarter of a century in a comfortable, companionable marriage to Minnie Cushing Astor, a union that allowed both partners the freedom to pursue their own interests within a more or less traditional framework. The marriage had worked relatively well for Jim and Minnie, enabling him to paint when so inclined without having to seek out a slot in academia and her to pursue her lifelong goal of becoming the greatest twentieth-century salon hostess and patron of the arts. The couple complemented each other without making great emotional demands.

In 1977 Fosburgh had come to the tragic realization that his days were limited; his cancer was inoperable. Minnie, also suffering from cancer, fell and broke her hip in August of that year. Clearly, weekend trips to their cozy country home, Cantitoe, in Katonah, had become a physical impossibility. And so it was that Minnie and Jim decided to sell the property to art dealer Richard Feigen. According to a friend in the art world, "Jim drank a lot and was sedated for cancer during this time. He was very hard to communicate with." The negotiations for the sale of Cantitoe were extremely difficult. At first Jim wanted to sell the contents of the house for $300,000, but Feigen declined because Jim could not make up his mind about precisely what he wished to include. Finally, Jim sold the house without the contents for $60,000.

Truman Capote continued to visit Jim and Minnie, the sole Cushing sister who would receive him socially. True to her gentle character, Minnie had never been able to bear a grudge. She had forgiven the impish author for his *Esquire* bombshell. Of course, Minnie had not found herself under personal attack from Capote's pen, as Babe and at least to some extent Betsey had. In any event, Minnie was undoubtedly glad to have Truman's company, for the long months of Jim's illness, coupled with his drinking and sedation, had made him less and less communicative. His final days were lonely and painful ones for her.

On April 23, 1978, at the age of sixty-seven, Jim Fosburgh succumbed to his cancer in New York's St. Luke's Hospital. He left behind an estate that totaled $767,542, a legacy of good if not great paintings, and a terminally ill widow. Minnie took the loss in typical Cushing style— stoically. This was not to say that she did not grieve for him; theirs had been a close, if not a sexual relationship, and Minnie now found herself very nearly alone in the world, too ill to go out or entertain.

Babe could give little more than moral support through a daily telephone call and an occasional visit when she herself felt up to venturing beyond her Fifth Avenue apartment. Betsey was nearly always occupied with the full schedule of being Mrs. John Hay Whitney and matriarch to her daughters, sons-in-law, and di Bonaventura and Haddad grandchildren. She did stay in daily touch via telephone. When in town from Greentree, she would visit Minnie's East Sixty-fourth Street apartment to give sisterly solace. One close friend of the Fosburghs maintains that Minnie suffered from Alzheimer's disease and also a drinking problem. An equally close friend disputed this claim on both counts, saying merely that Minnie was "very frail."

While Minnie dealt with her lonely widowhood and her own devastating illness, Babe's health had taken a decided turn for the worse. Finally, on Easter Sunday of 1978, she took to her bed, and the death watch began in earnest. What little entertaining had gone on at Kiluna and at 820 Fifth Avenue ceased completely. Only family and longtime intimate friends were permitted to see Babe in her Sister Parish–Albert Hadley bedroom, a room filled with exquisite French furniture and other pieces so typical of Babe's eclectic sense of style—among them the Chinese vermilion lacquer tea table and the dozens of interesting bibelots she had collected over the years. Dying as fashionably as she had lived, Babe was always perfectly made up and dressed in exquisite nightgowns and bed jackets.

On just one occasion did she leave her bedroom—to make her final journey to Kiluna, the beloved country home to which she had traveled so hopefully thirty-one years before. That last trip to Kiluna took place in June of 1978. Bill, Tony, and Amanda accompanied Babe in a golf cart for a last look at the magnificent gardens, with their dell and pristine pond—the gardens she had created with the help of gifted landscape architect Russell Page. Never having found the happiness and fulfillment she had sought throughout her life, Babe was determined at the very end to take with her the memory of beauty that she herself had created. This last view and bittersweet memory were hers forever. It had been in this garden in the years before her illness that she had spent hours, a colorful straw hat on her head and white cloth gloves on her hands, pruning, digging, and planting—totally free and totally herself.

In the course of this weekend, according to author Sally Bedell Smith, Betsey came over to see Babe, but instead of lending a sympathetic ear to her dying sister, she reportedly spent the entire visit carping about her own servants. This scene between the sisters was described to Smith by Babe's daughter Amanda, who was amazed to learn that the two sisters didn't get along too well. Although the middle and the youngest Cushing sisters had been in almost daily contact throughout their entire lives, they did not enjoy the special closeness that characterized Babe's relationship with Minnie. Even as Babe's life was slipping away, Betsey continued to feel intimidated by her still beautiful younger sister.

Returning to Manhattan for the last time, Babe again took to her bed. According to a member of the Paley household, during the last years of her life

she just stayed in bed. She slept most of the time (regularly medicated with morphine, although refusing to be hooked up to tubes) or listened to the radio or looked at old movies. She liked the old Sherlock Holmes films. She also liked the old films of Paul Newman. Anyway, that's what she did most of the time. She just slept or listened to music, which I'm not sure she even heard, and

eventually she gave up on the television. Entertaining was altogether over. Mr. Paley's family came by almost every night to have
dinner with him. His daughter Hilary was around. Jeff [Paley] was
up in New England, I think. Certainly Tony came by, and his wife,
Siri, was just wonderful during this difficult period.

Referring to Babe's children, this same close observer of the Paley
household stated,

I don't want to discuss [them]. There were six of them. The most
devoted was Tony because he came by every single morning on his
way to work and every single night on his way home. Tony was
truly fond of his mother. I think the others all had dollar signs in
their eyes. Rich kids . . . on their way to becoming richer.

This may indeed have been how at least some of Babe's children and
stepchildren felt. They may well have rationalized that the inheritance—
the money and other worldly goods—that they would ultimately receive
from their parents was a sort of compensation for all the affection and
attention that they had missed out on during their childhood in the Paley
household. Of the six offspring only Tony can be said to have had a
really loving relationship with his mother; so it is little wonder that the
others could not and did not suddenly become close to Babe as she lay
on her deathbed. But perhaps there were feelings of regret, regret for the
relationships that might have been but never were.

As the last weeks wore slowly on, and Babe's life seeped away little
by little, she was more often than not in a semiconscious state. In her
cogent moments she continued to receive close friends and family for tea
or drinks at her bedside. In true Cushing style, Babe never allowed
conversation to dwell on her illness. Nevertheless, everyone—including
Babe—was well aware that she was approaching the final moments of
her life.

July 5, 1978, was Babe's sixty-third and last birthday. Needless to say,
it was not a festive occasion. According to one of the Paleys' longtime
staff members,

The family began to gather late that afternoon and they maintained their vigil until early the next morning, when she died attired in an imported lace bed jacket, her bald head beautifully wrapped in a silk turban and her face made up to perfection (a chore she herself took care of the previous night).

True to her image to the very end, Babe Cushing Mortimer Paley went out in style. Her daughter Kate, who had for so long kept her distance, arrived just in time to witness her mother's last hour of life.

The family summoned Steve Ross, who at the time was dating Amanda Burden (they would marry in December 1979, only to divorce less than two years later). Brooklyn-born Ross started his business career in his then father-in-law's funeral-parlor business before becoming a media mogul in his own right. Out of nostalgia he retained his mortician's license, thus proving invaluable to the Paleys at the time of Babe's death. Ross helped to make arrangements for Babe's body.

On the Saturday following Babe's death, services were held at Manhasset's Christ Episcopal Church. Some five hundred mourners, led by a stooped and saddened Bill Paley, were in attendance. After the service, guests gathered for a beautiful al fresco luncheon, completely orchestrated by Babe herself, almost as if her perfectionism had reached out from the grave. For months prior to her death she had planned every last detail of this farewell to her family and friends. A corps of white-coated waiters stood on the porch at Kiluna, serving Babe's favorite wine, a Pouilly-Fume de Ladoucette, as well as champagne. Babe's fine and stylish touch was evident in every morsel and decoration: the beautiful flowers, the elegant menu, the lovely place settings—silverware wrapped in napkins fashioned to look like flowers and arranged in wicker baskets on the tables that dotted the vast lawn. Spiritually Babe was present, presiding over one of her finest entertainments, complete with all the elegant details that were her trademark.

Thousands of condolences continued to pour in for weeks, but none of the kind words of admiration and praise would have pleased Babe more than the comments by the fashion professionals. *New York Times* columnist Enid Nemy wrote,

In that decade, she was to many the ultimate symbol of taste and perfectionist chic, the inspiration for manequins that lined the windows of Lord & Taylor and countless sketches, photographs and articles in magazines and newspapers throughout the country.

Babe would no doubt also have been very pleased to know that Monsieur Marc, her hairdresser, who had shared so many lunches and traded so many recipes with her, reminisced about her warmth rather than her glamour. "Everyone imagined her to be very stiff and snob-bish," he recalled. "But she wasn't like that. She remembered everyone's name, and she was always interested in their families." And this, no doubt, was just the sort of eulogy Babe would have wished for. Her fashion image was her vocation; her warmth and kindness were her essence. And in the long run friends and friendships were what mattered most to her.

She must have been aware that her perfection could be intimidating, could create an unjust but understandable impression of coldness. As Truman Capote had so aptly written in an essay published in *Harper's Bazaar*—surely with Babe in mind—

> The advent of a swan into a room starts stirring in some persons a decided sense of discomfort. If one is to believe these swan allergies, their hostility does not derive from envy, but, so they suggest, from a shadow of "coldness" and "unreality" the swan casts. Yet isn't it true that an impression of coldness, usually false, accompanies perfection?

Boaz Mazor recently reminisced about his first impression of Kiluna, based more on the warmth than the obvious wealth and glamour:

> [An entire room painted in faux malachite] sounds terrible when you say it, but it was beautiful. The whole atmosphere was com-fortably elegant. They were very cozy people; nothing stuffy. Food was always the best. There were always masses of servants, but always invisible. You hardly noticed them. They did not make a fuss.

Toward the end of her life, however, Babe worried less about one-upmanship and more about the quality of her friendships. She became very close to writer Patrick O'Higgins because, Mazor maintained, she "became fond of anyone who had cancer . . . O'Higgins was invited to every Paley dinner party, and she talked to him for an hour each day on the phone." Clearly, in those last days she desperately needed to confide in someone who would understand what she was going through—and she no longer had Truman Capote's shoulder to cry on. While Babe did speak daily with Minnie, it is doubtful that the younger sister would have unburdened herself to the elder, who was just as ill at that time and was also suffering from the loss of her husband to the same disease. O'Higgins, on the other hand, was extremely upbeat, and his humor coupled with his empathy were just what Babe must have needed.

She did not just lie on her bed of affliction and wallow in self-pity, crying on every available cancer victim's shoulder. That simply was not her style. Always so busy, creative, and organized throughout her life, she somehow managed to perfect the art of dying. In addition to dotting every "i" and crossing every "t" in her elaborate plans for her al fresco luncheon, Babe took great pains to spell out in great detail exactly what she was leaving to whom. Considering the size of her estate—especially the huge number and variety of personal effects—this was no mean feat.

Babe left an estate totaling more than $8 million—all of it acquired during her tenure as the wife of William S. Paley. Of that amount $4.2 million was in stocks and bonds, $3.8 million of which was in CBS stock alone. Another $1.6 million consisted of tangible personal property, mostly jewelry ($1.1 million). It is important to note that these figures were quoted in 1978 dollars—and so were far lower than they would be today.

Babe established trust funds of approximately $235,000 apiece for her children and stepchildren. In the early 1960s she had set up separate trust funds for Tony and Amanda totaling nearly $300,000 each. To her seldom-heard-from brother, Henry Kirke Cushing, she bequeathed $50,000. She also remembered her private secretary, Adelaide Wallace, to the tune of $35,000, and her personal maid, Winifred Dooney, with $15,000. Babe's alma mater, the Westover School, got $30,000.

Friends and family had their suspicions as to whether Bill Paley faithfully honored Babe's wishes and followed precisely her plan for distributing her jewelry and other valuables. Before her death she had carefully and thoughtfully allocated every single item, fastidiously noting each selection on a file card. In fact, she had even managed to wrap many of the gifts in colorful paper and place them on the shelf of her dressing room closet.

As was expected, Tony and Amanda came away with the greatest share of Babe's exquisite jewelry collection. Tony received a total of $182,500's worth, including spectacular earrings by Babe's favorite jewelry designer, Fulco di Verdura, set with two pear-shaped emeralds weighing in at approximately 44.48 carats and thirty-four round diamonds ($22,500). Also on Tony's list was a Van Cleef & Arpels ring, with a magnificent 30.92-carat cabochon emerald surrounded by thirty-four round diamonds weighing approximately 7 carats ($150,000). To her favorite child Babe also left a Camille Corot painting, *L'Atelier de Corot,* which was to remain with Bill Paley during his lifetime ($60,000). Tony's wife, Siri, a great favorite of Babe's, was a recipient of her mother-in-law's largesse. Siri's share of the jewelry came to a whopping $240,500 and included, among other items, a $2,000 Verdura-designed "blackamoor" clip and two pearl bracelets—one of natural black pearls with a platinum, diamond, and black and white pearl clasp, and the other of white cultured pearls with a similar clasp. Each of these bracelets contained sixty-two rough diamonds weighing approximately 5 carats ($7,500). Babe also left Siri a fabulous Australian cultured pearl necklace by Cartier, with twenty-eight pearls, an assortment of pear-shaped, marquise, and round diamonds, and a dazzling clasp set with fifty round diamonds ($45,000).

Amanda's portion of her mother's jewels came to $275,950. Among the items Amanda received was a $125,000 Harry Winston necklace of gold and diamonds—18 old mine-cut diamonds totaling around 25.57 carats and 20 old mine-cut diamonds weighing in at a total of 128.13 carats. Babe also left her first daughter a unique Verdura canary diamond ring, valued at $65,000. The huge 21.25-carat yellow diamond topped a special gold and diamond crown setting. Also in Amanda's bequest were Danos-designed earrings encrusted with 72 sapphires and 322 canary diamonds weighing about 22 carats ($11,500).

Hilary Paley Byers received a total of $68,000 in jewelry, which included a Cartier ram's-head bracelet set with coral and 58 baguette diamonds weighing roughly 6 carats ($8,000) and a Van Cleef & Arpels necklace of 18-carat gold, 27 baroque pearls, and 157 diamonds ($20,000). Babe also left Hilary one of her blonde Russian sable coats, valued at $3,500. Hilary's daughter Brook received $46,500's worth of her step-grandmother's jewelry, all to remain with Hilary until Brook reached her majority. Among these items were a clip of 18-carat gold and platinum with 7 reversible diamond leaves, with 175 round diamonds totaling 10 carats ($5,000), and an 18-carat gold and platinum Schlumberger "starfish" clip, with a pear-shaped emerald weighing around 3.33 carats, 118 oval sapphires weighing approximately 41.20 carats, 97 diamonds totaling about 3.24 carats, and 20 pear-shaped diamonds coming to 2.30 carats total weight.

Babe had originally decided not to leave any of her jewelry to her daughter Kate, but just before her death, Babe relented and decided to leave Kate a bequest worth about $30,500. The major portion of this gift was a stunning Schlumberger turquoise, gold, and diamond necklace set with 660 diamonds weighing about 1.72 carats ($22,500). Kate also received a gold and coral Panos choker worth $2,500 and a James Fosburgh painting entitled *Mittens,* appraised at $400. Billie Paley came away with even less—only $3,600 in jewelry, including a stunning but relatively modest Verdura ring of gold and cultured half pearls set with 32 diamonds totaling around 1 carat. Babe also left Billie a $1,000 gold and enamel bracelet.

Always so concerned about her friends, Babe did not forget them in her will. Diana Vreeland, who had befriended Babe early in her fashion career, received a $5,000 gold and enamel Faberge powder box. The round box was enameled in white and bordered with ciselé laurel. To Gloria Guinness went an ivory and tortoiseshell jewelry casket ($3,500). Natalie Davenport got a pair of carved and painted wood busts ($500), and Lady Anne Evelyn Beatrice Tree, wife of the Duke of Beaufort, received a magnificent Italian gold and green enamel horse pendant on a gold chain ($10,000). To Sister Parish went a pair of gilded carved wood Regency consoles ($1,000) and also a pair of Meissen porcelain lions on gilded bronze bases ($2,500). For her niece Sara Roosevelt Wilford Babe reserved $4,000 worth of bequests, including a jade bead bracelet with a diamond clasp ($2,000) and a plaster female figure by Eli Nadelman ($2,000), as well as miscellaneous clothing. For her other niece, Kate Roosevelt Whitney, there was a platinum ball bracelet with a twisted lapis lazuli fringe and a clasp with one carved 15-carat emerald, forty-two diamonds totaling approximately 2 carats, and twenty pear-shaped sapphires weighing around 6 carats ($2,000). In addition, Kate received a bronze-finished brass elephant cart with enamel panels painted with butterflies ($850), a small decorative watercolor of an anemone ($100), and other items that brought her total inheritance to $3,800. Socialite Jean Stein Vanden Heuvel got a Bulgari Oriental gold coin on a gold snake chain ($500). C. Z. Guest received a Chinese porcelain box decorated with trailing vines in red and green and yellow ($1,000). Longtime friend Susan Mary Alsop was left a necklace of carnelian and black onyx beads, pearls, gold, and enamel ($1,750). And to Jane Engelhard Babe left a gold "Little Prince" perfume bottle with caliber emeralds and sapphires ($1,800). Slim Keith's small bequest consisted of a pair of Japanese ceramic crab tureens, valued at $200. The cognoscenti speculated that this minimal gift might have been Babe's way of voicing her long-held suspicion that her husband and Lady Keith had enjoyed an on-again, off-again dalliance over the years. Babe also left a Chinese porcelain figural group to the doyenne of New York society, Brooke Astor. Apparently Babe and Betsey did not see eye to eye on the subject of Brooke Astor.

Bill Paley received such tangible personal property as furniture, silver, china, jewelry, a number of decorative objects, and two paintings: a still life by Berthe Morisot ($35,000) and an Edouard Vuillard entitled *The Windows* ($45,000). Paley and Tony Mortimer were the executors of Babe's estate.

Much of the magnificent furnishings of the Paley apartment at 820 Fifth Avenue went under the auctioneer's hammer at Sotheby's on October 4, 1991. Babe and Bill Paley, long known as discerning collectors of both decorative and fine art, would have been pleased to know that most of the items offered at auction went for far more than the reserve price on each item.

The Paley art collection, containing masterpieces by Picasso, Matisse, Gauguin, and Cézanne, was bequeathed to the Museum of Modern Art, which plans to exhibit the collection in early 1992.

On October 24, 1991, Sotheby's auctioned off a very modest assortment of jewelry owned by both Babe and Bill Paley. Perhaps the highlight of that offering was a fourteen-karat-gold money clip with a sketch of CBS star Jack Benny, given to the media mogul by the famed comedian. Its reserve price was $500, and it went for $2,640. The sales proved that the mystique surrounding both Babe and Bill Paley was still with us.

True to the old cliché, Bill Paley only began to appreciate what he had had with Babe after he lost her. Although he never lacked for female companionship, he was often very lonely and depressed. Even at Babe's funeral a handful of elegant, mercenary ladies—many of them Babe's friends—began to maneuver into position to capture the bereaved widower. They were not particularly circumspect about their intentions, but try as they would, they could never replace the remarkable woman who had catered to her husband's every whim while maintaining her glamour and dignity. That hers was a tough act to follow did not discourage the determined husband hunters. These predatory ladies went to great lengths in their attempts to snare the wealthy, powerful Bill Paley. So avid were they in their pursuit that Taki, the *Esquire* columnist, wrote about them in the January 1979 issue, noting:

> Jet Set vamps are locked in mortal combat for CBS's chairman. . . .
> However natural it is to wish to tread in Babe's elegant and expensive footsteps, it is not easy. But since greed is the second most powerful emotion after fear, there is a swarm of plutocracy-mad ladies eager to try. Ironically, though typically, the pursuing females are all very rich. But the difference between say $20 million and $500 million is what the game is all about.

Taki chose to give these aggressive women fish names. Jackie Onassis and her sister Lee Radziwill were tagged the barnacle sisters. Francoise de la Renta (late wife of Oscar de la Renta) was the barracuda. Marjorie Downey, owner of the Houston branch of Ciro Jewelers, was given the title of stingray, while Helen Rochas, the elegant owner of Rochas perfumes, was simply the shark. "Goldfish" Evangeline Bruce, widow of former ambassador to Britain (who got his fortune from his first wife,

Ailsa Mellon), was the top contender. Paley particularly admired Evangeline's patrician background, strikingly similar to Babe's. At around this time a close friend of Bill's commented wryly, "Bill is lucky. If it weren't for Evangeline's widowhood he would have turned gay— just to get away from all those women."

Evangeline did not make it to the altar with Paley. He continued to pursue feminine companionship as strenuously as he was pursued. Another serious contender in the Paley claiming race was Grace Dudley, the third wife and widow of the Earl of Dudley, who had left her a considerable fortune. In the end, Grace decided to hang on to her title and coronet instead of taking a chance on a footloose commoner like the peripatetic Paley.

Within a month of Babe's death, Bill Paley was seen everywhere and was entertaining nonstop to fill the void in his life. He enlisted the aid of Francoise de la Renta in planning the dinner parties and sorting out all the minute details he had always burdened Babe with. While Francoise lacked Babe's social credentials, she had always been a quick study. Many people credited her with having masterminded her husband's success in the fashion world. She had long since taught herself the fine art of entertaining and had become an accomplished hostess. Now, with Francoise serving as Bill's substitute hostess, people who would never have passed muster at Babe's table began turning up at 820 Fifth Avenue. It was no secret among those in the know that, during Babe's reign, an invitation from the Paleys meant instant acceptance into top-drawer New York society. Francoise began to see that invitations went out to a whole new crowd, including Barbara Walters, onetime model Barbara Allen, art gallery owner Bill Acquavella, CBS executive Thomas Wyman, and Frank Sinatra. The tart-tongued Lady Slim Keith was also a frequent visitor, often serving as an alternate hostess for Bill Paley.

According to Paley biographer Lewis J. Paper, it was a difficult period for the seventy-seven-year-old widower:

To help cope with the depression, Paley began to drink. He had never been more than a social drinker, sometimes having cocktails before dinner or wine with dinner. But now, as one friend commented, "He began to put down a lot of vodkas." There were embarrassing moments for colleagues and friends, but no one had the courage to say anything to the chairman of CBS—until a female friend bluntly told him that he was drinking too much. Paley was incredulous. When Paley casually asked a longtime servant whether he thought he might be drinking too much, the servant replied, almost casually, "Why, of course. Don't you remember that I had to put you to bed last night?" Paley did not remember, and it scared him. That was the end of his drinking.

The tragedy of Bill's life during the period following Babe's death was not so simply corrected. He successfully fought off forces at CBS who wished to push him into retirement, remaining at the helm for another six years, not retiring until the age of eighty-three. Although he had more female companionship than he wished for, Bill Paley was a lonely, unhappy man. Paper provides additional insight into Bill's problems during this difficult period,

> Babe filled a need that no one else could, and he felt lost without her. He would call friends and say, 'I can't be alone, can you please come out to dinner?' There were many people who cared about Bill Paley, and they were disheartened by what they saw. Babe actually thought he'd marry within a year.

For nearly two years after Babe's death he was very disoriented. He never did remarry.

Bill found that he could not return to Kiluna, so much Babe's creation and so filled with memories. He wound up selling the property to developer Ed Klar for $6 million. Klar put up a group of ninety middle-class commuter homes, in a development that he named Stone Hill. According to Boaz Mazor, Bill had promised Babe years earlier that he would never sell Kiluna and that the dell with its pond and magnificent surrounding woods would become a national park in her memory. The original white clapboard house and the children's cottage burned down in a blaze set by arsonists in February 1990. So between the sale to a developer and the fire, Kiluna became only a memory for Bill Paley, the children who grew up there, and the legion of friends who over a thirty-year period were the recipients of Babe Paley's legendary hospitality.

As Bill Paley pursued and was pursued by a bevy of high-profile international beauties, mourning in his own unconventional way the loss of the woman who had been his mainstay for thirty-one years, so Mary "Minnie" Cushing Astor Fosburgh was becoming more and more reclusive, largely because of her own illness. Her cancer, like her late husband's, was inoperable. She saw no one but close family members and such longtime friends as Mr. and Mrs. Edward Warburg, Dorothy Dillon Eweson, Jerry Zerbe, and her neighbors, the Alan Grovers. On November 4, 1978, she died in her Manhattan apartment—just four months after the death of her favorite younger sister. Services for Minnie Fosburgh took place at St. Thomas Church on Fifth Avenue at Fifty-third Street.

While Minnie may have lost her hold on a great fortune, she did not die impoverished. In fact, according to her will, which was filed for probate on June 15, 1982, nearly four years after her death, she left a gross estate of slightly over $9 million, actually topping the total dollar amount of Babe's will. Compared to her incredibly wealthy sisters, Minnie had lived on a shoestring, and yet she had managed to live well and wisely, enjoying those luxuries that really mattered to her while tripling the divorce settlement she had won from Vincent Astor. Part of that settlement—$800,000—reverted to his foundation upon her death, per the agreement at the time of the divorce. Even so, Minnie left a whopping estate, and not surprisingly, she was as generous in death as she had been in her lifetime, providing handsomely for her family, friends, and favorite charities.

Niece Leila Wilson Brown received $76,000, as did Amanda Burden. Minnie also left slightly over $70,000 to her brother, Henry Kirke Cushing, and the same amount to each of his three sons, Kirke, Michael Reed, and William Harvey. Her other Fosburgh nieces and nephews each inherited $74,000, while her favorite nephew, Tony Mortimer, got the nice round figure of $100,000. Kate Paley did not do nearly so well, and her brother Billie came out even worse; she inherited only $11,000, and he received only $2,700—far less than Minnie's maid, Maude Herlihy, who wound up with $10,000. Sister Betsey's bequest totaled $97,000, while that of her daughter Kate Roosevelt Whitney Haddad came to $4,000. Minnie's sister-in-law Leila Fosburgh Wilson was left $35,000. Minnie was also very generous with a number of institutions—principally City Center of Music and Drama ($367,000), New York Hospital ($200,000), the Metropolitan Museum of Art ($2 million), and Yale University ($3 million).

While her jewelry and personal effects were not nearly in the same league as Babe's, Minnie did leave some nice pieces to family and friends. Amanda Burden inherited gold, pearl, and diamond earrings. Truman Capote, persona non grata to so many of Minnie's socioeconomic class, received a painting entitled *Painting of a Cat,* by H. Shikler, and a dark brown Japanese porcelain rabbit. To her sister-in-law Mrs. Henry Kirke Cushing, Minnie left her cultured pearls—a single strand, a double strand, and the extra pearls, which she had kept in a safe. For niece Kate Roosevelt Whitney Haddad there was a pearl, diamond, and gold mermaid, and for niece Kate Paley, the less favored of Gogsie's namesakes, Minnie left a topaz necklace and earrings and the set of six black lacquer and gold Regency chinoiserie side chairs, which had originally belonged to Gogsie. Minnie's favorite nephew, Tony Mortimer, inherited a gold cigarette box with a jeweled train, a Sargent watercolor entitled *Peter Harrison,* and a painting by Babe, which she had called *Small Fry.* Betsey received a gold and blue enamel snuffbox with a diamond initial and a drawing of Gogsie by Raymond Crosby. Jock was remembered with a green Faberge picture frame containing a photo of Betsey. Babe, who had predeceased Minnie, had not been removed from the will. She was to have received a gold snuffbox with enameled flowers and a James Fosburgh painting, *Blue Towel.* According to reliable sources, these items went into Babe's estate.

Minnie's numerous friends received lovely personal items, too. Designer Main R. Bocher got a handsome pair of turquoise cufflinks with tiny rubies, which had formerly belonged to Minnie's mother. To Kitty Carlisle Hart went green enamel, gold, and diamond ivy leaf earrings. Henry and Drue Heinz received a gilt bronze toad and a jeweled fish clip, and Minnie even remembered Helen Lytle Hull, the first

Mrs. Vincent Astor, with a pair of white and gold Frankenthal porcelain sauce boats. To the Viscountess Lambton Minnie left a pink topaz ring in a gold setting, and to her friend Annabella Power (Tyrone's ex) a pair of earrings, each with one white and one black pearl and diamond accents. Mary Warburg inherited a round quartz clock with diamond hands, while actress Irene Worth got a gold Greek coin mounted on a gold, blue, and green enamel clip. And finally, the Duc di Verdura was left a pair of marble and bronze ram's head candlesticks and a painting of two ladies by an unknown artist.

The bulk of Minnie's estate consisted of art, and among those works that went to the Metropolitan Museum of Art were Cézanne's *In the Valley of the Oise,* Toulouse-Lautrec's *Portrait of Monsieur Grenier,* Manet's *Spanish Dancers,* and Constable's *Landscape.* The Yale University art gallery received Corot's *Plain of the Beauce,* Homer's *Dunes at Marshfield,* Renoir's *Petites Roses,* Gainsborough's *Rustic Landscape,* and Sevres's *Bust of Jefferson.*

Minnie had followed her mother's plan to the letter of the law, marrying one of the wealthiest and most socially prominent men in the United States. Although she had then broken the mold by renouncing Astor and his multiple millions, she had nevertheless managed to invest her relatively small divorce settlement wisely, so that she could live as well as she wanted to, enjoy the freedom of pursuing her own direction in life, and leave an estate that would be considered enormous by anyone but an Astor, Paley, or Whitney. With great diligence and a connoisseur's eye, along with the astute judgment of her second husband, she had built a fine, although not enormous, eclectic art collection. This collection, plus an infinite number of fond memories of her great gentleness and staunch loyalty, would create a fine monument to the eldest of Kate and Harvey Cushing's fabulous daughters.

22

THE SURVIVORS

*W*ITH Babe and Minnie gone, Betsey was the sole survivor of the legendary trio of Cushing sisters. As young women, they had stormed out of Boston and without so much as a tiny skirmish secured a favored spot in the loftiest ranks of blue-blooded American society. Definitely upper middle-class young debutantes, the sisters had, with a subtle shove from the velvet glove of their iron-fisted mother, taken the fateful step upward to live the incredibly wealthy and glamorous lifestyle that every red-blooded American woman of their era dreamed of. The famed sisters' phenomenal marital success stories had begun with Betsey—and with her it will eventually end. From that June day in 1930 when she wed Jimmy Roosevelt, she had left no doubt about her social and financial aspirations. Of all Kate Crowell Cushing's children, Betsey was the one who most closely adhered to her mother's ambitious game plan, the one who came nearest to perfection by those exacting standards.

Some keen observers of New York society in general and the Cushing sisters in particular formed the habit of referring to them as "the East-

Side Gabors." But others more accurately compared the Cushings to the glamorous and intriguing Soong sisters of China—the supreme dragon ladies of the twentieth century, famed for the brilliant marriages they had made.

Ai-ling Soong wed banker-politician H. H. Kung. Of the three sisters, she had the most spontaneous and kindly manner. Elegant and with a great interest in her surroundings, she was in many ways like Babe Cushing. Ching-ling Soong married Dr. Sun Yat-Sen, the most important revolutionary leader of modern China and its first president. Ching-ling, a woman of great self-control and austerity, with a harmoniously integrated personality and a quiet way of dressing, was the most independent-minded of the sisters—and the most like Minnie. Also like Minnie, Ching-ling had eventually opted for power and freedom over wealth and glamour. And Mei-ling Soong, who wed Generalissimo Chiang Kai-Shek and whose great beauty was concentrated in her wonderfully expressive eyes, was often compared to Betsey. Mei-ling, like Betsey, was a woman of quiet chic which stemmed from a natural quality rather than from effort. She also had a tremendous sense of loyalty to her family.

Now that both Babe and Minnie were dead, Betsey turned her undivided attention to her ailing husband. Her life centered around the ongoing tasks of making Jock's final years as comfortable as possible and tightening her hold on the Whitney millions. Jock had never really recovered from the massive coronary he had suffered in 1976 at Greenwood Plantation. His only hope for recovery was rest. This, of course, meant limiting his countless activities, a herculean task for a man who had always been so active and who had always had so many interests. Although he and Betsey hoped he would be able to resume nearly normal routines, the sad truth was that the life of John Hay Whitney was slowly but surely ebbing away.

His famed Greentree Stable had not had a winner in a number of years, and sadder still, the day came when he had to close down his beloved *New York Herald Tribune*. Of all his many business roles, that of publisher was the one he cherished most; he loved the daily meetings in the Front Page Session Room, where he and editor James Bellows, along with the other top editorial staff, congregated at 3:30 to put together the next day's front page. Jock Whitney had given such youthful stylists as Dick Schaap and Jimmy Breslin their first real opportunity to sound off, and under Jock's aegis political gossip columnists Rowland Evans and Robert Novak had become household names. Now Jock could only reflect on his past glories, especially on the many, many philanthropic deeds he and his vast fortune had effected. Unlike many multimillionaires of his generation, the Dodge brothers of automobile fame or F. W. Woolworth, the dime-store baron, for example, Jock Whitney had committed much of his wealth to good deeds and had dedicated his life to public service; he was not only a philanthropist but a humanitarian. The John Hay Whitney Foundation had, almost from its inception, been in the forefront of the civil rights movement, working to provide equal opportunities for people of all races long before such ideas had become fashionable.

In 1970 the foundation had begun to change its direction, largely due to the leadership of its new president, Archibald L. Gillies, a liberal Republican and onetime close aide to Nelson Rockefeller. Under Gillies's guiding hand and with the full support of Jock Whitney, the foundation began to broaden the scope of its programs, phasing out the Opportunity Fellows program, which provided grants for the humanities, in order to face the challenge of eradicating inhumanities. The new focus was on helping individuals—from low income and minority groups—who were trying to make institutions, such as schools and governments, work better for the people they serve. With these changes set into motion, Whitney and Gillies brought in directors from outside, including two very high-profile black leaders—Vernon Jordan, of the Urban League, and Franklin A. Thomas, who had made his mark in the public sector as head of the Bedford-Stuyvesant Restoration Corporation, which had been set up in 1967 to rebuild one of Brooklyn's sorriest slums.

Recently Gillies reminisced about the early years at the John Hay Whitney Foundation:

> There was a nine-member board, which included in addition to Jock, Betsey, daughters Sara and Kate, Jordan and Thomas and a number of well-known names in the field of education. Betsey was

definitely an active member of the board. She was not without her own opinions; nor was she just deferential to Jock.

Sara and Kate were also very committed board members, according to Gillies. "Kate's interest in the field of education lent itself to many of the foundation's projects. Sara [was less engaged than Kate], but then, she had a lot going on in her life; her divorce from di Bonaventura . . ." Gillies went on to say,

> Let me take a moment to point out that it was very challenging to work with Jock. He did not worry about the unconventional aspects of what people were doing as long as they did it well. He wanted genuine results. No project was ever turned down because it was deemed too risky. . . .
>
> Another element that contributed to Whitney's progressive thinking, I believe, was being exposed during his capture by the Germans during World War II to all kinds of people from all kinds of backgrounds and social strata. He was democratic. He did not judge people by their appearance. He was a gem to work with.

Of course Gillies was too modest to mention the fact that much of the adventuresome attitude was a result of his stewardship, as well as the progressive thinking of Esther N. Raushenbush, former president of Sarah Lawrence, the college that both Sara and Kate had attended. Esther served for twenty years as senior consultant to the foundation.

The Whitneys were no longer able to live in their red brick, black-balconied townhouse on East Sixty-third Street. Prior to being posted to London, Jock and Betsey had purchased two adjacent townhouses, gutted both, and joined them together. With the help of decorator George Stacey, Betsey turned that home into a cozy residence. The entrance hall, with its great sweep of a curving stairway and its walls of crimson flocked paper, was stunning, with the comfortable elegance, the feeling of leisure, and the quiet order that typified all Whitney homes. Beautiful furniture, fabrics, objects, paintings, and flowers in great abundance from the Manhasset greenhouses gave off an aura of welcome and comfort. What Betsey brought to each Whitney house from the very first days of her marriage was harmony and genuine affection. She never went in for dazzle or fads but rather aimed for a certain prettiness and a touch of amusement. Nothing was ever overdone. And Jock Whitney was always grateful for the wonderful comfort he found in each of his homes. A friend once said, "The Jock Whitneys are just about as 'down-to-earth' as any people can be with a quarter of a billion dollars."

But soon the charm and coziness of the East Sixty-third Street townhouse and its overall tranquility was broken by the constant roar of jackhammers below ground where the city was doing extensive construction work on the subway system.*

Betsey and Jock moved from the townhouse to a duplex apartment on Beekman Place. Jock's health was so poor that he seldom ventured beyond his beloved Greentree estate. His love of racing continued, but he was not up to going to the track, let alone to Saratoga for the August racing season, where in the past he had always celebrated his birthday with an uproarious party. The sad fact was that he was reduced to watching the races on television.

Betsey maintained a vigil at her husband's side during his final illness, canceling all social activities when he was not well enough for them. At the very end only family members were there to add to Jock's few pleasurable moments. Of course, Sara and her five children and Kate and her three made for lively times at the Greentree household. Whitney was an indulgent but prudent grandfather. When each of his grandchildren graduated high school, he gave the graduate a new car—but a good, practical American car, not a luxury model. He dearly loved his adopted daughters and their children, and their presence brightened his final days.

The end came on February 8, 1982, in the North Shore Hospital in Manhasset, one of his principal charities. The seventy-seven-year-old financier and philanthropist succumbed to congestive heart failure after a long illness. His legacy, in addition to vast sums of money, beautiful

---

*It seems ironic that this would occur to the Whitneys, in that the founder of the family fortune, William C. Whitney, had begun establishing that fortune as a result of his investments in the New York City transit system.

property, and fabulous art, consisted of fond remembrances and good works. The funeral service for this kindly gentleman took place at Christ Episcopal Church in Manhasset.

When Jock's will was probated, six weeks after his death, it revealed that he had indeed left most of his vast estate to his wife of forty-three years. Publicly it indicated a bequest of only $5 million outright, plus the 500-acre Greentree estate, the Beekman Place co-op apartment, the flat in London, Greenwood Plantation in Georgia, the place at Fisher's Island, and the racing cottage at Saratoga. She also received Jock's first-rate art collection. In addition the will established three trust funds, one of which was to contain $10 million to provide Betsey with an annuity of $500,000. Daughters Sara and Kate each received $1 million in cash, and each of the eight grandchildren inherited $25,000. A full $17 million of his huge fortune was left to a charitable trust Jock had created in 1959. No total dollar value was ever placed on the estate, but reliable sources conservatively estimate the figure to have been in the range of $200 million. Among Jock's personal bequests was his boathouse in Plandome, Long Island; this he left to John Simms "Shipwreck" Kelly. Kelly had been Jock's boon companion and part-time court jester, who unlike Truman Capote never gossiped about Jock nor introduced his multimillionaire friend to the legion of girls who always seemed to gather around this affable Irish-American.

Betsey's financial triumph did not temper her immense grief. She had adored her husband and was devastated by his death. In true Cushing style, she did not air her feelings publicly but rather bore the pain in stoical silence. Even though she had inherited Greentree, that grand seventy-six-room house she had come to as a bride in 1942, and had become the sole possessor of very nearly all her late husband's multimillion-dollar estate, she made few changes in her lifestyle. She did make some changes when it came to those interests of Jock's she had never shared. Horse breeding and racing had never really caught her fancy. The Greentree Stud in Lexington, Kentucky, was among the first casualties of Betsey's reign. This 600-acre horse farm, which had bred and raced two Kentucky Derby winners, had been the pride and joy of Jock's mother, Helen Hay Whitney, as well as of her two children. Once Betsey had made the decision to rid herself of the magnificent farm, she made the following statement:

Times have changed and amendments to the tax law, coupled with
increasing costs of doing business, require a much more active role
in operating of farm management than I or other members of my
family can spend, particularly from out of state.

The fact that one of Betsey's di Bonaventura grandsons had reportedly
done an admirable job of running the Greentree Stud seemed not to
influence her decision. Once she had made up her mind, that was
that—the Greentree Stud had to go.

According to Jock's biographer, E. J. Kahn, Jock had wondered
during his last days whether the foundation that bore his name would
live on after his death. And his concern seemed to be well justified, for
within months of his death, the John Hay Whitney Foundation ceased
to exist, and the Greentree Foundation came into being. Not only the
name but the focus of the foundation changed radically. Its expenditures, once so generous and even a bit whimsical due to its founder's
quixotic nature, were somewhat curtailed. A recent look at the foundation showed that its assets were slightly in excess of $7 million, while its
annual average in grants seldom reached $500,000. In addition, the new
thrust of the foundation was to reduce "educational, social and cultural
deficiencies in urban areas [primarily in the New York Metropolitan
area], preferably through programs initiated by local communities."
This new agenda reflected the increased influence of Franklin A.
Thomas, longtime companion of Kate Roosevelt Whitney. No one
knows why the name of the foundation was changed; it seems quite
peculiar that anyone would want to eradicate the name of the man
whose great personal wealth enriched the lives of so many. Perhaps the
name *Greentree* would allow for broader interpretation of the identities
of the benefactors, while preserving the influence of Jock Whitney,
through reference to his beloved estate.

Though *John Hay Whitney* may have disappeared from the office
door and letterhead, no one could ever obliterate the memory of this fine
patrician gentleman who had not only served his country with great
distinction but aided his fellow human beings with his true generosity
of spirit and his great philanthropic works. He was the product of fine
tradition, but he lived by the simple philosophy that tradition should be
responsive to new ideas. Fairness and decency were at the heart of all

his beliefs and actions, and his popularity crossed social and economic lines. Jimmy Breslin, who prides himself on being the salt of the ethnic, urban earth, once said of this great man, "Jock Whitney is the only millionaire I ever rooted for."

A comparison of Jock's sister's foundation with the Greentree will point up a number of differences. Among them the assets of each foundation vary widely, the thrust of their grants are totally different, and disbursements annually are nowhere close. In 1947 Joan Whitney Payson had established the Helen Hay Whitney Foundation, honoring her mother. Recent statistics from that foundation showed assets in excess of $26 million and annual grants totaling close to $1 million. Its thrust is toward supporting beginning postdoctoral training in basic biomedical research through fellowship to residents of the North American continent. All recipients must be under thirty-five years of age. Joan had set up very specific goals and guidelines for her philanthropy.

Despite the havoc Betsey had wrought with the foundation and the "for sale" sign up at Greentree Stud, her day-to-day life continued as it always had. Most of her attention focused on Sara and Kate and their maturing brood. Both of Betsey's daughters followed what seems to have become a tradition among Cushing women, divorcing their first husbands and remarrying or at least entering into another, longer-lasting relationship. In addition, all the Cushing women (except Minnie) seemed to be attracted to strong, highly motivated men—possibly an ideal based on Harvey Cushing and passed down from generation to generation. Sara's second husband, Ronald Wilford, is an extremely determined man and a successful, capable businessman. Kate divorced William Haddad and has as her companion the dynamic Franklin A. Thomas, who is now president of the Ford Foundation.

Betsey continued to live at Greentree alone, or as alone as one can be with a houseful of servants. She did pare her staff down considerably, as she no longer needed the seventy-odd employees who had kept things running smoothly in the Whitneys' heyday of entertaining. Nevertheless, it still takes twenty or so full-time workers to run the massive house and maintain its enormous grounds.

Now an octogenarian, Betsey is quite infirm. She rarely travels beyond the grounds of Greentree. When she does venture forth, it is usually in the company of one of her daughters or grandchildren who, miraculously, have been able to avoid publicity of either a positive or negative sort. She often uses a wheelchair, and on those rare occasions when she goes out to a social function, she invariably has a nurse at her side. She does still manage to grace special events with her presence. Big evenings, like the dedication of the John Hay Whitney Gallery at the Museum of Modern Art or a major event at the Metropolitan Museum of Art or the North Shore Hospital, can generally draw her out of her Manhasset home. Despite her frailty, her presence still bespeaks the indomitable spirit and quietly elegant manner that has made her so celebrated, especially so when we measure celebrity today in so instantaneous a fashion. Betsey has acquired another distinction with her listing in the 1990 edition of *Forbes*'s "rich list," stating that Betsey Cushing Roosevelt Whitney's wealth was estimated at $700 million. Within the near future it may even reach the $1 billion mark.

The other survivor among the Cushing sisters and their high-profile mates was, until quite recently, Bill Paley. Although a goodly number of women had set their sights on him even before the singing of the last hymn at Babe's funeral, he proved to be a slippery catch, unwilling to take a third walk down the aisle. In his post-Babe years he managed to be seen everywhere and, with the help of a couple of these women friends, to entertain frequently. All the while, forces at CBS were intent upon unseating him as chairman, and the company was in a state of severe turmoil. It was at this juncture that he suddenly took up with actress Lois Chiles. Apparently they complemented each other very well. She was pretty and very kind to him, and he in turn was most indulgent toward her. She appeared with him at numerous social functions and at the small, chic restaurants that he favored, and even spent time with him at his Nassau retreat. But the romance did not last even a year. Soon he had his old pal, Slim Keith, in tow again.

Late in the winter of 1987, while vacationing in Lyford Cay, Bill came down with pneumonia. The CBS plane had to come to shuttle him back to New York. During this illness, Kate Paley, apparently having resolved much of the anger she had for so long harbored over her parents' rejection, took an active interest in her father's health and sought to relieve his discomfort by spending hours reading to him from the Bible. At last he recovered from this bout with ill health, but by early fall of the same year he had developed a severe circulation problem in his legs and could only get around in a wheelchair. He had nurses attending him twenty-four hours a day, accompanying him on his daytime and evening social rounds.

Throughout the late 1980s, William Paley suffered constantly from gallbladder and kidney problems. Then, in what may well have been the final blow, the beginning of the end, the proud and headstrong Paley lost the one true love of his lifetime—CBS—in a takeover by hotel and insurance magnate Laurence Tisch. Despite his failing health and his overthrow at CBS, Bill made a heroic effort to keep up his appearances on the Manhattan-Southampton social axis. He still gave small dinner parties at his Southampton home, with Slim Keith as his hostess. When in Manhattan, he entertained at 820 Fifth Avenue, but on a small scale, and he would occasionally appear at large social functions. On one occasion during those twilight years, Jacqueline Onassis honored him at a fete given by the Municipal Art Society. With his daughters, Hilary and Kate, and his stepdaughter, Amanda, gracing his table that evening, he was in a rare state of peace and contentment.

Paley's health problems continued to plague him, and the loss of his closest friends no doubt compounded these problems. He was sorely grieved by the death of Walter Thayer and then Loel Guinness—and in the spring of 1990 his faithful pal Slim Keith died of chronic heart disease. Paley's sister, Blanche, also died that spring. Since he had never forgiven her for having been their mother's obvious favorite, he hardly noticed this loss. The old hurt had festered in his soul for too many years to be exorcised.

With his daughter Kate keeping the death vigil, William S. Paley expired quietly at his Manhattan apartment on October 26, 1990. He had outlived Babe by a dozen years, and despite constant female companionship and the six children who survived him, he had always been an essentially lonely man. He had never really been able to share his innermost thoughts and feelings with anyone, had never really been able to love or accept love.

A memorial service was held at Fifth Avenue's Temple Emanu-El, built on the site of what had been former brother-in-law Vincent Astor's childhood home. Those who eulogized him included Henry A. Kissinger, former secretary of state, and family friend and CBS board member Marietta Tree. According to Kissinger, "Mr. Paley would never allow anything to interfere with his love affair with CBS." Ms. Tree, reflecting on her forty-year friendship with Bill, spoke of his "zest for life and zeal to achieve perfection." The ushers included designer Oscar de la Renta and Steve Ross, former undertaker, cochairman of Time Warner, and ex-husband of Amanda Burden. It was the kind of high-profile send-off that Bill Paley would have appreciated and a grand last hurrah for Mr. Television.

Paley's last will and testament came as a great surprise to his six children, each of whom received $20 million (or perhaps $30 million, as Boaz Mazor recently claimed they'd gotten). Could Paley possibly have had regrets for the lost opportunity to form close bonds? Could he, in the only way he knew how, have been asking for his children's forgiveness? Or could he merely not have known what else to do with the vast fortune that had never really bought him happiness? Or perhaps the disposition of his will was simply his way of going out in style, as Babe had.

POSTSCRIPT

What the Cushing sisters accomplished socially and economically was a phenomenon that is highly unlikely to repeat itself in the future. That all three sisters married three of the wealthiest and most powerful men in the country was one of the major coups of the century. Author Michael Thomas put it very well in a recent interview, "They were great ladies, real leaders, not just someone some rich man picked up along the way. You don't talk about the Gayfried Steinbergs of this world in the same breath as Babe."

Each of the sisters found her own unique and highly individual niche in life, thus sharpening an image that had been developing since early childhood. Minnie Cushing Astor Fosburgh found her reward being among artists. Her friend the late Count Lanfranco Rasponi once said of her, "She has moved farther and farther away from society to dedicate her time to the intelligentsia, seeing very little of anyone who is not an actor, director, writer, or artist." And in following this path Minnie became an astute collector of art and a renowned salon hostess. As Babe said of her, "Minnie is everyone's friend; you may warn her that a particular person will bite her sooner or later but Minnie won't take your advice until she feels the bite."

Money, a cynic once wrote, is life's report card. But nowhere is it written that you have to earn your final grade yourself or that, even if you do, an A-plus will guarantee happiness. Nevertheless, the Cushing sisters' marital successes triggered America's forty-odd-year love affair with that glamorous trio. What made the public's ardor so lasting was the fact that the Cushing sisters fit perfectly into their time. They were role models for an age, they mirrored a culture, and they expressed values for people who needed to believe in fairy tales.

Babe, on the other hand, thrived in her splendid lifestyle. As decorator Albert Hadley said recently, "Babe was passionate about fashion and decorating." She adored media attention, the grand entrances and exits into and out of all the glamour spots around the world. Most of all, she enjoyed the mystique that surrounded her great beauty and flair for style. As Betsey once told E. J. Kahn, "Babe was always the glamour girl and I was always the crumbum except when I was away from her. Babe was a perfectionist. Compared to her I always felt insecure."

If Babe embodied glamour, Betsey embodied upper-crust restraint. Publisher John Fairchild once dubbed her "Queen of the WASPs," and that was truly the way she would have wished to be seen. She had hobnobbed with kings, queens, and prince consorts, and when not in the actual presence of royalty, she gave a decidedly royal appearance herself. Betsey loves the regal splendors of Greentree. According to a source who has known Betsey for nearly thirty years, "She has many broken bones, is now quite lame, socially reclusive, [but] has an extraordinary inner reserve of strength even now. You can feel it when in her presence."

SELECTIVE BIBLIOGRAPHY

Asbell, Bernard, ed. *Mother and Daughter: The Letters of Eleanor and Anna Roosevelt.* New York: Coward, McCann & Geoghegan, 1982.

Astor, Brooke. *Footprints.* New York: Doubleday, 1980.

Baldwin, Billy, with Michael Gardine. *Billy Baldwin: An Autobiography.* Boston: Little, Brown & Company, 1985.

Beaton, Cecil. *Beaton in Vogue.* New York: Potter, 1986.

Birmingham, Stephen. *The Right People: A Portrait of the American Social Establishment.* Boston: Little, Brown, 1968.

Capote, Truman. *Answered Prayers: The Unfinished Novel.* New York: Random House, 1987.

Chase, Edna Woolman, and Ilka Chase. *Always in Vogue.* New York: Doubleday, 1954.

Clarke, Gerald. *Capote: A Biography.* New York: Simon & Schuster, 1988.

Cowles, Virginia S. *The Astors.* New York: Alfred A. Knopf, 1979.

Curtis, Charlotte. *The Rich and Other Atrocities.* New York: Harper & Row, 1976.

Denzel, Justin F. *Genius with a Scalpel.* Englewood Cliffs, New Jersey: Messner, 1971.

Fairchild, John. *Chic Savages.* New York: Simon & Schuster, 1989.

Gates, John D. *The Astor Family.* New York: Doubleday, 1981.

Hart, Kitty Carlisle. *Kitty: An Autobiography.* New York: Doubleday, 1988.

Kahn, E. J., Jr. *Jock: The Life and Times of John Hay Whitney.* New York: Doubleday, 1981.

Kavaler, Lucy. *The Astors.* New York: Dodd, Mead, 1966.

Metz, Robert. *CBS: Reflections in a Bloodshot Eye.* New York: Signet, New American Library, 1976.

Morgan, Ted. *FDR.* New York: Simon & Schuster, 1985.

Paley, William S. *As I Saw It.* New York: Doubleday, 1979.

Paper, Lewis J. *Empire: The Life and Times of William Paley*. New York: St. Martin's Press, 1987.

Roosevelt, James. *My Parents: A Different View*. New York: Playboy Press, 1976.

Seebohm, Caroline. *The Man Who Was Vogue*. New York: Viking/Penguin USA, 1982.

Selznick, Irene Mayer. *A Private View*. New York: Alfred A. Knopf, 1983.

Smith, Sally Bedell. *In All His Glory: The Life of William S. Paley: The Legendary Tycoon and His Brilliant Circle*. New York: Simon & Schuster, 1990.

Thompson, Elizabeth H. *Harvey Cushing: Surgeon, Author, Artist*. Canton, Massachusetts: Watson Academic Publications, 1981.

PERIODICALS AND NEWSPAPERS

Capote, Truman. "A Gathering of Swans," *Harper's Bazaar*, 10/59.

Smith, Liz. "Truman in Hot Water," *New York*, 2/9/76.

Taki. "Panting for Paley," *Esquire*, 2/79.

Thruelsen, Richard. "The Fabulous Jock Whitney," *The Saturday Evening Post*, 5/57.

Avenue
The Chicago American
Fame
Forbes
Fortune
House Beautiful
House & Garden
The Ladies Home Journal
The London Times
The New York Daily News
The New York Herald Tribune
The New York Journal-American
The New York Post
The New York Times
The New Yorker
Newsday
Newsweek
The Palm Beach Daily News
Paris Match
The Saturday Evening Post
Time
Town and Country
Vanity Fair
Vogue
Vogue (British)
Vogue (French)
W
The Washington Post
Women's Wear Daily

INDEX

PERMISSIONS
ACKNOWLEDGMENTS

Grateful acknowledgment is made to the following for permission
to reprint previously published material:

CURTIS BROWN, LTD.: Excerpts from *As It Happened* by William S. Paley. Copyright ©
1979 by William S. Paley. Reprinted by permission of Curtis Brown, Ltd.

DOUBLEDAY: Excerpts from *Footprints* by Brooke Astor. Copyright © 1980 by Brooke
Astor. Excerpts from *Always in Vogue* by Edna Woolman Chase and Ilka Chase.
Reprinted by permission of Doubleday, a division of Bantam Doubleday Dell Publish-
ing Group, Inc.

HARPER'S BAZAAR: Excerpt from "A Gathering of Stars" by Truman Capote. Reprinted
by permission of *Harper's Bazaar* magazine.

INTERNATIONAL CREATIVE MANAGEMENT, INC.: Excerpts from *Jock* by E. J. Kahn, Jr.
Reprinted by permission of International Creative Management, Inc.

LITTLE, BROWN & COMPANY: Excerpt from *Billy Baldwin: An Autobiography* by Billy
Baldwin with Michael Gardine. Copyright © 1985 by The Estate of Michael Gardine.
Reprinted by permission of Little, Brown & Company.

MACMILLAN PUBLISHING COMPANY: Excerpt from *My Favorite Things: A Personal Guide
to Decorating and Entertaining* by Dorothy Rodgers. Copyright © 1964 by Dorothy
Rodgers. Reprinted by permission of Atheneum Publishers, an imprint of Macmillan
Publishing Company.

THE NEW YORK TIMES COMPANY: Excerpts from "Observer: Truman Capote's Gift to
Literature" by Russell Baker, "William S. Paley Obituary" by Jeremy Gerard, "Bar-
bara Cushing Paley Dies at 63 . . ." by Enid Nemy. Copyright © 1966, 1978, 1990 by
The New York Times Company. Reprinted by permission.

RANDOM HOUSE, INC.: Excerpts from *Answered Prayers* by Truman Capote. Copyright
© 1965, 1976 by Truman Capote. Reprinted by permission of Random House, Inc.

SIMON & SCHUSTER, INC., AND INTERNATIONAL CREATIVE MANAGEMENT: Excerpts from
In All His Glory by Sally Bedell Smith. Copyright © 1990 by Sally Bedell Smith.

Reprinted by permission of Simon & Schuster, Inc., and International Creative Management.

ST. MARTIN'S PRESS, INC., AND SCOTT MEREDITH LITERARY AGENCY, INC.: Excerpts from *Empire: William S. Paley and the Making of CBS* by Lewis Paper. Copyright © 1987 by Lewis Paper. Reprinted by special permission of St. Martin's Press, Inc., New York, N.Y., and Scott Meredith Literary Agency, Inc.

THAMES & HUDSON LTD.: Excerpt from *Beaton in Vogue* by Josephine Ross, published by Thames & Hudson Ltd. in 1986. Copyright © 1986 by Josephine Ross. Reprinted by permission of Thames & Hudson Ltd.

ABOUT THE AUTHOR

DAVID GRAFTON is the author of *Red, Hot and Rich: An Oral History of Cole Porter*. A member of New York's Café Society during its heyday in the fifties, he lived for a period of time in Puerto Rico, where he created the magazine *Talk of the Town*. He has written articles for *Forbes, Paris Match, Interview* and *Elle Decor*. He lives in Chicago.